EAST
COAST
TOAST

Walker Newton

EAST COAST TOAST

Walker Newton

Published by Wahoo Publishing House
St. Augustine, Florida
Copyright by Walker Newton
Cover Photo by Phil King
Author Photo by Bonnie King

All characters appearing in this work are fictitious. The basis for any character may be drawn from real life, but all dialogue, actions and appearances are only in the mind of the author. Real locations may have been altered to fit the story. Authors do that.

By Walker Newton
TRACKS
ST. AUGUSTINE SET
EAST COAST TOAST
DAYTONA DIRT
SAND CRABS AND SHARKS
DIVE DARK WATER

EAST
COAST
TOAST

A horse misused upon the road
Calls to Heaven for human blood.
–William Blake
"Auguries of Innocence"

I never wonder to see men wicked,
but I often wonder not to see them
ashamed."
–Jonathan Swift

EAST
COAST
TOAST

It was a lot harder stabbing someone since the accident, but Mick wasn't complaining. The same wreck that left him slightly injured, set him free. He rubbed his sore shoulder as he walked slowly down the aisle of the little Louisiana country store. Ragley? Ragley, Louisiana? It was no surprise that he'd never heard of it.

Mick was beginning to feel his age. He turned sixty last year in the prison at Galveston. He was still strong, though, and he had a full head of sandy brown hair, buzz-cut short. He was tall, six feet, and pale. His eyes were a washed out blue that were attractive until you realized that there was only darkness behind them.

Late morning sunlight came through the windows. It highlighted thousands of dust motes in the air. There were tin signs on the bare wood walls advertising products like soap powders, Dr. John's Cure-All Medicine, and Coca-Cola. Wooden shelves held the "everything" that a farmer living miles from nowhere might need. It was fall, so most of the feed and fertilizer had been sold, but there were a few bags of each in a pile at the end of the first aisle. A faint, musty smell hung over the crowded shelves. They were filled with canned goods and general merchandise. He picked a child's backpack up off a wooden display table. It was decorated with a large picture of a flying super hero. Mick was born in

1

a city and had never been in a real country store. The odd assortment of products for sale amused him.

He unzipped the backpack. As he wandered the aisles of the store, he put items into it that he thought he might need. The unlucky truck driver's clothes were too small for him. They were tight and splashed with blood. He had to get rid of them, so he picked up a pair of new Levi's jeans and a flannel shirt. He grabbed two pairs of socks, and two of underwear. These items went into the pack. He added a bottle of dark brown hair dye and a weak pair of reading glasses. He picked up a green, John Deere ball cap and put it on his head.

Mick was nearing the back of the store when he heard a noise coming from behind a closed door. "Who's there?" he shouted. His defenses were on full alert. "I've got a gun and I'll use it. You better show yourself!"

I wish I had a gun, he thought. Even the pocketknife he took off the trucker was out of reach, still stuck in the throat of the old man. If anyone gave him trouble, he would have to rely on his hands.

It wouldn't be the first time.

There was a shuffling noise, and then a cute young girl in her early teens opened the door and stood in the doorway. She was thin, but beginning to develop. She stood about five feet tall, and had a tangled, dishwater blonde ponytail. She wore a dirty, Denver Broncos T-shirt and cutoff blue jeans. Black, high-top tennis shoes were on her feet. Her fingernails were ragged and needed cleaning.

She looked him straight in the eyes. "Did you kill him?" she asked calmly. Mick didn't reply. "There's another one hiding back in the storeroom," she said, pointing over her shoulder.

2

Mick took the girl by the arm and moved her out of the way. He stepped into the back room and found a stocky Latino man, pock-marked, mid-thirties, trying to hide himself behind some empty cartons.

"Get out of there, dumbass," Mick demanded. The man was crying softly. He shielded his face with his hands. Mick kicked the cartons away from in front of him. The man fell to his knees, pleading.

"Please don't hurt me, senor! I have three kids. I didn't see nothing and don't know nothing. I just work and go home. I won't never say a word to no one!"

The girl standing beside Mick gripped his arm. "Kill him, mister," she urged. "You got rid of Charley, my granddad, didn't you? I heard him scream. This one's name is Santos. He needs killing, too."

"Your granddad?" Mick glanced up the aisle. At the end of it beyond some feed sacks, a shoe and a lower leg were visible, stretched on the floor. From his angle, the blood around them just looked wet.

"Yeah, my granddad. I don't know what you got planned for me, but I want to see both these bastards die."

Mick studied the girl a minute, then said in his gravelly voice, "Could be you're too late for the old man. You're welcome to check, but I'm pretty sure he's finished. What's it all about between you and this guy?" He grabbed the Latino by the arm, pulled him to his feet, and jerked him out of the storeroom. He tripped him so he fell face forward on the floor.

"Never you mind," the girl said. Mick stood there thinking things over. In a surprise move, she reached right past him and snatched a bone-handled hunting knife from a counter display that he hadn't noticed. Mick raised his arms and jumped back, but the girl didn't give him a glance.

3

She stepped forward, and rammed the seven-inch knife into the center of the crying Latino's back. She then backed away, leaving the knife sticking there, blood gushing out around the hilt. The man's sobbing turned to a gasping, then a gurgling sound. The girl used her foot to carefully spread the man's legs and then, with all her power, kicked the dying man in the crotch so hard that he lifted several inches off the floor. He fell back, flat out and silent. She turned to Mick and smiled.

Mick relaxed his hands and looked the girl over. What the hell?

"You did it wrong," he commented. "Should have kicked him first. I bet he hardly felt it with that knife in his back." He picked up the backpack where he had dropped it, and stepped over the man to walk the last aisle.

"I've been working here," the girl said. "I can help you find stuff. Just tell me what you need."

"Oh, I could use a couple of those hunting knives, I guess, and a gun. You sell guns here?"

"No, we don't sell them, but Charley keeps one under the candy counter. It's up by the cash register."

Mick walked to the front of the store, careful not to step in the pool of blood around the old man. As he looked for the gun, he called, "I guess you didn't like them much, either one of them." The girl didn't reply.

He found the handgun where she said it would be. It was an old, thirty-eight Smith and Wesson. It was loaded. He raised the gun and sighted it on a bottle of ketchup halfway up the aisle. "Pow," he said. He set it on the counter and picked up a Snickers bar. He unwrapped the candy bar and took a bite.

4

"They're in hell, both of them. That's right where they ought to be," she replied. "They should have been there a lot sooner."

"You're mighty young to be doing such serious things," Mick observed.

"Well, they didn't think so." She hesitated, and then asked, "You going to kill me? You're going to have to kill me if you think you're going to fuck me. I'll put a knife in you just as fast as I did to Santos. I swear I will."

"Oh, you're too young, and maybe too mean, for me to fuck. To tell you the truth, little girl, I haven't decided about killing you yet. I'm kinda up in the air about that. You might help me out some while I'm making up my mind. Like, where are the shells for this pistol?"

"Back in the storeroom."

"Well, go get 'em." The girl turned and went through the doorway. She returned with a small cardboard box of ammunition in each hand. "There's an axe and a shovel back there, too. I mean, if you want to bury the bodies."

"That would be real nice, I guess, but I figure I've only got a limited time around here before someone starts rattling my cage. I've been locked up for the last twelve years, and I kind of like being out."

"How did you manage it? Getting out, I mean."

"Just crazy luck." Mick looked the girl straight in the eyes. "Every damn day of the past twelve years I've been planning to escape. I would have done anything to get away. I mean anything. I did get close a couple of times, but nothing ever worked out. Then, real early this morning, I'm in a van being transferred from the prison in Galveston to the maximum security prison up in Killian County. The driver makes the right mistake at just the right time. We get T-boned by a semi out on the two-lane. The van rolls.

The truck driver is killed. The guards are both knocked out. Whoop-ti-do. The van is split open, and here I am. It was just crazy luck.

"How'd you get to Ragley?"

"I caught a ride out of Texas with a Good Samaritan. That's his Buick out there. But I know half the country is looking for me now. I need to make tracks and fast. The Buick driver was expected at a sales meeting about eleven o'clock in Beaumont. Someone will be looking for him. Pretty soon the law will get it sorted out."

"Will anybody find him?"

"Not unless they look in his trunk." Mick grinned. "I'm banking that they'll figure I'll run for Mexico. They'll put all the cops and roadblocks on the western route. That's why I'm heading east on this two-lane. I need to hide the Buick and get another car. What about our friends here?" He gestured at the bodies on the floor. "One of them must have had a car."

"Charley has a Chevy pickup in the equipment shed out back. It's old, but it runs good. You could put the Buick in the shed and take the truck. He keeps the store keys and the truck keys on a nail by the door."

"Well, that's pretty helpful, young lady." Mick paused. "I'll tell you what. I won't kill you just yet. You can ride along with me. The law won't be looking for a man with his granddaughter. We'll be family. Take a ride and see the country."

Mick walked up the aisle to the Latino's body. He wiped the bloody handle of the hunting knife off with a bandana. Then he firmly grasped the handle, but left the knife in place. "That should get rid of your prints and leave mine. I'm guessing you haven't killed a lot of people. I have. One or two more won't make much difference to me."

6

"How many you killed?"

"Shit, girl, I lost count a long time ago. Now listen, granddaughter, you put together a few clothes for you and some food for the both of us. Do what I say, and we'll see how things go."

2

Before leaving the old store to check out the shed, Mick dragged the girl's grandfather behind a stack of grain sacks. He then lowered the curtains on the door and the front window. He scribbled a note on a shirt cardboard, "Closed for family emergency. Back Saturday," and taped it to the window, face out. That might buy them a few days, and in a few days, he planned to be looking at an ocean.

Mick took the wallets off the two bodies and put them in the pack. Then he cleaned out the cash register. There was only seventy-five dollars in it. He filled a paper sack with peanuts and candy bars. He took a blanket off a stack of bedding on a back shelf. There was an old guitar leaning against the wall. After thinking a minute, he picked that up, too. He wrapped the instrument in the blanket. The girl handed Mick two nice, long-bladed hunting knives in their sheaths.

The girl then took another backpack and filled it with canned stuff: baked beans, tuna fish, Vienna sausage. She added a small cooking pot and a jar of instant coffee. As they left the store, she grabbed a handful of Snickers bars, two big bags of potato chips, and a loaf of Wonder bread.

Mick locked up the store, and they started to get in the Buick. As the girl was climbing in the car, Mick grabbed her blonde ponytail and jerked her back towards him. He spun her around, and pulled another hunting knife she had hidden from the waist of her cutoffs.

"Nasty, nasty, little girl. You're messing with me." He slapped her hard across the face. The sound was like the crack of a breaking branch. "You mess with me one more time, and I'll be doing my traveling alone. When I leave, you'll be nothin' but a wet stain on this asphalt." He unsheathed the knife and held the point to the girl's throat. "You get it?"

"OK, yeah, I get it." The girl's cheek was bright red where Mick's hand had landed, but she didn't cry. She didn't beg or whine either. She met his glaring eyes full on. "I just thought I needed some protection. You're a murderer, you know."

"And you are, too, sweetheart. Don't you forget that part. You best remember who's the boss here, and who's on shaky ground." He sheathed the knife and slipped it into his work boot.

Mick let the girl's arm go. He pushed her into the car. As he walked around to the driver's side, he noticed the small pool of blood spreading on the pavement beneath the trunk. Yeah, time to get rid of this car.

They drove around the right side of the store. There was a large steel building shaded by a huge hickory tree behind the building. The metal shed had a sliding door that took up most of the front of it. Mick parked the Buick and he and the girl got out. The sliding door wasn't locked. It slid open easily. Inside, there was a riding mower, a bunch of scattered farming tools, and an old brown pickup with one primer-gray fender.

The Chevy pickup didn't look like much, but the tires were good. It cranked the first time Mick turned the key. He backed the truck out of the shed and then put the Buick in its place. Mick got out of the car and glanced around the shed's interior. He stripped off the trucker's uniform, and threw it under the car. He began putting on his new clothes. His body had several gray scars that striped his back. His right shoulder was one large bruise from the van wreck. He rubbed it absently.

He was zipping up his stiff new Levi's when he noticed the army cot. It was in the far corner of the gloomy space. There was a rumpled sleeping bag spread on top of it. He walked over while buttoning his plaid flannel shirt. He saw that there was a cardboard box of clothes and other items under the cot. There were some outdated magazines, a white pair of flip-flops, and an old transistor radio in it. The radio was pink plastic and covered with grimy fingerprints.

Above the end of the cot, attached to a bolt through the wall, there was a length of number ten chain. There was a single steel handcuff welded onto the end of it. Mick could smell something that was beginning to rot.

He walked out of the shed wearing his fresh new clothes. He motioned for the girl to get into the truck. He pulled the shed door back into place, and then got into the truck's driver's seat. "I'm heading for the east coast," he said, looking straight ahead. "I'll take you with me if you want. I'll have to kill you if you don't."

The girl nodded her head. She didn't look frightened. "Not much of a choice. How far you going? Do you know?"

"I'm going until the cops or the ocean stops me," Mick answered. "Can you drive?"

"Charley never wanted me to learn, but I'll try anything. I can drive a tractor. I'm a fast learner."

"Better be." He put the truck in gear and set off. "I think we can start out on state 190. The law will find the bodies here in a day or so. Once they see our friends inside, they'll know it's me. They'll figure out which way I'm heading. Then they'll re-focus the search. We'll have to stick to the blue line highways and drive non-stop. You watch me while I'm driving. You're going to have to spell me somewhere down the line. You can ask questions, but not about anything but the driving." He gave her a dead serious look.

They made pretty good time that day. The old Chevy didn't have a radio or air conditioning, but it was proving reliable. There didn't seem to be any special activity on the part of the law. Mick stayed right on the speed limit, changing his driving hand occasionally to rest his sore shoulder. They passed bags of chips and junk food back and forth without sharing a glance. They made a couple of pit stops, and by nightfall they were past Mobile, Alabama. They had only exchanged a few words the whole day.

"Aren't you tired yet?" the girl asked. She was eating potato chips again.

"Course I am," Mick replied, "but being a serial killer is hard work. It's not for just anybody." That got a smile out of her. "Since it looks like we're going to spend some time together, why don't you give yourself a name?" he asked. "It doesn't have to be your real name. It shouldn't be. Call yourself whatever you want. Have some fun. It'll make things easier."

The girl turned away from him, and looked out the window. She ate a few more chips. After a few minutes she said, "You can call me Sunny. I always liked that name." She turned back to look at him. "What about you?"

"Michael Jason Parsons, and that's the real one. You'll see it in the papers and on the news soon enough. Yours will be there, too, you know. Your real name." Sunny frowned at that, but didn't comment. She brushed some crumbs off of her T-shirt and put the chip bag on the floor.

"Well then, if we're going to have to get rid of our old names, shouldn't we make up some good ones that we like?" Mick nodded his OK. "I guess I can tell you, my real name is Brenda Rose Martin. Don't you laugh at it. I hate it. I'm going to be Sunny Cathleen Cantrell. I've been dreaming about that name for a long time."

"OK, Miss Sunny. So who should I be?" he asked. The girl was enjoying the game.

"Well, who do you like? Isn't there someone you like a lot?"

"I guess so. Maybe this guy named Ted."

They were passing the "Welcome to Florida" sign. It had a huge palm tree under a setting sun painted on it. Smaller script said, "The Sunshine State."

"Wow, we're in Florida!" Sunny exclaimed. She was excited and distracted by the state line. "I haven't been out of Ragley in four years."

"Four years, huh? Where were you before Ragley?"

"Up in Little Rock."

"Why'd you leave?"

"What's it matter? Especially to you. I left, that's all." She stared straight ahead. "I was eleven years old. I got put on a Greyhound bus. All I had was thirty dollars, the clothes I was wearing, and a ticket to Ragley. My mother sent me off to live with this loving grandfather that I had never met." She turned to the window again. "Just drop it, mister. Mister Ted no-last-name."

Mick was worn out. He had only slept four of the last seventy hours. Sunny had been watching him drive. She kept asking for a chance to try. Thankfully, the old Chevy was an automatic. He knew it was either take a chance on her wrecking the truck, or take a chance on stopping somewhere and maybe getting spotted. He decided he would feel a lot better if they could get another five or six hours of road underneath them.

"Sunny Cantrell, your time has come. You think you're up to it?" She grinned at him. She had a nice grin. Her lips pulled back and you could see the white of her teeth.

"You know I don't have a license, don't you?"

"Girl, I saw you stick a great big knife through a man's spine. I think I can forgive you for your lack of a driver's license." She gave a shy nod, and smiled.

They were on a lonely stretch of highway 98 between Panacea and Perry. The road was good, and there was hardly any traffic. The sun was about to break over the horizon, and an orange glow filled the windshield.

Mick pulled the truck onto a lonely side road and stopped. The surrounding cypress trees were covered with Spanish moss that gave them a little cover. The smell of the Gulf hit him as he opened his door and stepped out. It was seaweed and oyster shells, tidal ponds and fiddler crabs, dead fish and thick mud. Mick breathed in deeply. He remembered the familiar smells from his childhood on the Texas coast.

Sunny slid into the driver's seat. Mick took a last deep breath, and then got back into the truck on the passenger side.

"Now remember, girl, you've got both our asses in your hands. No fooling around. You keep your shit together." He told her to leave the gearshift in park and turn the key. She did, failing to let off when the engine caught. The starter produced a loud grinding sound. Mick grabbed her hand and twisted it until the grinding stopped.

"Hey!" she started to protest.

He was so tired. "Look, just shut up. I'll start the truck. You watch." He turned the key and the engine started perfectly.

"Now look behind you. See anything? OK, put your right foot on the left pedal. That's the brake. OK, now put the gearshift in 'R.' That's reverse. Ease your foot off the brake, and we should start backing up."

Sunny did as she was told. The old truck backed slowly onto the deserted highway. Mick talked her through braking and going into drive. Then he taught her about the gas. Sunny paid attention. Damned if she didn't quickly have them moving down the road at a solid forty-five. That was just fine with Mick.

"It's not a lot different than a tractor," she said, "just faster."

Mick nodded, and tried to stay awake, but soon his eyes closed. Even Sunny's erratic driving couldn't keep him from falling into oblivion.

3

"Oh shit!"

Sunny's scream woke Mick up. At the same time, he felt a jolt pass through the truck. He struggled to fight his way free from the fog in his head. The truck was swerving wildly across the two-lane highway.

"What happened? What happened?" he yelled. "Hit the brakes!"

Sunny slammed on the brake with both feet. The old truck swerved sharply one last time. It skidded sideways to a stop. There were two wheels on the pavement, and two on the edge of a deep drainage ditch. Sunny slumped over the wheel. She was hitting her thighs with her fists. "Holy cow!" she managed. "It ran right out in front of me. It was a fucking monster. Something huge!"

A monster no less. Mick reached over and pulled the keys from the ignition. He'd had enough of Sunny's first driving lesson. His short rest had revived him somewhat. He opened the door of the truck to go check for damage. As he stepped out, "God damn!" He jumped back in the cab and slammed the door. He jerked the thirty-eight out from under the seat and cautiously looked out the window. Directly below him, Mick saw an injured alligator at least nine or ten feet long. It was crawling slowly past the truck. The huge reptile hissed and growled, snapping its gaping jaws and whipping the asphalt with its tail. As he watched, it moved slowly past the truck and slid into the weed choked, drainage ditch. Sunny must have hit the gator with the truck as it was crossing the road.

He turned to her and laughed. "Damn, girl, you're even trying to wipe out the alligators. You're just a natural born killer."

"Screw you! That thing could have killed us both. I've never seen a gator that big. It nearly turned us over when I hit it. It crawled out of nowhere."

"They're moving around this time of year, looking for a good place to sleep through the winter. He's gone now. I feel wide awake. I'll drive on from here."

"You better believe you will. I don't want any chance in hell that I'll hit another one of those things. You get out and go around. I'm not setting foot outside this truck."

Mick got out on the passenger side. He walked around the rear end of the Chevy. He could smell the musk of the surrounding swampland where gators love to live. He kept the thirty-eight in his hand just in case there were more of the reptiles close by. As he opened the driver's side door, he noticed that the front left fender was crumpled onto the tire. He looked around, but didn't see a handy tool. Glad he was strong for his age, he grabbed the fender and managed to bend it away from the tire. Now, if the tire wasn't too badly damaged, they could get back on the road.

The sun was fully up when Mick got to Perry, Florida. He could smell the mixed fragrance of bar-b-que meat, oyster shells, and azaleas. At the main intersection in the little town, he decided to take highway 27 straight east. He made the turn, and drove towards the coast. Sunny was dozing off and on, content to have him drive her anywhere. The sun was glaring into the windshield as he drove. The truck heated up quickly. Mick rolled up the sleeves of his heavy shirt.

They would have to stop somewhere for the night. He had to change his appearance and decide what to do about the girl.

"Where'd you get that?" Sunny was awake. Her voice was husky from sleep. Her finger pointed at the tattoo on Mick's forearm. The green and red image was of a three inch heart, pierced by a dagger. Mick glanced at it, and then returned his eyes to the road. He said nothing.

"Come on, tell me. I like tattoos. I'm going to get one of my own one of these days. I've been thinking about either a butterfly on my shoulder or a little cartoon devil on my calf. That one on your arm is cool. A heart with a dagger. What did it cost you?"

"Twelve years, little girl. Twelve long years."

"Huh? Did you get it in prison?"

"No. I got it in Nam."

"What's Nam?" Sunny asked.

"You're a kid. You're too young to even know about it. Nam was Viet Nam. A war, a nasty war that happened long before you were born."

"What kind of war? Were you a soldier? Were you in any action?"

Mick gave her a scathing look. He never talked about Nam. He never talked about much at all. After his years in solitary, being with another person felt awkward. Still, this kid didn't make any real difference. What the hell. He was probably going to kill her anyway.

"Yeah, I guess you can say I was in action. I was a nineteen year old wise-ass. I needed to get out of an assault charge hanging over me in Galveston. Joining up kept me out of jail. Once I was in, I got pretty good at it."

"At soldiering?"

Mick looked at her and grinned.

"At killing."

They rode along in silence for several miles. Sunny looked out the window and Mick concentrated on the road. They were passing through some of central Florida's cattle country. Bright green pastures held groups of large grey Brahmas and Black Angus cattle. All of the cows had small white birds standing around them as they grazed. They were egrets. The birds ate the ticks and parasites that fed on the cattle. The smells of fertilizer and cut hay drifted into the truck windows.

Sunny turned to Mick and asked, "Who broke your heart?"

"What do you mean? No one's ever broken my heart." He paused. "No one's ever even had a chance at my heart."

"But what about your tattoo, the heart with the dagger through it?"

"Oh, shit, little girl. I got that tat the weekend after I stabbed my first man to death. I shoved my knife right into his heart, and then watched his eyes gray over as he died. That's when I knew how I was going to live my life." His gravelly voice seemed to fill the cab of the old truck.

"Is that why you went to prison?" Sunny looked pale.

"Hell no. That's how I won my first medal. Killing that slant-eye made me a hero." He chuckled. "I think the army saw the psycho in me, even before I did. I was assigned to a sniper unit right out of boot camp. I already knew how to shoot, so that part was easy. Watching a brain explode never bothered me either, but some guys couldn't hack that. After sniper school, they picked two of us to go to another 'special' school. This one didn't even have a name. The other guy and I were flown down to Honduras.

18

When we got there, they put us on a chopper and flew us into the jungle."

"Gee, that sounds so cool!"

"Yeah, it was cool all right. It was a hundred degrees. The humidity pulled sweat out of you faster than you could put water back in. It was a hell hole, and meant to be. I was there fifteen weeks; fifteen weeks of Uncle Sam's most intense training. Make you a killer, or kill you trying. That was their mission. They did a good job. That's where I got some real education. I learned how to kill a man a hundred different ways."

Mick's mind slipped back to that jungle. He could hear the buzzing of the mosquitoes. He could feel the sweat dripping into his eyes and smell the decay of damp, rotting vegetation. He could feel the crawling insects and the blood-sucking leeches on his skin. Mick could hear his sergeant yelling in his ear and feel the slaps against the back of his head. He remembered the powerful urge to kill that grew minute by minute.

That urge became a part of him. They shipped him off to Nam and turned him loose. That was the first time he used his new skills. On that first solo assignment, as he saw the light of life fade from a North Vietnamese commander, he accepted death as a purpose for his life. It was not something he would seek, or something that he would avoid. He lost any value he might have placed on life. He had no feeling concerning it. From that day on, killing would simply make his life more pleasant to endure.

So be it.

During his two tours in Nam, Mick had twenty-six confirmed kills. He knew there were more, but you couldn't take credit for killing an obnoxious bartender, or a fellow soldier that cheated you at cards.

"You feel anything when you knifed that guy, little girl?"

Sunny's eyes welled up, but she didn't allow herself to cry. She picked up the bag of chips from the floor. She didn't open it, but clutched it in her hand.

"Yeah, I felt a little sick, but it was a good sick. I was happy, too. I've wanted to kill those two for so long. Then you showed up, and I had my chance. At least I got Santos. Sick or not, I'm still glad I did it. I'd do it again."

"See there, that's the difference, little girl," Mick explained. "When I kill, I don't feel nothin' at all."

4

The worst part was just getting there. The creaking and groaning of metal under stress assaulted his ears. It constantly reminded him that he wasn't supposed to be in this steel cocoon, hiding under cold dark water. He was surrounded by stale air and the reek of diesel fuel, the hiss of hydraulics, and the barking of strange orders. He hated the clanging noises, and the deck that was always shifting under his feet.

Mick was squatting on the floor of the torpedo room going over his equipment one last time. He was oblivious to the comments and conversations of the submariners around him. His body rocked, adjusting automatically to the tilt and slightly increasing movements of the sub. A man had to be nuts to voluntarily climb into one of these tin cans, and then to sink it on purpose.

The submarine had to be getting close to periscope depth. Down deep there was hardly any motion. Now, the deck beneath him was moving. The inflatable raft he was going to use was in good shape. The tiny electric trolling motor checked out perfectly. He wore his wet suit over his camouflage clothing. His underwater lantern, oxygen bottle, mask, fins, and snorkel were laid out on the deck in front of him. There was a plastic bag with the map and a picture of the target. He touched a button on his two-way radio and heard the squelch. Left of this gear was a water tight pouch that held two grenades, a smoke flare, a small backup Beretta, and a pill bottle. He felt along his hip on the left and found the K-Bar knife that he thought of as part of him. His forty-five was on the right. The waterproofed sniper rifle rested in its sling across his back.

"You're up, soldier," a skinny boson's mate, first class told him. No one was allowed to use names on these missions. That suited Mick fine.

"Then let's get me the hell out of here." Mick packed and arranged his gear like he had practiced so many times before. He put everything on in its proper place. Loaded down, he waddled to the ladder leading to the escape hatch. The boson's mate already had the lower hatch open. Mick managed to work himself and his gear up the ladder and into the small compartment.

"Adios, motherfuckers," he said, as the boson's mate swung the hatch closed and dogged it down. Almost immediately water began to pour into the sealed space. In less than a minute it was up to Mick's waist. He banged three times on the side of the compartment with the K-Bar. The water continued flowing in until it was up to Mick's chin. He banged the signal a second time, and the water stopped. With a loud hiss, the rest of the compartment was filled with pressurized air

Mick put his rubber mouthpiece in, and opened the valve on his oxygen bottle. A regular scuba tank would have been too bulky, but this little fellow worked fine. It held two hours of air, and was only eighteen inches long. He turned on his waterproof lantern, reached above his head, and opened a valve that allowed a stream of seawater to enter his enclosed space. Mick waited until there was enough water above him to equalize most of the pressure. Then he grabbed the latch handles and using all of his strength, turned them until he could force the outer hatch opened. Black water rushed into and filled the remaining space. He swam out into the cold and dark. He adjusted his airflow, and rose slowly up to the surface.

Seventy-two hours passed. Under a dark, cloudless sky, a small rubber raft was floating in an unusually calm Yellow Sea. A voice came over a low frequency radio. "Turtle, this is Bamboo, Turtle, this is Bamboo. Come back."

The man lying flat in the raft smiled. He keyed his radio and replied, "Bamboo, Turtle is over Bamboo. I say again, Turtle is over Bamboo. Turtle is ready to nest."

Four nights later, Mick was in an expensive brothel in Bangkok on Pat Pong Road. This world famous street welcomed soldiers and travelers by offering the wildest of exotic foods and sex offerings. His weekend pass was a bonus from his captain for a job well done.

Mick shifted the pretty teenage prostitute on his lap so he could reach his drink. He took a long swallow. The girl was tiny, naked, and laughing. She playfully kissed his neck, not knowing she was spending her last night alive.

The part on land was always easy.

It was a night to celebrate.

5

Traffic was picking up. They were still about ten miles west of Gainesville, but the college town had spread enough to outgrow its borders. Subdivisions had eaten into the adjoining countryside. Spreading oaks dripped moss and touched branches over the highway as they neared the city limits.

Gainesville was home to the University of Florida, one of the state's premier institutions of higher education. The university is famous for its academics, its athletics, and its "Let's party!" atmosphere. Over twenty thousand freshman students study, or at least enroll there, every year. By their second year, six or seven thousand are gone. About eleven or twelve thousand survive to become juniors, and nine thousand of these might eventually graduate.

Mick missed his turn at the bypass. He found himself caught in the swirling college traffic on University Avenue. The sidewalks were jammed with young people strutting around, feeling superior. Sunny kept her eyes glued to the scene, amazed at the crowds of young people that were actually attending college. They sported great suntans, weird haircuts, and orange and blue T-shirts and jackets. They were smiling and laughing their way through the day.

While he was stopped at a traffic light, Sunny asked Mick, "You ever go to college?"

"Not a chance, little girl. My only schooling was in the Army and on the streets. How about you? Are you any good in school?"

"I don't know. I haven't been a single day since Charley took charge of me. He never would let me go." Sunny looked down meekly. Hank saw her rubbing her right wrist. It looked scarred.

"Did you cut your wrist there?" he asked her, as he pointed. "Try to do yourself in?"

"That's none of your business, mister, but I would never do that." Her eyes flashed. "You're an idiot," she hissed.

"Hey, watch out now. I'm still deciding about you. I've got to stop somewhere tonight. When I do, you can be with me or not. It makes not a shit of difference. There are plenty of places to lose you along the road."

There was a traffic jam a few blocks ahead. Mick saw a large crowd gathering around an intramural soccer field. He made a quick decision, and pulled the truck into a parking lot beside it.

"What are you doing?" Sunny squealed. "We can't stop. Are you crazy?"

"Here's a lesson for you, little girl. When you're hiding out, you want to be around no one, or everyone. Now, we're going right into the middle of this crowd. I'm going to try and sleep for a half hour. I've got to get some rest. You're going to sit beside me and wake me up if we have a problem. Grab the blanket and that guitar in the back. Let's go."

Mick put on his reading glasses and pulled his John Deere cap a little lower on his forehead. He locked the truck cab and gave a five dollar bill to the kid working the parking lot. He and Sunny walked down the sidewalk to the soccer field among the crowd. They were ignored. Most of the people were college age, laughing and joking as they walked. They were wrapped up in their own world and paid little attention to anything else.

When they got to the field where the game was being played, Mick guided Sunny to a spot in the middle of the growing crowd. The game was in progress. The teams were on a large green grass expanse with no sideline seats or bleachers. The ·crowd stood along the chalked boundaries to watch the game and cheer. Mick spread the blanket on the ground, and they sat down. The onlookers were mostly students. None of them paid any attention to the pair.

"I've got to get a little sleep, Sunny. Keep a sharp watch out for trouble." With that, Mick lay back on the blanket, pulled his cap over his eyes, and went instantly to sleep. It was a skill he had learned in prison. When he needed to sleep, he could block all distractions from his mind. Noise, light, physical comfort, none of it mattered. He could bar them from his consciousness. For twelve years he slept as much as fourteen hours a day in the midst of screaming, loud music, slamming steel bars, flashlight beams, hot and cold, wet and dry. Sleep was his one way to escape.

Sunny sat on the blanket in awe. The lean players in their bright uniforms ran up and down the field. They were kicking a ball with no real purpose that she could figure out. There were many people in the crowd, all talking to each other and laughing and cheering. There were couples that held hands, and hugged and kissed when a good play was made. It was all so new to her.

Sunny hadn't been this close to any human beings except Charley and Santos for the past four years. When she was working in the store, if a customer came in, she had to go to the storeroom. This soccer game was just great, the whole thing. The sun was shining, the crowd was fun, the sights were new and exciting.

And she was in Florida!

She absently rubbed her scarred wrist.

Mick woke up as the game ended. From beneath his cap, he watched Sunny idly pick at the strings of the old guitar. She held it on her lap like a shield. The instrument made for good cover.

The pair stayed immersed among the crowd as people began to leave the field. They slowly made their way to the parking lot. Sunny wrapped the guitar in the blanket again. She put it back in the bed of the pick-up. The trusty Chevy started easily, and they merged with the cars that were turning east.

Mick managed to drive through the rest of Gainesville without incident. He watched the road while Sunny looked out the window. Mick drove carefully, always keeping to the speed limit and obeying every sign or signal. About thirty miles east of Gainesville, he saw a large sign by the side of the road. It said,

STARKE STATE PRISON, 5 MILES
DO NOT PICK UP HITCHHIKERS

Oh shit, Mick thought. It would be just my luck if some other con breaks out of this joint today. If that happens, I could get caught up in another guy's net. Wouldn't that be the shit?

"Oh, look. It's like your homecoming," the girl said, pointing to the large sign. She turned and smirked at him.

"Shut up. I'm far enough away now that you aren't much help to me. There are plenty of deep ditches along this road where you can spend forever." He turned his eyes towards her. There was gray smoke in them.

Those eyes, and the tone of his grinding voice convinced Sunny he was dead serious. Yeah, dead serious. She crossed her arms across her budding chest and looked straight ahead. Her feet tapped rapidly on the floor of the truck. "I didn't mean anything."

"So shut up."

Mick drove down the highway with both hands on the wheel, his eyes constantly sweeping the road ahead. In a few minutes, the prison came into view on their right. It was a large piece of land, maybe fifty acres, totally surrounded by a twelve foot, barbed wire fence. Razor wire wrapped the top few feet. Inside that fence was a ten yard space, and then another fence. The inside one had large signs on it every twenty yards or so. The signs had writing in both English and Spanish, but they were too far away for Mick to read. He knew from his prison experience that they would say, "Danger! Electrified Fence," and have a picture of lightning bolts striking a stick figure.

A big parking lot occupied by a few cars served a large, two-story brick building. This building was attached by walkways to a series of smaller buildings joined by concrete walls. Men in denim coats played basketball in one open area. Others in undershirts lifted weights in another. There were tall wooden towers spaced throughout the property. Guards with guns stood inside the towers.

"Take a good look at that place, Sunny. That's what hell looks like. You never want to see the inside of a place like that."

"You were in prison for twelve years. How was it just because of a tattoo?"

"Yeah, I did all that time, and I'll never go back. I was in a bar fight in Corpus Christi. I cut a wise guy's throat. I was behind him when I did it. I got away clean, but a friend of his spotted the tattoo and remembered it. That's how the law found me, and that's how they convicted me. When I get somewhere safe, I'm going to get rid of it."

Sunny sat quietly. She thought about the way it felt when she stabbed that hunting knife into Santos. She could feel it glance off the bones. It felt fresh, and good.

They drove on past the prison without incident. Mick gave the place the finger when he knew they couldn't be seen.

"Fuck you all," he mumbled.

It was nearing sundown when they passed through the town of Starke. Mick decided that highway 100 was the most direct route to the east coast and the Atlantic. He would never admit it to Sunny, but he had never been to Florida either. In fact, other than during his years in the Army, he had never been out of Texas.

6

Less than an hour later, they were passing through the small riverside town of Palatka. It was a pretty place with lots of stately, two-story houses situated beside the wide winding river. Old brick and stucco buildings anchored the center of the town.

Most of the food from Charley's store, the tuna and the other canned stuff, had been consumed along the way. Mick was hungry. On impulse, he pulled into a little diner a few blocks before the bridge that crossed the river. The place was called "Angel's," and the sign said, "The World's Best Milkshakes."

Sunny was asleep, her head resting against the window. She looked very peaceful and childlike. Mick tried to remember ever seeing a sight like that, but he couldn't. Well, maybe there were some in the art books he got from the prison library.

"Wake up, little girl." Mick shook her shoulder gently. She opened her eyes and smiled shyly. She looked around, exploring.

"Wow. What's this place? It looks nice."

"Just another town, but we're getting close to the ocean. I swear I can smell it from here. You know, I lived near the beach when I was about your age." He thought briefly of those times. "How old are you, anyway?"

"Charley told me I was eleven when I came to him. I don't know for sure." She frowned. "I've never known my birthday. I was in Ragley for about four years. I think I'm probably fifteen or so by now."

"I'll tell you what. I'm starving. Let's just say today is your birthday. You can be sixteen. We'll get some burgers and fries to celebrate. A big milkshake, too. What about it?"

"Sixteen, huh? I like that. You think stopping's safe?" she asked.

"You never know when you're safe when you're on the run. You just figure out things the best you can. You take care of situations as they come up. We've gone just about as far as we can go. In less than an hour, I'm going to look at the ocean. Then tonight, I'm going to get a motel room and sleep in a real bed. I'm going to dye my hair and trim my beard so it will grow out nice. I'm going to get me a bottle of whiskey, get drunk, and put the TV on any damn thing I want. All we've spent getting here is gas money. We've been eating crap and sleeping sitting up. Between the guards, the trucker, the Good Samaritan, Santos, and Charley, I've got over four hundred dollars in my pocket. When that's gone, I'll get some more. Now, you want that birthday party or not?"

Sunny clapped her hands. "Hey, OK! I'm sixteen years old today, and I'm in Florida. Let's go!"

They went into the tiny diner and got their treats. After a few days of just eating canned crap and potato chips, a good fatty burger really hit the spot. Sunny ate two cheeseburgers with fries, drank a strawberry milkshake—it was great—and ate a piece of pecan pie. Mick had the same, but for his pie he chose Dutch apple with ice cream. The tired looking waitress was friendly. She chatted with Sunny while they gobbled the meal. Mick left her a five dollar tip. She smiled and waved at them as the two walked out of Angel's. They were full of tasty food and great expectations.

Next stop, the east coast.

Mick drove the truck out of Angel's and past a bronze statue of a World War One soldier. The highway carried them onto a beautiful bridge that spanned the St. John's River. Beneath them, the dark water stretched in both directions. Boats moved randomly, leaving white wakes behind them. Fishermen leaned against the bridge railing lazily tending their lines. The scene looked like a travel poster.

The pick-up passed over the bridge and into East Palatka. The land began to turn rural again. After a mile or so, Mick turned left on State Road 207. The Chevy began to move through large farms growing potatoes, cabbage, soybeans, and all manner of vegetables. Huge green tractors moved across the dark sandy soil doing their part to feed America. They passed through an intersection at the small farming community of Hastings without having to slow down.

"I'd like to live on a farm one day," Sunny said. She was watching a huge machine pull an arm of plow points through a gray dirt field.

"You can have that farm crap, little girl. I've had all the dirt digging I can stand. I was on the Galveston county farm for eighteen months. I can still smell the pig shit when I think about it. That was my job, taking care of the pigs. Every morning I had to be up and at the back of the mess hall by five o'clock. I'd load all the garbage from the day before onto a four wheel cart, and then pull it to the pens. I had to sort out the stuff the pigs could eat, and then make sure each pen got enough. Those pigs squealed like a weak man getting stabbed. That's how I finally got out of the job."

"You killed a pig?"

"Sort of," Mick grinned. "I killed the guard that liked watching me stink myself up."

Sunny frowned at him. "Whatever," she mumbled. She studied a road map that she had picked up at Angel's. "We're getting real close to the coast now. We take a right off 207 onto 206. Then a few miles down the road, we hit the interstate and cross under it. From there, our next stop is the Atlantic."

And she was right. After the turn on 206, it was a three or four mile drive to an underpass beneath interstate 95. Several miles later, they came to a beautiful arching bridge that crossed the Intracoastal Waterway. As the trusty pick-up topped the rise of the bridge, both the travelers took a deep breath, stunned by the beauty that surrounded them. The truck's open windows seemed to scoop in the smell of sweet saltwater and the sound of gulls and waves. It was low tide, a time when scattered flats made tens of islands. They saw exposed oyster beds and bright green clumps of sea grass. Heavily tanned fishermen stood balanced in short flat boats trying their luck. There were attractive homes facing them along the waterway. The eclectic houses had gray docks and sleek boats in slings waiting for the next lucky person's ride. Pelicans seemed suspended in space as they rode and dove in invisible wind currents. A few boats sped beneath them, throwing white foam behind, and leaving fragile patterns in their wakes. Sunshine accentuated the scene as if it was a posed portrait. Straight ahead, they could see beyond the narrow width of Anastasia island to the ocean.

"This is really something," Mick mumbled.

"I couldn't imagine anything like this. It's like a magazine." Sunny stared in amazement. She turned to the window so Mick couldn't see her tears.

They crossed the bridge and made a right turn. They only had to go a block or two to find a couple of restaurants, a small shopping center and a gas station. There was also a large municipal parking lot. The sign at the entrance said, "Welcome to Crescent Beach."

Mick pulled in and shut off the engine. They got out of the truck. Sunny took the blanket out of the back. She put the guitar and the few other things they had in the cab and Mick locked it. They walked across the lot to a walkway to the beach. When they got there, they skipped down the wooden ramp like a couple of kids.

Suddenly, there it was before them, the deep green of the Atlantic. They were standing on the east coast.

7

Sunny dropped the blanket at the end of the ramp and ran on ahead, her face feeling the sun, and her toes digging into the soft white sand. There were mini-whitecaps on the green of the ocean. The sound of the waves hitting shore was music to her ears. She had never smelled the ocean. She gulped in huge breaths as she ran. She was thrilled.

He didn't want to show it, but Mick was just as excited. He struggled to get off his sweat-soaked, flannel shirt. He untied his work boots and kicked them off. He left the clothes in a pile on the blanket on the sand, and set off for the water, still wearing his stiff, new Levi's.

It was getting late in the afternoon and many of the tourists had left the beach for the day. There were still several small groups scattered around, lounging on aluminum chairs or lying on blankets. There were lots of kids busy building sand castles, splashing in the tidal pools, or searching for sea shells. Their squeals of delight amused the adults as they read, or just relaxed in the sun. The gentle breeze that washed over them smelled of sunscreen and drying seaweed.

The bravest people, both young and old, were out cavorting in the sea. That's where Mick found Sunny. She was dancing in the surf, still wearing her T-shirt and cutoffs, now soaked. She was laughing with delight as wave after wave smashed into her spindly legs. After a really strong one knocked her over, she stood back up and waved to Mick. "Come on!" she shouted. "This is fantastic!"

What the hell, he thought. He took off across the beach and ran full speed into the water. He dove into the first wave he encountered. He came up on the other side, just barely in time to duck the next one. She was right. This was the real ocean, and it was fantastic.

They played in the water long enough to satisfy their immediate needs, and then they walked back onto the beach and sat on their blanket on the sand. The view before them was one Mick had read about, but one that Sunny had never even dreamed existed.

"You know," Sunny began, as she dribbled sand through her fingers, "I don't care what you think of me. I don't care what you do to me. I don't care what I've done, or even the price that I'll have to pay for it. I don't care that much if I see tomorrow. This is the best day of my whole life." She blushed.

"Well sure, little girl. It's your birthday, and it's not over yet." Goddamn. Mick felt strange. He wondered if he could ever learn to care for anyone. What was feeling supposed to be like?

Mick stood up and offered Sunny his hand. He pulled her up easily, and then shook out their blanket. They went up the walkway, stopping at the public shower to wash some of the sand off their legs. Mick eased back into his clothes. Sunny dripped dry, and then let the sun dry her hair. She kept running her fingers through it and smiling. Further on, there was a family in the parking lot getting into a van next to their truck. "Excuse me," Mick said as they approached, "can you folks recommend a decent motel around here? A cheap one?"

The father was wrestling with a folding chair and trying to shake a toddler off of his leg. He looked at them and smiled. "Crescent Beach is more condos and long-term rentals. You'll have better luck getting a motel room a few miles north in St. Augustine."

His wife nodded her agreement. "There are several nice ones along Beach Boulevard." She pulled the bathing suit off another giggling child. Pounds of sand spilled from the wet suit.

"Thank you, folks," Mick smiled back. He unlocked the truck and helped Sunny get in.

"You know who Saint Augustine was?" he asked. Sunny was soaking in the scenery. She didn't bother to answer. She spilled some potato chips on the floor of the truck as Mick pulled out of the parking lot heading north. He answered his own question.

"He was a guy that started out pretty bad, and ended up pretty good."

"What's that mean?"

"Just what I said. He was a drunk and a gambler and a whore fucker. Then he decided to go straight. He ended up a Bishop, and then after he died, the Catholic Church made him a saint."

"How do you know all that? Are you smart or something?"

"Not really smart, but twelve years in prison helped me learn a few things." Mick thought back for a second. "My first two years inside, I just played the man's game. I shuffled and 'yes bossed,' and kissed enough ass to make my lips bleed. I was constantly looking over my shoulder, waiting for some shithead to try to take me out. I was playing it safe and letting them make me over. But why? For what? I was doing life without parole. What was the point? I walked the yard alone, kept my head down, followed all the rules. I even took some classes to pass the time. I studied history, government, Spanish. I even tried to learn how to play the guitar."

"Wasn't all that good?"

"It could have been, but the screws used that stuff against me. It just gave them more to hold over my head. There was always a god-damned 'if.' Sure, I could keep the guitar an extra hour in my cell, 'if.' Sure, I could play through exercise time, 'if'. Need a pencil, some more paper? Another 'if.'"

The island was narrow here and the winding river was very pretty on the left side of the road. The sun was setting in golden streaks. Covered docks and mangrove islands competed for their eyes. A red speedboat moved rapidly down the river throwing a white rooster tail behind it. The air was hot and sweet and smelled of flowers.

Sunny saw the anger in Mick's eyes that prison memories were fueling. She stopped looking at him.

"I finally wised up. Even in prison, I wanted my own life. I've never needed company. I had to toss a guy off a third floor cell block, boil another one, and then flush another one's head down his own toilet. It took biting a guard's finger off to finish that last guy," Mick chuckled, "but after two years inside, I got my permanent cell in solitary. After that, life was OK. I was just killing time and looking for a chance to escape."

"I don't see what that has to do with this saint." Sunny was puzzled, but she was paying attention.

"While I was in solitary, I read. Books, lots of books. Books were the only things I was allowed to have in my cell, and I could only get them one at a time. No visitors. No radio. No TV. I was locked up twenty-three hours a day. At first, trying to get the words to make sense was a pain in the ass. I couldn't read very good. But there was nothing but push-ups, living in these crazy mind games, and jacking off to make the minutes tick by. I tried harder with the words, and slowly I got a little better. One ordinary day, just like all the rest, I realized I was beating them. They wanted me to go crazy and I wasn't. I was getting stronger. I began to get better and better at the books, and I started to enjoy them. The reading gave me freedom. I could read my way out of that cell."

Sunny turned to look at Mick's face.

"Once I got started, I finished every book of fiction in that crappy little library. It took me a little over twenty-one months. The year after that, I hit non-fiction, the good stuff. I started reading about people with real brains. A guy I knew had been helping to improve the library. The books got better. I started to feel myself getting smarter. It took me three years to go through that new shit. After that, I knew that information, this new knowledge, was giving me power."

Sunny was paying attention. Maybe with a library, she wouldn't have become a teenage murderer on the run.

"About my sixth year in solitary, I started reading the encyclopedia. It was a brand new one. My 'pal' arranged to donate it. The stuff I learned from it was like treasure to me. You're a kid." He smiled at the girl. "Yeah, I know. Now you're sixteen," he touched her forearm, "but still a kid." Mick looked into her eyes. "You can't imagine that kind of life, the 'no' life. There's a kind of starvation that comes with it. Then for me there came a day, just another pass-the-seconds, pass-the-minutes, hours, days, when I knew. I knew what would get me through. I started with fucking 'A'. Fucking book 'A'. There were twenty-six fat fucking encyclopedia volumes waiting for me. Each one took its turn sitting on my one shelf just daring me to finish it.

"Want to know the president of the Confederacy? Jefferson Davis. The inventor of the telephone was a guy named Marconi. Magellan sailed around the world in fifteen-twenty and made maps no one believed. Pompeii was a city covered in volcano ash from Mount Vesuvius. It happened so fast that people were smothered in place, still holding spoons up to their mouths. Romans wore white togas when they wanted to get elected to some kind of office. Chess was invented in India. I learned stuff, all kinds of stuff, and I liked it."

"OK, smarty, but I don't read so good," Sunny said.

"Maybe I'll teach you a little."

"Yeah, sure, I bet you will. Do me a favor first?"

"I'm not too big on favors. What do you have in mind?"

"Well, you know you never did pick a name for yourself."

Mick was slowing down as the road narrowed ahead. They were passing through a group of condos and entering a more commercial area. There were shops on both sides of the road.

"I told you I liked Ted."

"Yeah. I know, but you've got to have a last name, too. I thought maybe you could use mine."

"Martin?"

"No, man, come on! That 'Martin' shit is over. I mean you could use my new name. You could be Ted Cantrell."

The girl sounded excited.

"Just think about it. It sounds cool and it suits you. People would be more likely to believe you're my granddad if you used it."

He looked over at her. She looked so small, but she was tough. It was easy to forget she was just a kid.

40

"Ted Cantrell, huh. I guess it's as good as any. Hello there, miss. Name's Cantrell, Ted Cantrell. What do you think? Does it sound all right?"

"Why Mr. Cantrell, I just love your name." They both burst out laughing.

"You know, Sunny, if I'm going to be your granddad, you're going to have to clean up your language." He was joking with her.

She looked up at him. "OK, I will," she said earnestly. He realized she was taking him seriously.

"Hey, look up here." The new Ted pointed at a large store on the right with all manner of gaudy stuff in the windows. The aqua-colored building had concrete waves cresting six feet high along its roof. Orange neon signs offered T-shirts, beach towels, and great sale prices on tourist stuff.

"Let's take a look."

8

"Ragley? Where in hell is Ragley?"

Bonnie Fitzgerald was one of the top reporters at one of the nation's most respected newspapers. She was standing in front of the desk of the Editor in Chief of the New Orleans, Times-Picayune. She was slapping a stack of papers against her palm, and pacing back and forth as much as the small area of her boss's designated space in the newsroom would allow.

Bonnie was a very attractive redhead in her mid-thirties. She had green eyes that flashed when she was angry, which she was right now. She pushed her half glasses more firmly on her nose. Her full lips were quite comfortable with curse words, and she used a few as she brushed her shoulder length hair out of her eyes. "Goddamn it, Jack, you know I've got a head start and good leads on the FEMA story. If you'll get out of my way, I can have half of those bastards indicted in less than six months. It will be great for the paper, and great for the city, too. Not to mention, the story will win me a Pulitzer."

"Calm down, Bonnie. I'm not killing the FEMA story. I want it done, and you're the right reporter to do it. But it's not going anywhere, and this new thing in Ragley could turn into something big. I've got a feeling about it."

Bonnie had shared plenty of drinks and even a bed with Jack Tingsley on a few playful occasions. She knew him well. He had done good investigative work to earn his editor spot, and she admired his judgment. Of course she did. Jack was the one that had lured her over from Atlanta four years ago. He used the promise of a great bump in salary and the freedom to follow her instincts. He was a straight shooter. He had delivered so far.

"Well, what's so special about a double murder in Ragley?" Bonnie asked. "I can look out the window and see one here on any sunny day."

"That's just it," Jack said, "there hasn't ever been a murder in Ragley. Not ever. It's just a little crossroads with a few farms and this general store. Now we've got the double murder. There's a possible kidnapping, or even a *third* murder, and guess what recent escapee left prints at the scene."

"No! You're shitting me. Is it Parsons?"

"You astound me with your intelligence, Bonnie dear. Michael Jason it is. The cops all thought he would be on his way to Mexico or back to Texas, but Mick fooled them again."

"Michael Jason Parsons. One of the most notorious psychos ever. Escaped, and on the run... Yeah, I like it." Bonnie could smell the impact of the story. She slapped his desk. "OK Jack, you've got me. I'm on it. I'll let Colleen know that I'm leaving right away. I'll have to go back home to pick up a few things. I should be on the road in an hour." She turned, and then turned back. "What do people wear in Ragley?"

"They wear the same sort of things you wear, Bonnie, but they get their fancy shirts at K-Mart, and their jeans cost ten bucks instead of the four hundred you pay."

"I'll ignore that dig, and what about my first question?"

"What was that?"

"Where in hell is Ragley?"

Bonnie went back to her desk in the bull pen. Her status at the paper warranted an office, but the noise and hustle of the newsroom energized her. She liked working in the middle of chaos.

Colleen, her assistant, was standing by her desk. The young woman was twenty-four, blonde haired, with brown cow eyes and a complexion that was radiant. Her cheekbones were high, and they framed a perfect nose. She was beautiful and refused to accept it. She held a small stack of pink phone slips out for Bonnie.

No time for those.

"I'm out of here in five minutes, Colleen. You've got to help me. Call anybody important in that stack, apologize, and let them know I'm on assignment for several days. I won't be available. Trash the rest. I'm going to some town named Ragley in Louisiana, but that is only for you and no one else to know. I'll be taking my second phone so I can call in, but I don't want anyone calling me unless the president's been shot, or the Saints win the Super Bowl. Now, precious one, find me a map, and tell me how in the hell I get to Ragley."

Bonnie watched Colleen scurry off, and then sat down behind her desk. She looked briefly at some of her notes on the FEMA story. You lucky bastards, she thought. Don't you worry, I'm coming for you assholes just as soon as I take care of Parsons. She put the notes in her desk drawer and locked it.

Bonnie grabbed her purse from the top of a file cabinet. She took out a brush and ran it through her thick red hair. She pinned the loose tendrils behind her ears. She took out a small compact and checked her face. OK, but no prize. She touched up her lipstick, and put her tools away. Oh, to be twenty again.

Colleen was holding a map when she got back. "Ragley is pretty close. It looks like it's about three hours straight west on highway 90." That was good. Bonnie decided to take her own car instead of renting one.

"Thank you, sweetheart. You're the best."

Colleen sat down in Bonnie's extra chair. That was usually a sign she wanted something.

"Good morning again, Colleen. Are you here to enlighten me about something?"

"Not quite, boss. You remember the bonus you gave me for the city inspector story?"

"Yes, I certainly do." I thought it was pretty damn generous, too, she thought, and don't try to hit me up for more.

"Well, I would like some time off."

"You haven't had a vacation in over a year. That sounds fair enough. You planning on taking a trip?"

Colleen blushed, and that rarely happened. "No. I'm using the bonus to get new boobs."

"Gee, honey, why do that? You have a terrific figure."

"I guess it's OK, but I want to fine-tune myself a little. I want to turn heads when I come in a room. You know, the way you do." Bonnie soaked up the compliment as Colleen knew she would.

"If you're really sure about this, I'll let you have the time off. But you know I think you're beautiful just the way you are. There's not a man I know that wouldn't give one nut to use the other one on you."

"Boss, you're very sweet, but I'm sure about this. It will make a difference. I'll only need a couple of days and a weekend. If you're leaving town, I can have the operation while you're gone."

"OK, sweetheart. Fine. Now, besides taking good care of yourself, I want you to keep that call-in phone with you at all times. I'm never sure what I'm going to run into, and if I can't reach Jack, you'll have to be my go-to girl."

"Oh Bonnie, you're great! I'm so excited! Thank you, thank you, thank you." The women stood up and they hugged. Colleen went back to her desk with a huge smile on her face. Bonnie just shook her head. The things we do, she thought. We are all crazy. With that, she picked up her laptop and hurried from the newsroom.

When she first moved to the Big Easy from Atlanta, Bonnie stayed in a small boutique hotel in the French Quarter. She loved the flavor of life in New Orleans, and she couldn't wait to be a part of it. The food was scrumptious, jazz and blues music could be heard everywhere, and the thick Cajun accents enthralled her. She was seven years divorced. The many available men were a nice feature, too.

Bonnie loved her little house. It took her six weeks to find the little 1920s cottage off of Desire Street. It was only thirteen hundred square feet on two levels, and its floors had a definite tilt to them. The clapboard exterior needed painting. The property was in an estate when she bought it. Bonnie managed to keep some of the more comfortable antiques that were in the house as part of the deal. Since then, she had added some more pieces that she found in the yard sales that occur on the weekends in New Orleans. At night, she liked to stand out on her tiny balcony. She sipped bourbon on ice and watched while the world strolled by.

But today she was in a hurry. She pushed through the wrought iron gate, and took the three porch steps in a single leap. She had her key ready, and opened the oak door without slowing.

Bonnie always kept a packed bag in her bedroom closet for just such emergencies. Still, Ragley would require adjustments. She put the bag on her cherry, four-poster bed. She took out two drip-dry suits, a silk dress and her suede high heels out of it. She threw them on the floor, and substituted a second pair of jeans, a short sundress, and two simple cotton blouses. She put a pair of running shoes in her bag, and then kicked off her heels and slipped on a pair of sandals. She checked to make sure her extra makeup kit was in the side pocket, and it was. That should do it. She zipped the bag closed, picked up a pair of sunglasses, and headed for the door.

As she was locking the front door, her neighbor Collin called out to her. "Bonnie dearest, what are you doing home during the day? Would you like to share a wonderful toddy?"

Collin was in his early fifties. He was handsome, gay, an alcoholic, and a great neighbor.

"Thanks Collin, but I've got to leave town for a couple of days. Will you watch the house for me?"

"Of course, my dear. No one shall storm your castle while I maintain the watch."

"You're a dear, Collin. Why aren't you straight?"

"I'm just too much for a woman to handle, sweetheart. Oh, the pity." He raised a glass to her. "You take care now, you hear?"

Bonnie lugged her bag up the block to a garage she rented. She unlocked it and swung the double doors open. She threw her bag in the passenger seat of her 2008, Mustang convertible. She started the engine, and backed her car into the street. This was tricky, but there was no traffic on the road. She got out quickly, and locked the garage doors without blocking anyone. Then she got back in the Mustang and drove away. She could feel her excitement building.

Ragley?

9

"These T-shirts are three for ten dollars! How much will you let me spend?" Sunny was going through a pile of brightly colored shirts on a big display table.

"How much do you think you've earned?"

She came close to him and whispered, "How much do I get for killing Santos? And don't forget, I drove the truck some, too."

"That first little job didn't mean much. You weren't hired for it. I was going to take care of him myself. Besides, it probably kept you alive." He picked up one of the T-shirts. "Still, you did drive a couple of hours, and you checked the map for me. Let's call it about forty buck's worth. I'll throw in a ten dollar birthday bonus, too."

"Wow, granddad, that's great!" Sunny rushed off searching for the perfect clothes for her Florida adventure. Ted strolled through the big store, taking his time, stopping occasionally to touch a fabric, or to hold something up. Wearing anything but an orange jumpsuit was going to be a total change for him. He finally picked out a yellow golf shirt with a dolphin on the pocket, and a Hawaiian shirt with surfboards and hula girls. After paying for his selections, he put the golf shirt on in the dressing room, and put his damp flannel shirt in the bag. When he came out, Sunny was waiting by the cash register.

"Granddad, look what I found!"

Damn, the granddad shit was going to get on his nerves. Ted looked at the small pile of clothes on the counter. "What's all this gonna cost?"

"Sir, if you'll allow me, I think your granddaughter would like for you to see the clothes on her before she makes a final decision." The clerk behind the counter smiled at Sunny. The friendly look was gratefully returned.

Ted began to sort through the clothing. A pair of sandals was on top of the pile. There were three T-shirts with crazy sayings on them, two pairs of short pants that looked chopped off, a sundress, a floppy hat, and a very small, two-piece bathing suit. He held the suit up, looking doubtfully at Sunny. He shook his head, but put the suit back on the pile.

"So, little girl, you like this stuff?"

"Yeah, I do. It's neat, granddad. This is great stuff for Florida."

Ted turned to the clerk. "Like I said, what's the price?"

"The pants are on sale, and with the rest of the items and the tax, the total will be fifty-three fifty." Sunny looked at him hopefully.

He met her gaze. "Happy birthday," he said. And then to the clerk, "I don't need to see her wear this stuff. Go ahead and wrap it up."

Ted paid, and the goods were put in a plastic bag. Sunny squealed with delight. She took the bag from the clerk and clutched it with both hands.

When they left the store, the pair looked across the street and saw a clump of palm trees surrounding a turquoise sign. The golden script read, "Welcome to St. Augustine Beach." They got in the truck, and Ted turned back onto the beach road. They passed a large grocery store, a shopping center, and then several restaurants. They passed beauty salons and real estate offices, ice cream shops, and a tattoo parlor. There were souvenir stores and surf shops, too.

Ted passed several chain motels, but he knew that they would demand a credit card. He had the one from the Good Samaritan, but it would be red flagged by now. He might as well get rid of it. About a mile down Beach Boulevard, he spotted what he was looking for, the Shallow Dive Motel.

The Shallow Dive was obviously an independent operation. The motel was an "L" shaped, concrete block, nineteen fifties building. The structure framed a blacktop parking lot. Patches of grass spotted the ground where it wasn't paved. There were a few dying palm trees scattered about, and a couple of hibiscus plants that needed tending. The doors to the rooms were painted in fading tropical colors. The few cars parked on the lot were old and in rough condition.

A picnic table sat on a piece of bare ground that looked as if it had once held a swimming pool. There were two men drinking beer at the table. There was a ragged hammock strung between two scraggly palm trees nearby. Someone was sleeping in it.

"Here's home," Ted commented. He parked the truck and went over to a glass door at the nearest end of the "L." There was a neon sign above it that wasn't working, but Ted could still make out the lettering. "Office".

He entered a dark room. Ted realized that someone was watching a TV set on the other side of the space. He leaned against a stained pine counter and tapped a bell sitting there. "Hello?"

A loud voice barked back, "Hold your horses there. I'll get to you. You ain't the only person in this world, you know." A tall, bent old man with thin gray hair stood and turned to face Ted. He was wearing thick eye glasses. "What do you want?" he said.

"I was hoping to get a room for a couple of nights. You have any vacancies? I've got my granddaughter with me. I'll need one with two beds."

"Vacancies are about all I got. There's sixteen rooms out there. You can have your pick of ten of them. They all have two beds. Two have broken AC units. There's no TV in two, and the TV doesn't work in two more. Another one has a roof that leaks as fast as the rain can fall. You still want one?"

"How much?"

"Nineteen a night and a ten dollar key deposit."

"I'll take the best one. Which is it?" Ted counted out forty-eight dollars on the counter.

"Probably fifteen," the old man said. "It's back off the road, and the AC and TV both work. Not great, but they work." He reached up on a varnished board and retrieved a key on a rubber band. "You'll have to sign in." He pushed a spiral notebook across the counter.

Ted took the pen that was tied to it with a string. He signed his new name. Then he passed the notebook back to the old man.

Welcome to the Shallow Dive, Mr. Ted Cantrell.

Sunny was standing by the old Chevy when Ted went out to the parking lot. He was going to have to ditch that truck pretty soon. The girl, he still hadn't decided.

The sun fell beneath the horizon as Ted moved the truck to a spot at the end of the building. He parked, as Sunny walked down. They gathered their things from the cab and the back of the pickup. The key unlocked the room door after a little jiggling, and they went inside.

The room was just what you would expect. It was about 12 feet square with a tiny bathroom and a closet off to the right side. The only furniture was a wooden chair, a dresser, and two standard sized beds with a nightstand between them. There was a portable TV sitting on the dresser, and a lamp on the nightstand. The place smelled of mold and stale smoke. It was stifling. Ted moved to the far wall and turned on the AC unit. It started with a clatter that slowly settled into a buzz. A faint stream of tepid air emerged.

"This is cool," Sunny said with a smile. "I've never stayed in a hotel before."

"This isn't a hotel. It's a motel, and it definitely isn't cool."

"Well, whatever it is, it's cool to me." She threw herself onto the far bed. "Can we watch TV, granddad?"

Might as well get used to the granddad shit. "Yeah, I guess, but I thought you might want to look around. You know, scope out the place."

"Is that OK? You don't care?"

"Naw, I don't care. Just remember that every move you make, somebody is watching you. You are a cold-blooded murderer, a wanted woman. The cops would love to get their hands on you. Before you go out, we've got a few things we need to do." Ted opened the child's backpack. He took out the hair dye and began reading the instructions.

Fifteen minutes later, Ted was sitting on the john with a towel wrapped around his head. His scrubby beard was now a nicely trimmed goatee, and he held the reading glasses in his hand.

Sunny was on her tip-toes. She was standing beside him, looking in the mirror. Her blonde ponytail was on the floor at her feet. The girl that looked back from the mirror had short, spiky brown hair. Sunny was turning back and forth, changing her expressions. "I think I look older," she said, "more mature."

Ted chuckled. "You look like Liz Taylor."

"Who's that?" Sunny asked.

"Oh, forget it. Try on some of your new Florida clothes. Then you can go see what the east coast looks like."

10

It wasn't hard to find the store in Ragley. The store was all there was in Ragley.

As Bonnie was pulling up in her convertible, a pretty, heavily made-up, blonde TV reporter was speaking into a camera near the front door. There were three TV vans with their big dish antennas scattered around, and enough cop and sheriff's cars to have an auction. She parked beside a black and white patrol car and quickly ran a brush through the tangles in her hair. She checked her makeup, and opened one more button on her silk blouse. She wasn't stupid. She knew her looks opened a lot of doors for her. It only made sense to take advantage of her assets.

Bonnie took a notebook and pen from her laptop case, and started for the front door. She only made it as far as the first deputy sheriff before she was stopped.

"Sorry, lady, no one goes any further than here." The large, dark haired man looked to be in his mid-twenties. It was probably his first murder scene, but he wasn't too nervous to take a good look at Bonnie's cleavage. She smiled brightly.

"I wouldn't want to break the rules, officer, but I just have to get some information on this situation or I'm going to lose my job. My boss is an asshole. He knows how to make a single girl's life just miserable." Bonnie shyly looked up at him.

The deputy took her arm and began to move her to the side. "Come on," she pleaded, "I really need something. I can't afford to lose this job. You've got to help me."

The deputy looked over the scene. Everyone was occupied with one task or another. Two deputies were stringing crime scene tape. Another was keeping back the growing crowd. Several state troopers were moving slowly across the ground in front of the store, searching every inch of it. The whole area around the front door was filled with representatives of various law enforcement agencies, sparring with each other for access and control.

"What do you need to know?" the deputy asked, speaking out of the side of his mouth. He kept his eyes staring straight ahead.

"Just break it down for me. You know, the victims, motive, any clues." Bonnie moved so her breast brushed his elbow.

"Just this once, one tip, and then you're out of here." He looked around. No one was paying any attention to them. "Victim number one; Charles Martin, in his sixties, owned the store, stabbed in the throat with a pocket knife. Victim two; Santos Garcia, about forty, illegal, worked odd jobs for the owner, stabbed in the back with a hunting knife. The ME found a good set of prints. The cash register was emptied, but there couldn't have been much in it. It looked like a few small items might have been taken. Victim one had an old farm truck he kept in a shed out back. It's gone, and there's an unidentified 2002 Buick in there. A ripe body is in the trunk, likewise unidentified. There were some bloody clothes found under the Buick that we think might have been taken in a prison break."

A shout came from one of the men in suits near the door. "Whitman! Get that woman outside the line and get over here!" The deputy took her arm and led Bonnie to the crime scene tape. He held it up so she could walk under.

"Thanks," she whispered. "I owe you one." The deputy blushed.

Bonnie started for her car, and then changed her mind. She decided to join a crowd of gawkers across the road. There were about twenty people standing in a loose group, pointing and gossiping among themselves. Bonnie spotted an overweight woman with a basket in her hands and a distraught look on her face. The woman had on a plain gingham dress and unlaced, men's work boots. Her hair was hidden under a bandana. A bit of smooth maneuvering let Bonnie slip through the crowd until she was standing by the woman's side.

"Did you know them?" she asked.

"Know them? I've known Charley for my whole life. I've known the Mex for three or four years."

"What do you think happened?"

"I think the little bitch did it. Probably took Charley's gun and shot them both. He told me she was gonna be trouble on the first day she showed up here."

"There was a girl there? Living there?"

"Well, I guess she lived there. I never saw her come or go. Charley would drive up in the morning with Santos in the truck. He'd pull around back. Then they would come back around front and open the store. The little bitch would be between them."

"Did you know Charley well?"

"Know him? I was married to the bastard for eleven years. If he hadn't been such a pervert, I'd probably be married to him now. I wouldn't be a Goddamn cleaning woman either."

"What can you tell me about the girl? Did she work in the store?"

"Nobody knows much about her. She hid out in the storeroom when people came in. As far as I know, she never went to school, or out anywhere much." The woman raised her arm and scratched beneath it. Rolls of fat hung down and jiggled with her movement. "Charley was probably fuckin' her. He had a strange side to him. That's one reason I divorced him. I never did want to do the crazy stuff he liked to do."

"What did he like?"

The woman faced Bonnie with a scowl on her face. "Who the hell are you, anyway?" The woman stamped her foot like an animal. "My sex life is my business. Not yours or anyone else's. Get your fancy ass away from me."

Bonnie turned and walked toward her car. She was making some notes when someone called out to her. It was the young deputy, Whitman. He was standing next to the crime scene tape border. She walked over and stood beside him. She was careful not to look directly at the officer. She didn't want to get him in trouble.

"There was a girl living here," he said without looking at her.

"I know, but what can you tell me about her?"

"Young, maybe fourteen or fifteen. She was small, a hundred pounds or so, blonde hair, brown eyes. No one knows if she was here when the shit went down or not. Looks like she lived out back in the shed. The killer either took her with him, or maybe wasted her and dropped her body off somewhere down the road. He left here in the old man's Chevy pickup, but we don't have a plate." He touched her forearm lightly. "You want to get a drink later?"

Bonnie gave him her best smile. "I'd love to, but I have to be back in the Big Easy by deadline. Give me your number. I'll be coming back. I'll call you."

The officer slipped a card out of his shirt pocket and handed it to her. "Don't call the home phone," he said, and actually winked at her. God, what a jerk. No wonder she preferred one night stands.

When Bonnie got back to her car, she sat for a minute, then she called Jack. She used his private number. He answered on the second ring.

"Yeah, this is Jack."

"Hi boss, I'm in beautiful downtown Ragley. It's a shithole, but I think this story may be a keeper."

"What's up?"

"I've got a good feeling now that I'm here. Everyone in media is going to have the stuff on the murder, but the real story is Mick and some kid that was here. Now, the two of them are gone. No one knows if he killed the girl or what. Jack, this story is going to have legs. I want this one with no leash."

A reporter rarely asked for this kind of OK. It meant an unquestioned expense account, no controls on their movements, and total investigative freedom. It also meant they were putting their ass on the line. They were guaranteeing a major story. Not a below-the-fold re-cap. A major story.

"Bonnie, you sure about this? What about your FEMA scoop?"

"I'll get those assholes, too, but this is big, Jack, and this is happening right now." She pushed her hair back from her eyes. "I'll make it worth your while." She was pulling out all the stops. "Remember Miami? That was a good weekend, Jack."

"Yeah, I remember. We're definitely good together." She could tell he was smiling. "OK," he said, picturing her waking up next to him, "you've got a few days to run with it. Keep Colleen in the loop, and save your receipts. You better be as good as I think you are, and you better be as good as I know you are down the road." He hung up, grinning.

"Now the fun begins," she mumbled, "and he damn well knows how good I am."

11

Ted watched a snowy picture on the TV for over an hour. Damn, he really hadn't missed much in solitary. Sunny was still out somewhere exploring. He decided to get some real whiskey and get drunk. In the can, he had only had two drinks in twelve years. They were nothing to get excited about, just prison bug juice made from rotten fruit. Having a real drink would be a celebration.

Ted put on his ball cap and the reading glasses, and stepped out of the room. The early evening was gray and damp, but the ocean smell and the soft breeze made it pleasant. There were four men sitting at the picnic table. Two rusty bicycles lay on the ground beside them. A half bottle of rum sat on the table. Two of the men held red plastic cups. One of the men was strumming a guitar while another played softly on a harmonica. Ted walked over and stood by them without speaking.

"Hola, amigo," one of the men said. He was long haired, unshaven, and dressed in a wrinkled Hawaiian shirt. He and the other men all wore shorts or cutoffs. They were all barefoot or wearing flip flops.

"Yeah, hello," Ted responded.

"Like music?" one of the men asked.

"Yeah, sure."

"We do too, but we can't play for shit." He laughed. "Stick around, though, we usually drink ourselves good."

The man at the end of the table spoke. "You're staying here, so you're either local and broke, or from out of town and don't know what a dump this is." The others nodded in agreement. "These guys are Jake, Donnie, and

Lonny. They call me Poon. We're staying here until they tear the place down."

"Tearing it down, huh. When's that supposed to happen?"

"Next week some time," the one called Lonny said. He was bearded. His eyes were so bloodshot that the pupils were lost in red.

"So the end is near, then. Well, my name's Ted. Have you guys seen my granddaughter around?"

"If she's the little one with short hair and a big smile, she's probably down by the pier. She asked us where the kids hang out around here."

"Yeah. That sounds like her. Thanks. I'll look there." Ted started off, but stopped. "Say, you guys know where there's a liquor store?"

"Damn, Ted, what kind of question is that? Look at us. I'm pretty sure everyone at this table knows where every liquor store within three counties is. The closest one to the Shallow Dive is two blocks up. It's part of the Panama Hattie's restaurant, but the one you want is down the beach road a quarter mile past the curve. It's an ABC. It's got the best prices. If you're feeling generous, you might bring back something for us."

"Sorry pal, thanks for the information, but I'm not the generous kind. If my granddaughter comes back, tell her to wait here for me." Ted walked to the truck, started it, and drove off.

"Tight motherfucker," Poon said, "but he seems pretty smart."

Ted wasn't feeling too smart. He had to get rid of the old truck and get another vehicle quick, and where was the girl?

He found the ABC easily. It was next to a surf shop in a small strip center. He went into the liquor store and then realized he didn't know what he wanted. After all, it had been twelve years since he had been shopping for real booze. What was even available? He wandered the aisles, stopping often to look at the colorful labels and the enticing advertisements. He finally settled on a cheap fifth of Early Times Bourbon and a six pack of Busch beer. He kept his cap pulled low as he paid for the merchandise.

As he left the store, he noticed a McDonald's restaurant in the same group of stores. He walked over, entered the place, and joined a noisy line of customers. He stood a moment admiring the pictures. He read the offerings from a menu hanging on the wall, and when his turn came, he ordered two quarter-pounders with fries, and a large coke. The food was placed in front of him almost instantly. He smeared everything with mustard and ketchup. The meal was the best thing he had tasted in years. He finished it in ten minutes.

Damn, freedom was wonderful! Ted got a coffee to go and went back to the pickup. Now what?

He drove the truck to the parking lot for the municipal pier. He got out and walked to the small visitor's center at the pier's entrance. He couldn't see Sunny anywhere nearby. There were a few fishermen on the pier, but no kids that he could see on the beach. The place was certainly beautiful, though. There was a rising moon sending its multiple reflection over the waves. There was enough fading sunlight to make the sky glow. Pelicans skimmed the water. Very peaceful, he thought. He went back to the truck. He wasn't used to such calm.

When Ted got back to the motel, the picnic table was empty. The sun was down, and the light was on in room 15. As he got out of the truck with his purchases, a bright beam of moving light flowed over him. He ducked and almost started to run. The light was like the sweeping spotlights that had ended his first prison escape attempt, exposing him halfway up a twenty-two foot concrete wall.

As he watched the beam swing out over the ocean, he realized that there was a lighthouse somewhere close by. He relaxed slightly when he spotted the top of it over some trees.

As he approached number fifteen, he heard guitar music. He opened the door and found that the outdoor party had moved into his room. Two of the men from before were sprawled on his bed. The man named Donnie was playing the guitar, and Jake was blowing into the harmonica. They were both barefooted. Their grimy feet were on the bedspread. The third man, Poon, was sitting on the floor. He was singing what sounded like an old Jimmy Reed tune, holding a fist up to his mouth like a microphone. Lonny wasn't there.

"What the hell are you doing in here?" he demanded of the group.

Sunny was sitting on the floor by Poon, leaning against the wall. She was singing, too.

"Granddad! Come on in and join us. These guys are teaching me the old stuff."

12

"Join you? You little shit. You'll be sleeping on the beach if you don't get some smarts in that pea brain of yours." Ted was pissed off. Sunny had put them at risk. "Get your ass out of here while I think things over. Take these nut cases with you."

"Whoa there, amigo," the one called Poon said. He was older than the others, maybe mid-sixties, and he looked a little cleaner. "We weren't trying to bust up your party. You said to tell your granddaughter to wait here, and that's what we did. She just asked us in to keep her company. We didn't mean any harm."

"She should know better. You guys are strangers. You could be dangerous." Sunny smirked at that. She knew the real danger. "No one better invite you in here but me, and that's not likely."

The crew grumbled as they filed out of the room. Sunny was at the end of the line. As she passed, Ted grabbed her by the arm and pulled her back into the room. He slammed the door. Then he turned and slapped her hard across the side of her face.

"Don't you ever bring anyone around here, or *any place I am,* without asking me first. Put me at risk, little girl, and I will waste you without a second thought. You want to live to see morning?" Ted's voice was cold. His tone left no doubt that he was serious.

Sunny held a hand to her cheek. She said nothing. A few tears slipped past her fingers. Out in the parking lot, the men started singing again

"Go on. Get out," Ted told her angrily.

"OK, tough guy," she mumbled. She brushed past him and left. Ted had no idea where she would go. She wasn't much use to him now. He didn't really care.

Pressure was building up. Ted knew that if he didn't get rid of the truck and maybe the girl, he would wind up back in prison. There was only one person he could trust to help him, and he wasn't even sure that he was still alive. If he was, the man would know Ted was on the run. He would expect contact from him.

Ted opened the whiskey and poured a healthy measure into the cup closest to him. He turned on the old TV and flopped across the bed. The snowy picture was now accompanied by static instead of sound. Screw that, he thought. He looked around the room. There was nothing to read, and that was the one thing he was used to doing. There wasn't even a Bible in the nightstand. The Mormons must have given up saving souls. He drank the whiskey down, and savored the burn of it. The warmth felt terrific. He poured another cupful.

After his long sobriety, the liquor hit Ted hard. After his fifth cup, the bottle was close to empty, and Ted was flat on his back. He watched the ceiling spin around. He realized too late that he had put himself in a bad situation. He sat up to try to clear his head, but he was past that point. He fell back on his way to passing out. His last conscious thought was that he hoped he hadn't made an inescapable mistake.

Cheap sheer curtains did little to block out the painfully bright Florida sun. Ted woke up just after dawn, tangled in sweaty sheets, with a splitting headache and a tongue that tasted like drywall mud. The old TV was still on, bringing the joy of a blank screen and noisy static back into Ted's brain. He had to force himself to roll on his side so he could spit on the floor. Those assholes outside were still strumming the guitar somewhere. They must have been drinking all night. It didn't even sound like music.

As he struggled to get his eyes open, Ted realized that the guitar noises were actually coming from inside the room.

Oh shit.

He jerked himself awake, automatically grabbing the hunting knife under his pillow. He sat up, brandishing the blade in front of him. It was a protective move he had trained himself to perform during his first stay in prison.

There sat Sunny on the next bed, peacefully running her fingers over the strings of her grandfather Charley's old guitar. "Sleep well?" she asked. "The way you spit on the carpet was nice. Real classy."

Ted was flustered, but aware enough to relax just a little. His fear quickly turned to anger, then curiosity.

"What the hell are you doing back here? I thought I'd seen the last of you. You've got a lot of balls sneaking in here like this."

"Sneaking? A heavy metal band and a SWAT team could have come in here without you knowing it. Do you know your snore sounds like a street cleaning machine? And you smell like a wet possum."

Ted put the knife on the bedside table. "If I wasn't so hung over, I'd cut your throat," he said.

"And with you so drunk last night, I could have cut yours any time I wanted. You think you're so smart, but you make mistakes just like the rest of us." Ted looked at her. She was tiny, but there was a flash of bravado in her eyes that he had to admire.

"Listen. I don't think you know what trouble we're in. If you do something stupid, it's game over. We're both murderers. If we get caught, you'll go to prison for a long time, and I'll get the chair. We're wanted for first degree murder! Get it? Shit, you are likely better off on your own. I can give you a little cash. When that's gone, a cute girl like you can always make money."

"So you think I'm cute, huh? Then why haven't you tried to sleep with me? You haven't had a woman in years."

"Damn it, Sunny, you're not a woman. You're a little girl."

"I'm sixteen, and I'm no virgin." She tossed her head. "You must be gay."

"No, I'm not gay. I just want sex to be right, and with a kid, it's not right." The little piss-ant.

"Wow, you mean Mister Serial Killer has morals? Don't make me laugh." She leaned the guitar against the wall and then faced him. "I'd never let you anyway. Not in a million years."

"Shut up, and get some sleep. We've got things to do today. I feel like shit, and I'm going to need your help."

"Oh, now you need me."

"You better hope I keep needing you." Ted lay back flat on the bed.

"After you threw me out last night, I went out on this long pier. There was a pretty moon and lots of fishermen to talk to and watch, but there was no shelter out there. It was windy and I got cold. I couldn't come back here. You were such a shit—sorry—you were such a lousy person to me. I stayed on the pier until after three o'clock. I would have spent the whole night there, but one of the fishermen offered me his jacket. When he went to put it around me, he grabbed my crotch. He grabbed it like it was some wet, slippery fish he was catching. He was grabbing me and laughing.

"I wasn't going to take it. I stomped on his foot as hard as I could. I elbowed his eye, and then ran off of the pier. I had no other place to go, so I decided to come back here. You didn't even have the door locked." Ted said nothing.

"Tell me, Ted, are all men selfish perverts?"

Sunny leaned the guitar against the wall and lay flat on the bed. She closed her eyes. In minutes, her breathing became soft and regular. Ted could tell that she was asleep. The tough little girl rolled on her side and stretched her right arm above her head, her scarred wrist pressed against the headboard.

13

Bonnie was going nuts. She knew she had a terrific story somewhere, but where? Half of the country was looking for Mick. She had to find a way to locate him on her own, but she didn't have a single solid lead. The girl? She was most likely dead, but no one knew for sure. No body had been found. She could be somewhere hurt and terrified, still at that psycho Mick's mercy, or she could be just one more name on his long list of murder victims.

The noise and bustle of the newsroom seemed to point out that everyone was busy accomplishing things, while she twiddled her thumbs. She picked up the police report again. Nothing in it had changed. She looked at the map of the United States. It displayed a big country with lots of places to hide. She went over her notes from her day at the crime scene. Nothing.

Bonnie kept going back to the missing teen, Brenda Rose Martin, fifteen years old. The girl puzzled her. No one knew much about her. The only way Bonnie knew her name was a tip about a birth certificate found in the storekeeper's house. The local school didn't have her registered, and when Bonnie interviewed people that frequented the store, few even knew she worked there. The ones that did said she was very shy, and always went into the storeroom as soon as they began their shopping.

With little else to go on, Bonnie hired a Galveston P.I. she had worked with before to check out the prison that Mick had called home. The investigator didn't come cheap. Jack would raise hell, but she had to develop a lead somewhere.

While she waited on the investigator's report, she contacted all her sources in law enforcement. They included policemen, sheriffs, state troopers, and DA's. Even though Bonnie was known to reward those that helped her generously, none of her connections had much to offer. She only learned things that hadn't happened. No luck finding the storekeeper's truck. The girl's body had not been found. No more murders that could be tied to Mick, and show them where he was. No, no, no.

Bonnie opened her lower file cabinet and took out her flask. She didn't drink while working very often, but she didn't get stuck like this very often, either. She took a long pull. As the bourbon burned its way down her throat, the intercom on her desk buzzed. She hit the hands-free button. "Yeah, Colleen, tell me something good." She held the phone against her neck and picked up a pencil.

"I can't tell you much at all, but your man in Galveston is on line three."

"Thanks, honey." Bonnie flashed on Sam Jeffers, her private investigator. He was good looking in a cowboy kind of way. She liked his irreverence and lack of pretense. The two once spent a few nights together in a Corpus Christi hotel after a bad storm and a good story. This better be good, she thought, or this flask and I are both getting refilled.

"Handsome Sam, what do you have for me?"

"Damn, Bonnie, no hello? No small talk? No flirting? I thought you said I was your favorite man."

"Oh, but you are, Sam. Give me some good news and I'll prove it to you."

"I'm going to hold you to that, sweetheart." She could hear him shuffling some papers.

"First off, I went out to the prison today. I got a peek at Mick's cell. It was still empty. Administration is waiting for a transfer to come in. It was an eight by ten concrete box with a steel bunk and a stainless steel john. He had one shelf. Nothing else. Not a scratch on the wall, a poster, a painting. I asked the guards if he took a lot of stuff with him when they sent him down for transport. Only a few shaving things in a paper bag. No pictures, no books, nothing that would help us."

"And so? Come on, Sam."

"Mick hasn't received a letter in over ten years, Bonnie. This guy was totally cut off from the outside."

"Shit."

"Hold on. Being the super sleuth I am, I got the warden to give me a list of Mick's visitors. Guess what?"

"Don't fuck with me, Sam. Let me have it."

"I plan to, darlin'. Oh, do I plan to. But in the meantime, Mick hasn't had a visitor in the last nine years. Not one. Not a priest, a relative, or a friend. No one."

"And that's supposed to be good news?"

"Just hang on a minute. Let me frame it for you. No guard has ever been friendly with Mick. He ignores them all. In fact, for the last eight years, he's done nothing but sit in solitary and read. Our boy has read every single book in the prison library, *and* an entire encyclopedia."

"Sam, where are you going with this?"

"To my gut feeling, darlin'. No mail. No visitors. No friendly guards. Where does he go if he needs help—which we know that he will."

"Sam!"

"All right. He goes to the only person he's had any contact with on a regular basis, the prison librarian! Almost every day for years this guy delivered books to Mick in solitary. You know, a librarian would admire even a serial killer if he could read an encyclopedia. Plus, our librarian was released two years ago. Double plus, his last known address was 415 Talbot Street, Jacksonville, Florida. I do believe that's east of here."

She heard paper rustling. "Meet my hunch," Sam said. "Paul Mobley, once inmate number 28553. He did ten years for counterfeiting municipal bonds, and he could probably put together a reasonable set of ID if you needed one. He's pretty old, but our boy Mick is no spring chicken. I know it's a long shot, but what else you got?"

Bonnie was weighing Sam's report in her mind. She hated it, but in the end, he was right. His hunch was all she had.

"Good work, Sam. Send me your written report and your usual padded bill. I'll get Colleen to take care of it."

"What about me?"

"You I'll take care of later. I promise. Bye, Sam. Kiss, kiss." She hung up before he could press her, and headed to the city desk to talk to Jack. As usual, he had a stack of papers in one hand and a phone in the other. He held up the papers to get her to wait.

"Don't give me that crap," he shouted. "I want those pictures by four o'clock or you can stick them up your ass!" He slammed the phone down and smiled at Bonnie. "Just a little encouragement for one of the photo stringers," he explained. "What do you have for me, babe, and it better not be trouble or cost me money."

"Then I'm in deep shit," Bonnie responded. "Look, Jack, I hired Sam to go to the prison in Galveston."

"Bonnie, goddamn it, the last time you used Sam, it cost us over four grand for three lousy days!"

"Right you are, boss, and don't forget, I had to join him for a wet and wild weekend in Corpus Christi. But look what we got. That story brought down the number one crooked building inspection ring in the city. Our circulation and advertising went way up, and there had to be some lives saved somewhere. We were heroes. Now, just hear me out."

Bonnie went over Sam's phone call point by point. Jack listened, but with a frown on his face. Then she told him about the librarian theory. He perked up some, and actually smiled when she made her offer.

"Here's the deal, Jack. I haven't had a vacation in four years. Give me a week to check out this guy in Jacksonville. If I get a good story out of it, Mick or no Mick, but a good story, you pay for the trip and you pay for Sam. No story, it's all on me."

"On you isn't bad," Jack joked.

"OK. I'll throw that in, too." That statement sealed the deal.

Bonnie rushed back to her desk, shouting on the way, "Colleen! Colleen!" Her assistant met her as she fell into her chair. "Get me everything you can on an ex-con named Paul Mobley. He did time in Galveston Federal for counterfeiting. He was released two years ago. Get me a map of Florida, and rent me a very bland, mid-sized something for a week. Jack's going to pay. Quickly! Quickly!"

"OK, OK! But don't forget, Bonnie, it's new boobs week."

Colleen rushed off. Bonnie leaned back and closed her eyes. Yeah, this was a real long shot, but her gut was grinning.

14

As Bonnie rushed from the Times-Picayune building, she saw a large crowd at the corner of the block. She could also see the flashing lights of several police cruisers and hear the wail of an approaching ambulance. She thought of the early years when she was a cub reporter. Car crashes were big news stories to her then. Thank God she was past that now.

She turned in the other direction and searched for a cab. The staccato sound of an approaching helicopter drew her eyes to the sky. Damn, not now, she thought, but sure enough, the white Bell chopper grew near and hovered a few hundred feet above her. "WARM, today's news station!" was painted in large blue letters on its fuselage. The chopper briefly tilted side to side, and an arm reached out of the cockpit to wave. Doug Brady, the station's traffic reporter, was saying hello.

Doug had become a valuable source for Bonnie. Whenever a bird's eye view was beneficial, Doug was happy to give her one. He also could be counted on to let Bonnie know first if his station had news she might want to know about. Loyal he wasn't. Handsome and sexy he was.

Doug was blue eyed and over six feet tall. He wore a sandy crew cut he held on to after a tour in the Marines. Bonnie had become more and more attracted to him this past year. The two dated whenever their demanding careers allowed.

Bonnie waved at the helicopter, and pointed to the small park across the street. It was trashy. All the playground equipment was broken, so it was seldom in use. She hurried into the park and positioned herself between two rather scraggly bushes. The chopper moved directly over her. Hi Doug, she said to herself, as she waved both arms. As the chopper tilted its "hello," the down draft lifted some of the paper trash into the air. Bonnie quickly looked around. She was alone in the park. She grinned, and then lifted her blouse up over her breasts. She wasn't wearing a bra. The fresh air on them felt great. Before she covered herself, the chopper tilted enough for the pilot to wave again. He gave her a quick "thumbs up."

That should keep him happy for a while, she thought.

Bonnie adjusted her blouse. She started to cross the street again, but spotted a taxi and flagged him to a stop. "The Hertz rental lot," she told the driver. The drive took only about ten minutes. She spent the time looking out the window at traffic, and trying to imagine the coming challenge.

After picking up a dull gray, Toyota Corolla, Bonnie drove to her house and picked up some clothes for the trip. She repacked her suitcase with a digital camera, some shorts and light tops, extra sandals, and as an afterthought, two of her bikinis. Well, it was Florida. If nothing panned out, she could work on her tan.

She was locking the house when Collin called to her from his porch, "Darling! Are you rushing off again so soon? I'm beginning to feel downright discriminated against. I have the loveliest roses blooming in my garden. You must see them. There's also an ice cold pitcher of freshly mixed martinis that I'm dying to share with you. We could sit outside and catch up."

"You know I would love to, Collin, but I am borderline crazy for time. I'm going to Florida. What about Todd, sweetheart?"

"I never want to hear that terrible 'T' name again. If you stayed home and visited with your friends occasionally, you would know that he stomped all over my dignity and broke my heart."

"Oh, I'm so sorry, honey, but there will be other men. They will line up to get to be with you. You be brave, now, but I really have to go."

"In that?" Collin was pointing incredulously at the Toyota. "I didn't realize you were having such tough times. It must be a bad month for all of us."

"They happen, Collin. Bye." Bonnie blew him a kiss, threw her bag in the back seat, and hurriedly started the small car and pulled away.

Bonnie kept the road map in her lap even though it wouldn't be necessary until she hit the Florida state line. The Sunshine State was a little over three hundred miles away. The little Corolla didn't have anything like the power of her Mustang, but it purred along. She maintained a steady eighty. Passing was a little tricky, but Bonnie soon got the hang of it. Since she could end up paying for everything on the trip, the good thing was that the little car used hardly any gas.

About the time Bonnie was refilling the Toyota, Sunny was putting on her first bikini. She was going for a quick jump in the ocean before she had to help Ted. He was sitting on his bed, studying his map. Jacksonville was about forty miles north. He didn't know if Paul was still there, or if he was even alive, but he had no one else to go to. He had to get some ID that didn't show him as an established murder victim. He had an old phone number from a couple of years ago, but if it was still in service, the cops might have figured out his problem and tapped the phone. Mick decided to go to Jacksonville and look around. He needed to either see Paul in the flesh, or make a new plan and start killing again.

"What time do you need me back, Ted?" Sunny asked.

"Girl, you don't have a watch, so the time doesn't matter. Check the sun. I want to be where we're going a little after dark."

"Where are we going?"

"All you need to know is that it will take about an hour to get there, so you be sure to have your ass back here before sunset. Got it?"

"Yeah, I've got it, but tell me, Ted, you getting rid of me tonight? Killing me? Is that what this is about?"

"No. I told you, I need you to help me with something. Why would I kill you now?"

Bonnie paid for her gas, bought a bag of chips and a tall beer, and got back on the road. She was normally very careful about what she ate. After all, she wasn't a teenager anymore. Even though her body was holding up well, it couldn't stay in its current shape forever. Still, she was technically on vacation. Screw it. She popped the top on the beer and used it to wash down a mouthful of chips. The tall can felt good when she put it between her legs.

As Bonnie cruised along Interstate 10, she tried to imagine what a man that was suddenly and unexpectedly released from a long-term stay in prison would do. Of course, he would need money. After three and possibly four murders, Mick surely had some cash. Probably not a lot, but some.

He would want a weapon. Mick had a pistol and at least a knife or two, and he was trained to be deadly with his hands.

He would want a woman. Mick had the girl as his hostage. He could force her to give him all the sex he wanted.

Bonnie noticed the cool of the beer can between her legs. She lifted it and took a swallow. Without thinking, she had nearly finished the chips. She opened her window a crack. She could smell the hot asphalt and the pines along the highway.

Mick was smart enough to know that the IDs from his victims would be monitored. He would have to get new ID. But would he go for help to his friend, the librarian and counterfeiter? Or could he have another source that Sam didn't find out about? Then too, he could kill a stranger and try to assume their identity.

When she thought the whole situation through, Bonnie didn't like her chances of success. She finished her chips and drained the beer. She tossed the chip bag onto the back seat, but for some reason, she put the beer can back between her legs.

For all her talk, she really didn't get laid that often.

In her mind, she heard a helicopter approaching. Her hand wrapped around the beer can and pressed it hard between her thighs.

15

Colleen was sitting up in bed admiring her new breasts. She held a small mirror in one hand. She was examining them inch by inch.

Her chest looked great. The breasts were well balanced. The nipples were nicely in line, and just perky enough. All of the stitches were underneath her arms and nearly invisible. She put the mirror down and hefted her new beauties, one in each hand. Oh yes! She smiled. She was sore as hell, but well pleased.

At the last minute, Colleen had decided to go a size bigger than planned. She was now a thirty-six D cup. She was happy with her decision. She couldn't wait to put these puppies into action. She was going to turn heads all right. She picked up the mirror again. As she did, the private cell phone that only her boss used rang.

"Bonnie?" she answered.

"Bonnie? No, this is Sam. I was calling for Bonnie. Who's this?"

"Oh, hi Sam, this is Colleen, Bonnie's assistant. We met last year. I didn't think anyone but Bonnie had this number."

"Yeah, well I do. She gave it to me when we worked together last year. Look, I need to get in touch with Bonnie. It's important. Do you know how I can reach her?"

Sam was tall and husky with rugged features. He had a nose that had been broken several times and there was a small scar under his left eye. When you described him like that, he sounded scary, but his features all went together in a way that made him ruggedly attractive.

Colleen toyed with her right nipple.

"Gee, Sam. I don't know. If I did I couldn't tell you. You know Bonnie's rules." She hesitated. "Sam, guess what I'm doing now," she asked coyly.

"Come on, Colleen. You can give me her number."

"I'm touching my new breasts, Sam. I'm touching them all over. You should see them. They are magnificent."

"And I'm stroking my diamond hard johnson, too. Squirt, squirt. So now that we've got the phone sex out of the way, where in the hell is Bonnie? I really need to talk to her."

"Sorry, Sam. The best thing for you to do is to call Jack at the city desk. I put in the invoice you faxed, by the way. He was still screaming when I left for the hospital."

"Well, he's not done. Screaming is his way of life. When Bonnie calls in, Colleen, tell her to call me as soon as possible, day or night."

"That I can do." She paused for a second. "There are lots of things I can do, Sammy. You coming to the Big Easy any time soon?"

"Maybe sooner than you think, Colleen. You be good now, very good." He hung up. Women could be so damn stubborn.

"I always am," she said into the broken connection. She carefully checked each of her new breasts again. She smiled and planned their debut.

Sam wasn't excited about calling Jack. They weren't exactly buddies. Jack didn't like paying for anything, even top quality work, and he was also still pissed off about Sam and Bonnie's weekend together.

Well, fuck him. Sam placed the call.

After he did some pleading with Jack's assistant, the editor came on the line. "You're robbing me!" were the first words out of his mouth.

"Hello to you too, Jack. Listen, before you start your tirade, you've got to get some information to Bonnie. I know her and I know you, and I'll bet my ass right now she is on her way to Jacksonville. Am I right?"

There was a pause, and then Jack replied, "Cut the shit, Sam, what's this about?" He had to admit, the guy was good.

"After I got through talking to Bonnie. . ."

The editor interrupted, "At about a hundred bucks a minute."

"Jack, goddamn it, will you just listen! After I talked to her, I kept thinking about this librarian angle. There had to be a way to flesh out the theory. I decided to go back out to the prison—on my own dime I might add—and just go back over everything. If I was way off track, I wanted to know it.

"When I got there, I sat in Mick's old cell and went over all my notes again: the bare cell, the guard's statement, the visitor list with no visitors, the librarian. That's when it hit me. Mick never had any visitors, but maybe the librarian did. He was seeing Mick almost daily. He could easily pass messages to and from him. Sure enough, when I called the warden and got Mobley's visitor list, one person's name was showing up every three months, just like clockwork."

"So, tell me."

"One Barry Zimmer."

"Zimmer . . . no! Tony Cicarella's Zimmer?"

"That's the one. The top lawyer for the Galveston mob is visiting Mick's only connection every three months, and he's been doing it for over seven years."

"What the hell? Why would Tony Toes want to communicate with Mick?"

"There's the big question, but regardless of the reason, Bonnie needs to know she is not only chasing a certified serial killer, but she may piss off the mob along the way. She's could be getting in deep, Jack."

"But what if your whole theory is crap and Mick is in the Bahamas somewhere, sipping rum drinks, and porking black babes between kills?"

"That's a possibility, but there's a fair chance I'm right. You know it. That's why you let Bonnie take off for Florida."

Sam didn't wait for a comment. "After I got back from the prison, I called a friend of mine in the sheriff's department. He sniffed around in some old files for me. Listen to this. Before they lucked out and nailed Mick for the bar fight, they had him down as the prime suspect for six hits that had his name on them, but they couldn't get any evidence. Clean, professional jobs. Every one of those hits were contracts done for—guess who—Tony Toes."

"And? Come on, help me out here."

"And, before Mick is even indicted, three wise guys jump him in the county jail and try to take him out. They obviously didn't know Mick. He gets a minor shank wound in the arm, breaks one guys nose, round kicks another's knee so hard he walks in two directions, and hits the last guy with the flat of his palm in the forehead. The guy is lights out for twenty minutes, and drools for a week in the hospital. It was a great example of sending boys to do a man's job."

Jack could hear Sam light a cigarette, and then he continued. "Before you ask, here's my read. Tony hates loose ends. He hates 'em. I think he tried to have Mick hit before the trial. The three goons with the contract blow it. "Mick stays stand-up through the trial, sure, but Tony is still thinking, what if somewhere during the life-without-parole he's doing, he decides it's in his best interests to sing a little? There's no statute of limitations on murder. Tony thinks, I could still get the shit stick. Why take the chance? Yeah, why? Now it gets weird, but I like this part."

"Now?"

"The three guys that tried to take Mick out, the dumb shits? They all wind up in the same federal prison in Galveston with Mick. In less than nine months, one has taken a dive off a three story tier, one has been cooked like a lobster over a broken steam pipe in the prison laundry, and the last one Mick drowns in the toilet in his cell. He still has the last guy's head stuffed in the john when a guard walks by. The guard sees what's happening. He tries to pull Mick away. Mick bites his finger off, clean off! Then he finishes the toilet job while the guard runs off looking for mommy."

"Shit, this guy is a hard case," Jack said. "That's when he goes to solitary, huh?"

"Right, and I think he had that planned. At least in solitary he didn't have to look over his shoulder all the time. Mick doesn't like people anyway. To Mick, solitary is a vacation. But now, with no more chances to wipe him out, what can Tony do? Mick could still finger him at some point in the future. So, maybe Tony keeps him happy and insures his silence with a bribe."

"OK, Sam the investigator, that's where you go wrong," Jack said. "Mick's doing life without parole. He's got no family, no wife, no girlfriend. What good is money to him? None. None at all."

"Yeah, I get you, Jack. You're right, but in solitary, what *is* valuable to him? What would he want?"

"Sam, just spit it out."

"And who is his only connection?"

"Sam!"

"Do you know that the library in that prison is now the best in the state? It wasn't when Mick got sent up, not even close. Now it has three times the books of any other prison library. It has been buying a specified selection of new books every three months for years. Wonder how? Earmarked, anonymous, private donations. A different one showed up a few days after every one of Zimmer's visits.

"Now get this, the last donation, made two years ago, was for a full set of the best encyclopedias in print. After the set of encyclopedias was delivered, no donations or purchases since. I hope you can figure out all by yourself the 'who' that was behind those donations."

"Wait a minute, Sam, are you trying to tell me that Tony Toes kept Mick quiet with a few books? That's bull shit."

"Is it, Jack? They say water is priceless in the desert. Light is priceless in a cave. Air is priceless underwater. What's a new book worth inside four concrete walls where there's no radio, no TV, no mail, no human contact?"

Jack was silent. Could Sam be right? Maybe it made sense. The guy was crazy from the get-go, and Tony Toes is a wicked kind of genius. Maybe, just maybe.

"Besides," Sam went on, "Tony Toes wasn't buying Mick. He just wanted him comfortable so he wouldn't start singing. It didn't cost much or even take much effort, and it must have worked. Mick never once opened his mouth. He never ratted on a soul."

"OK, hold on." Jack was trying to process Sam's theory. "Let's just say there could be some truth to this. I'm not saying there is, but you're right about Bonnie. She left this afternoon in a rental car heading for the address for Mobley that you gave her."

"Oh, shit." Sam started hoping he was wrong.

"You know damn well Bonnie's not going to turn back," Jack declared. "King Kong couldn't stop her. So where do we go from here?"

16

When Sunny came back to the motel room, the sun was just about to fall into the horizon. She was in high spirits. She was dripping wet and her little swimsuit looked much too little to Ted. He threw her a towel, and she began drying herself vigorously. He noticed that the afternoon sunshine had added some pink to her pale skin.

"The old guys out there are having a bar-b-que. They said we could come if we want." The music and laughter floated into the room. They heard a beer can fall on the asphalt and roll a few feet. The smell of burning charcoal drifted under the door.

"Sure. Why not? We'll bring a dish. Maybe we can have a hootenanny."

"What's a hootenanny?"

"Forget it. We're not exactly in a position to socialize, Sunny. Remember? We're wanted. We're murderers." He was rubbing the tattoo on his forearm. He had to get rid of the heart and dagger. His new golf shirt was short-sleeved, so he folded a bandana and tied it over the ink. "Besides, I told you, we've got something to do."

"What do I wear, since I can't know where I'm going?" Sunny asked.

"Just put on some shorts and a T-shirt. It won't be a fashion show." He had been wearing his yellow golf shirt for two days, but it didn't smell too bad. He could wear it tonight and maybe tomorrow.

Sunny went into the bathroom to dress. Ted was checking over the old pistol when a knock came at the door. "Who's there?" he called loudly, holding the gun at the ready.

"Just me, Poon," was the answer. "Sunny said you two were going out tonight. Donnie just broke a second string on the guitar we fool around with. I wondered if we could borrow yours. I'll take good care of it."

"We're gonna be out late."

"No problem, man. I'm staying here in number nine. If you don't get back, I'll get it to you in the morning."

"If she wants to, Sunny can bring it to you on our way out. That's if you get away from that door and let us be until then."

"Yes sir, Ted. Will do, and thanks." Ted could hear the man move away from the door.

"Sunny! Get your ass out here. Let's go."

The teenager came out of the bathroom straightening the new T-shirt she had chosen. It was tight and pink and had a picture of a cartoon shark on it. The lettering said, "SWIM WITH ME!"

"You all set?" Ted asked.

"I guess, considering I don't have a clue where I'm going." She gave him a surly look as she picked up a hair brush. "I don't mind if the old guys fool around with the guitar. Do you?"

"Suit yourself. I just don't like them hanging around the room."

Ted checked the thirty-eight one more time. He slipped it in the back of his waistband. He needed to get some shorts if he was going to stay in Florida. Long pants stood out like a wedding cake at a fish camp.

He turned off the light. Sunny picked up the guitar, and they left the room. Ted locked the door carefully. He went straight to the truck. Sunny went over to where the usual group was sitting around the picnic table. There was a charcoal fire smoldering in a circle of rocks on the parking lot pavement. A refrigerator shelf was balanced on the rocks with what looked like hamburgers spaced across it. There was the smell of beef cooking and sound of dripping fat sizzling in the fire.

"Here you go, Mister Poon," Sunny said, as she handed the guitar to the group's leader.

"Thanks, Sunny. If you get back in time, we'll have a big juicy burger and some music for you." He handed the guitar to Donnie, and reached into a cracked Styrofoam cooler for a beer.

"The burgers look good. If I can, I'll take you up on that." Poon told her, "Have fun tonight," He winked.

"Sure will." She turned and hurried to the truck. Ted gave Sunny the map, started the old truck for what he hoped would be one of the last times, and drove north on A1A. The historic highway curved its way towards old St. Augustine. They passed the Alligator Farm and the mammoth, red-topped, black and white striped lighthouse. The lighthouse beam came on as they drove by, its sweeping light once again reminding Ted of prison.

After just a few miles, they crossed a short bridge guarded by two large, stone lions. As they crested the bridge, they saw the shapely spires of Flagler College pointing straight at the sky in front of them. A small park surrounded by colonial architecture was on their left. Their lane coming off the bridge guided them to the right along the bay front and through the historic district.

"Wow, look at this!" Sunny exclaimed, as Mick drove along beside the river. The harbor was filled with dozens of sleek, expensive sailboats at anchor. The current had the boats lined up like pieces on a chess board. They drove past a huge, ancient stone fort with guard towers like a prison. A man dressed in a suit of Spanish armor stood watch at the entrance. They passed milk-painted buildings that looked like they had been there forever.

The sun was down, but the brick streets were still full of tourists. People were lined up at the doors of pleasant looking restaurants. "This place is beautiful!" Sunny said earnestly, as they drove through the restored village.

"Oldest city in the country. In 1565 the Spanish started a settlement here." Ted could remember a good deal about St. Augustine from his readings in the encyclopedia. "This old town has been Spanish, British, Union and Confederate. That stone fort once held an Indian named Osceola. He was a Seminole chief. He was either the bravest or the dumbest man I've ever read about. They call this place the ancient city."

Sunny kept her eyes glued to the window, a big smile on her face. "Sure is a far cry from Ragley," she said.

"About anywhere is a far cry from Ragley," Ted said gruffly.

Highway A1A carried them through St. Augustine's historic district, and then turned east to cross another high bridge. From the top of this one, Sunny could see the town and harbor to the right. The green line of the river was to the left. The magnificence of the ocean was straight ahead. She fell silent as she contemplated the vastness of this new world.

After they crossed the bridge, they drove north. The highway led through the town of Vilano Beach. The road ran beside the sea. The waves produced a rhythmic percussion as they slapped the shore. The breeze smelled of drying driftwood and hibiscus. Gulls and pelicans flew above them. Eclectic beach houses lined the ocean side of the road. There were low clouds in shifting forms over the Atlantic.

"Sure is nice here," Sunny commented. "You think we'll ever get to live someplace?" She was enjoying every minute of the ride.

"I don't think about it, and you shouldn't be too sure you're going to live at all."

Sunny jerked to face him, her eyes flashing. "You know, you don't have to keep saying that. I know you don't want me around, and I've seen what you do to people that are in your way. Just shut up and do it if you're going to do it. I'm sick of you spouting off about it." She turned to the window. Her shoulders shook beneath the little T-shirt, but she didn't make a sound.

Ted glanced at her, but he didn't say anything. The little girl had a lot of guts. Not much sense, but a lot of guts. Hard to admit it, but he liked that about her. Sometimes she reminded him a little of himself back "when."

He could still remember. Damn, that was a long time ago.

Mick knew the routine at Juvenile Hall. The cop that was escorting him took him inside the gray brick building and down the hall to intake for administrative processing. When they got into the proper area, he unlocked the handcuff on Mick's left wrist and then closed it again around the last loop of a steel chain bolted to the wall. He pushed the kid into a metal chair, and turned to the uniformed woman at the desk. Mick gave him his snottiest smirk.

"Hi, Angie. I've got Parsons here for you." The cop straightened his utility belt and gave her his best smile. He had been trying to get a date with her for weeks.

"Him again, huh? I was hoping I'd seen the last of that little bastard." The intake clerk looked up from her paperwork. She was attractive. Coffee colored, with big white teeth, and huge breasts that rested on the desk in front of her. "His last visit he flooded his cell. When the guard opened the door, he tried to gouge his eyes out. I don't know what miracle keeps this kid from getting serious time."

"That's easy, our super intelligent government leaders. They think a fourteen year old kid can't be dangerous," the cop said. "How many times has Parsons here been to see you?"

The woman punched some keys on her computer. "This is number six. He's got a nice variety of charges, everything from burglary to assault, petty theft, carrying a concealed weapon. He's all over the board. What is it this time?"

"Another assault, this time with a deadly weapon."

"Fuck you! Fuck every one of you!" Mick shouted, jerking his wrist to rattle the chain against the wall.

"Want me to gag him?" the cop asked. He began to turn.

"Naw, don't bother." Angie said. "I've heard it all. Let him play tough. I'll just get him processed and send him off to sore-butt land. He won't be yelling like that back in the block, not unless he thinks it will keep the big boys off of him. Fat chance of that."

17

The road widened and the traffic picked up as they entered a pleasant town named Ponte Vedra. It was the kind of place where you could feel the money. Now, most of the cars they saw were expensive imports. There were no discount stores, but scores of boutiques and upscale restaurants. The subdivision entrances were heavily landscaped and gated. They passed several country clubs.

"Check that map again, Sunny. I don't want to miss the turnoff," Ted was uncomfortable in this highbrow area. He knew the old truck was standing out like a sore thumb. Why was he still driving the damn thing? He just didn't know. It was stupid. He had to concentrate on the business of staying free and alive.

They stayed on the highway until they found the turn-off to take them into the city of Jacksonville. Sunny wasn't much good at map reading, so Ted had to pull over several times to check their location. Finally, he was able to find Talbot Street. It was in a middle class neighborhood, where the occasional trees were full grown oaks, and the yards were kept in reasonable condition. The houses were ranch style, built in the seventies, with brick fronts and attached garages. The cars were mainly Fords and Chevys.

There were only a few street lights on Talbot Street. Ted strained to see the house numbers. He finally made out a faded "415" on the mailbox in front of yet another brick ranch. This one had a sagging screen door and a missing shutter on a front window. The yard was badly in need of attention. There were no lights on in the house. He parked the truck and told Sunny to sit tight. After looking around carefully, he went up to the front door.

Ted tried the doorbell, but it didn't work. He knocked once, and then a second time, harder. There was no response. Needing to know something for sure, he walked around the side of the house to the backyard. Among the weeds, there was a small concrete patio that was accessed by a sliding glass door. Ted wished he had brought a flash light, but where the interior curtains left a gap, he could see enough in the dim light to know the house wasn't occupied. There were cardboard boxes scattered on the floor, and there was no furniture. Shit. He had to find Paul somehow.

Ted went back to the truck. Sunny was leaning against the passenger door sulking.

"All right, little girl, it's time for you to earn your keep." Ted gave Sunny her instructions. The girl seemed to perk up. She wanted to be useful. She knew it was in her best interests.

The house across the street from 415 had a Ford pickup truck in the driveway. The lights were on behind flowered curtains. They could see the flicker of a TV through one of the windows.

Sunny rang the doorbell, and it took only a couple of minutes for a middle-aged woman dressed in a housecoat to answer the door. She opened it about six inches and peeked out.

"Yes?" she said tentatively.

A shout came from the back of the house. "Who is it, Dolly? Come on, the wrestling is gettin' ready to start." The woman yelled over her shoulder, "Give me a chance to find out, will you? I'll be there in a minute."

"Good evening, ma'am, I sure hope you can help me. I think my uncle Paul used to live across the street from you. That's the only address I have, but there's no one at the house. I'd really like to find him," Sunny lied confidently. "My daddy died two years ago. I haven't seen Uncle Paul since the funeral."

The woman looked the girl over carefully. She was young and tiny, with a cute smile, and a mild sunburn. There was someone else in an old truck parked on the street, but she couldn't see well enough to tell who it was.

"Tell me one more time, child. Why do you need to find Paul? Who are you again?" the woman asked.

"My name is Sarah. I'm sure Uncle Paul must have mentioned me. I'm visiting some family friends down in St. Augustine, and I sure would like to see him while I'm here." Sunny put on her best smile.

"Well, I'm sorry, honey, but Paul moved away just last month. He never spoke about you, but then he was a very private person. Me and my husband only saw him coming or going. We'd wave back and forth, but other than a little small talk, we didn't know him very well. If there's no note or anything at the house, I couldn't tell you where he moved. I wish I could help you."

"Well, at least I tried. I think of him lots now that daddy's gone. Thank you, ma'am." Sunny turned, and started down the walk.

"Oh, wait." The woman felt sorry for the girl, losing her father at that young age. "Is it Sarah? You might try checking at Paul's job, Sarah."

"Where is he working, ma'am?"

"If he hasn't quit, he's working at the New Life Print Shop. It's down on Barco Drive. They do all that religious stuff."

Sunny clapped her hands. "Gee, that's great. I'll try there. Thanks!" The woman closed the door and Sunny ran back to the truck where Ted was waiting.

"So, how'd you do, little girl?"

"You tell me, Mister Mysterious. This guy Paul moved a month ago. They don't know where. He didn't talk much, so they didn't know anything about him."

"So, no help, huh?"

"Just hold your horses, Ted. 'Uncle' Paul either still works, or at least he did work, at the New Life Print Shop, somewhere on Barco Drive. Now, is that good?"

Sunny watched in amusement as a generous smile made its way across Ted's face. She had only seen that a couple of times since they wound up together.

"That, little girl, is good."

There were no lights on at the other houses close to 415, so Ted decided to call it a night. He didn't want to hang around the neighborhood too long. Tomorrow was Sunday. A religious place, even if it was a front for something else, wouldn't be open on Sunday. He decided to go back to the beach. They would return on Monday. If Paul was working in a print shop, it was a good bet that a set of IDs would be an easy thing for him to put together.

But first, the truck.

Ted began to drive the subdivision's streets in a grid. He drove north for six blocks, east a block, south for six blocks. On his second turn east, he spotted a tan Safari van parked at the curb that looked about three or four years old. The street was fairly dark and deserted. Ted pulled the truck beside the curb about fifty yards past the van. He got out, leaving Sunny in the pickup, and strolled back. As he reached the van, he saw that the driver's side window was cracked open a few inches to release the intense Florida heat.

Perfect.

He went back to the Chevy and got in. "OK," he told Sunny, "this is what you're going to do. I'm going to boost that van. You have to follow me in the truck until we're far enough away from here to dump it. Maybe a mile or two. You have to drive slow. You have to put your lights on. Obey all the road signs. You have to stay on the road. Do you think you can do that?"

"I can do it."

"No running over anything, no dogs or gators or anything."

"Ha, ha. Aren't you the comedian."

"Let's do this. I'm trying to show my faith in you."

Ted didn't know where those words came from, but they couldn't hurt. He started the pickup, put it in neutral, and gave Sunny a serious look. He stepped out of the truck. Sunny slid over and took his place. He walked to the truck's rear end, used his knife to take the Louisiana plates off, and put them under his arm.

"Pay attention. Don't do anything but wait until I pull that van beside you," he said. Then he walked away. He wasn't used to working with anyone, much less a kid. She better not blow it.

18

Ted was pleased with Sunny's new-found abilities. She got the info on Paul from the civilians, and then she drove the truck without incident or accident, following him to a small strip center where she parked it and joined him in the van. The van now bore the pickup's Louisiana license plates. He would take them off as soon as he found some better ones, but they should be OK long enough to get them back to St. Augustine. All in all, the night had gone pretty well.

He pulled into a Tastee Freeze on the way back to the Shallow Dive. Without comment, he handed Sunny a ten dollar bill. She squealed, and happily jumped out of the van. She returned in a few minutes with a huge chocolate sundae for herself, and a double dip, vanilla and strawberry cone, wrapped in napkins for Ted.

"I didn't ask for anything," he grumbled, but he took the cone.

"You never do," Sunny commented, "but that doesn't mean you wouldn't like something nice every once in a while. Just eat it, and be quiet." Sunny held out the change, but he turned away.

"Keep it," he mumbled around his cone.

Within minutes, they had both gobbled their treats. Ted sopped up the dripped ice cream in his lap with a wad of napkins, and started the van. It sounded good. The engine was quiet and steady. There was a half tank of gas in the tank. The radio and AC worked, too. He set the AC on high and selected a jazz station on the radio. He calmed himself by listening to a moaning saxophone as he drove.

Sunny fell asleep on the ride back. She leaned the seat back as far as it would go in the van, and closed her eyes. She was out in seconds. Ted glanced at her, noting how fragile she looked when she was asleep. When she acted tough, it was hard to remember that she was only fourteen or fifteen years old.

Goddamn. Even he knew his birthday.

It was dark when they pulled back into the Shallow Dive parking lot. Something had to be wrong with the main lights. Even the neon sign at the entrance that usually read "SHAL W D VE" was totally blank. There were a couple of guys passed out on the ground by the picnic table, nested in various kinds of clutter. Remnants of the bar-b-que were visible in the van lights. There were beer cans and bottles on the table and in the weeds. Several cardboard boxes and paper bags lay on the ground. The Styrofoam cooler must have busted open sometime during the party. White chunks of it were scattered across the parking lot.

Sunny woke up when Ted stopped the van. "We home already?"

"Well, we're here, anyway. Looks like your buddies tied one on. There are two of them down for the count by the picnic table. Guess we've seen the last of that guitar."

Sunny remembered loaning the old guitar to the men. "Poon will bring it back. He's a straight shooter, Ted. He's staying in number nine until this place gets torn down. We can wake him up and get it if you want. I'd bet my butt on that."

"Naw, let it be. If he's the man you think he is, tomorrow will be soon enough. Neither one of us can play the damn thing anyway. I'm whipped, and I still have to steal another set of license plates for this van. You go on in." He gave her the key. "I'll be back soon as I can find some plates that will work."

An hour later, Ted returned. He had been searching the parking lots of local motels and tourist attractions. He found out-of-state plates from Mississippi on a similar van in the parking lot of the Holiday Inn. They were slightly rusted, and he had to pry the last screw out to free them. When he put the plates on the stolen van, they hung a little crooked. He wedged them as well as he could, and then headed for the Shallow Dive and bed.

He and Sunny both slept long and hard. It was well after ten when Ted opened his eyes. He saw the teenager in the next bed yawning and scratching her cheek. She saw him watching her.

"Morning, Mister Mysterious. Sleep well?"

Ted pulled the pillow over his head. "Don't call me that. You wanted me to be Ted, so I am. Call me Ted."

Sunny ignored his protest and jumped up on her knees. "If you don't have a secret mission for me today, granddad, I'm going down to the beach by the pier. There's a cute boy down there that can really surf. He said he would teach me." She started for the bathroom.

Ted moved aside the pillow. "Listen up, little girl, you just be careful what you do, and even more careful what you say. We're going to stay here today, then get some religion at the print shop tomorrow. I don't want to be worrying about you slipping up."

"Hey, It's my as—butt, too, isn't it? I'll be careful, granddad. I just want to have some fun."

"Have all the fun you want, just don't get too cocky. I'm going to pay for the motel through tonight. I don't want that old German prick going hard-ass on us. We need a new plan for tomorrow. I'll figure something out. Then I'm going to find a tattoo shop and get my arm fixed. If I'm not here when you get back, don't go wandering around, and don't let anyone, anyone at all, come in this room. Got it?"

"Yeah, I got it." Sunny went into the bathroom. Ted looked at his forearm. The heart and dagger had been with him since Nam. The ink had sentimental value. It marked his first legal kill. It was a shame he had to lose it, but he did. How could he change it or cover it up so the tat still had some meaning? That would take some careful thinking.

Sunny came out of the bathroom in her bikini. She looked young and carefree. She picked up the bandana Ted had been using to hide his tattoo. "Can I use this?"

"Yeah, go ahead." He was going to wear the long-sleeved shirt today.

She rolled the cloth into a twisted rope, and tied it around her forehead. It bunched up her short hair and made her look a little older. "I'll see you later," she sang out, as she went through the door. She immediately quick-stepped into one of those beautiful fall days so common in St. Augustine, and so rare a hundred miles either north or south.

Sunny walked across the parking lot, staring at the man called Lonny and the other one named Jake. They were lying in the grass by the picnic table. She was nearly past them when she heard someone call her new name.

"Hey Sunny! Over here. It's me, Poon."

She looked over to her right, and saw Poon sitting in a rusted lawn chair by the door of the motel office. He was barefoot, and had a two day growth of beard. The Hawaiian shirt he wore was wrinkled and torn at the pocket. He had the old guitar in his lap. He was lovingly rubbing the aged spruce top.

"I did you a favor last night," he said, smiling at her.

Sunny walked over to where he was sitting. She leaned against the block wall. "How's that?" Even from several feet away, Sunny could smell the alcohol fumes seeping through the old man's skin. Even so, for some reason she felt comfortable around him.

"You know Donnie, right?" he asked.

"Yeah. He's the one of your friends that's usually the drunkest."

"Right you are. He wanted us to steal your guitar last night. He was pretty fixed on it."

"Yeah? What for? What's the big deal? I'd probably give it to him if he asked for it."

"You're a sweet little girl, Sunny, but not too smart in the ways of the world. People don't usually do things without a reason." He paused to clear his throat and spit. "Where'd you get that guitar anyway?"

"Yard sale."

"Where at?"

"Where I came from, a while back." The lies came easily.

"I don't remember you telling me where you came from. Was it Louisiana? That's what the plates on your old pickup said. Or was it Mississippi? That's what the plates on your nice new van say." Poon locked eyes with the girl, and then he grinned.

"Look, darlin', don't be scared of me. I'm not gonna spill any of your secrets. I've got plenty of my own. I called you over here to talk about this old 'yard sale' guitar."

"What about it?"

"Last night Donnie was trashed when you loaned it to us. Nothin' new about that, but I knew when I handed it to him, he was getting big ideas. I could tell by the way he was looking at it. He kept turning it over, checking the neck, and looking inside the sound hole. After a time, he told me on the sly that he thought this guitar was worth real money. He wanted to take it with him when he left, but he was on a beach cruiser, so I convinced him to leave it here with me. When he wakes up today, if he remembers anything at all about last night, he's gonna want this guitar. When he comes over here and finds out I gave it back to you, he'll throw a total shit fit."

"Gee, Poon, thanks a lot, but what's so special about it? It looks just like any other old guitar to me."

"I can't tell you that. I don't know guitars that well myself, but if you'll leave it with me, and give me a day or so, I'll sure as hell find out. Donnie wanted it bad. That tells me it's worth something."

Poon continued. "I've got a friend, honest as the day is long, that owns a little music store past the ABC up near the lighthouse. His place is called Grandpa's Music. He'll either know offhand, or have a book or something that can tell us all about this sweet sounding hunk of beat-up wood."

Poon patted the guitar affectionately. "If I find out for you that this box is worth money, I expect you to throw a bar-b-que for us, right here. Burgers, beans, and beer for all the boys. Any friends of yours, too. We're all going to be homeless in a few more days. Why not? What do you say?"

"If this guitar is worth much at all, and you learn that it is and can sell it, you got a deal." Sunny reached out her hand to the old man. He shook it. She giggled, and started to walk towards the beach. After a few steps she turned back around.

"I'm going to the pier to make some of those friends to invite. Before I go though, Poon, can you tell me something?"

"That depends now, Sunny. We just agreed that most folks have secrets. What is it that you want to know?"

"How did you get such a funny name? Where did the name 'Poon' come from?"

Uh oh. The old man tried to think up a good story fast. A young girl like Sunny didn't need to know everything there was to know too soon.

"I got it years ago, little girl. I got my name when my family lived in Kentucky. Every Thanksgiving my grandma would cook up a big spread to feed an army of our relatives. She'd make turkey and dressing, country ham and biscuits, and five or six vegetables with a slew of pies for dessert. I mean it was a real feed for a couple of dozen of us." Poon reached down and picked up a bottle of rum from beside his chair. He took a drink. Then he continued his story.

"Well, when Grandma got ready to cook all of those pies, she'd tell me to go get the poontang. That's what people from Kentucky call a nice bunch of fall sweet potatoes. I'd run out to the bin in the spring house, pick out some of the best poontang, and bring it back to her. I got good at picking it out. Those pies were so delicious, folks started calling me Poon. That name has stuck to me ever since."

He took another swig. Shoot. It was just a little harmless lie. He chuckled a bit inside.

Sunny giggled, not fooled at all. "You're a funny man, Poon. Even though you're old, I think you're kind and handsome. I don't believe a word you just said, but you're a sweet, funny man." She bent down and kissed the old drunk on the cheek.

"See you later," she said, and she skipped off towards the beach.

Poon was happy with his story. What the hell. He was content playing his role as the town's lazy, country boy musician, with no money and a bottle problem. He pretended well.

He didn't have to pretend the bottle problem part. He leaned back in his lawn chair and thought about days gone by. Things were quite a bit different then. He was different then.

Atlanta was always a hassle. The traffic from the airport to the Riser Building was brutal. While his driver fought his way downtown, he sat in the back of the Mercedes stretch limousine and reread the reports on population growth, median income, and union activity. His Georgia advance staff had done a good job preparing the documents. He held a crystal glass of French champagne and sipped it occasionally as he read. He finished the last of the reports. With the figures fresh in his mind, he began to review and study the classified dossiers on the mayor and his chief of staff.

The company's investigative team was the best in the business. They did excellent work, and they knew the penalties for indiscretion. Not surprisingly, he would have plenty of leverage to work with today. It constantly amazed him the way smart men could reach positions of such power, and be such fools in their personal lives.

The governor, a stately, very married, black man in his early fifties, kept a twenty-five year old Caucasian mistress in a nice home in Druid Hills north of the city. She was a former featured employee of the Cheetah Club. That was where he planned to entertain tonight.

The governor's chief of staff was a closeted gay. He was having an affair with a twenty-two year old pre-med college student attending Emory University. The mayor had his secrets, too, but why not save them for another time? This negotiation should be easy.

The driver double parked the limo and quickly opened the door for him. He stepped out, smoothed his custom Italian suit, shot his cuffs to expose his emerald cuff links, and entered the revolving doors of the high rise office building. It was one of only three in the city with a heliport.

He was met by a staffer that tried to introduce himself. He ignored the man and went directly to the elevator. The ride to the top floor took only seconds. The governor and the mayor were already in the six passenger, Bell helicopter. It was warmed up and ready to lift off.

He held his briefcase with both hands and ducked as he ran across the roof to the chopper. The blades spun above him as he climbed inside and quickly fastened his seatbelt. He greeted the governor of Georgia and the mayor of Atlanta with a laugh and a handshake. He had to shout to be heard over the chopper's noise.

"Great to see you, gentlemen. You're going to enjoy this flight." He took a sterling silver flask from his briefcase and passed it to the governor. He purposely left the briefcase slightly open. There were banded packets of hundred dollar bills clearly visible.

The governor, a career politician, took a deep swallow and smiled in appreciation. He recognized the smoothness of Johnny Walker Blue, America's most expensive Scotch.

He settled back in his seat and relaxed. Sometimes it was booze, sometimes drugs, women, men, or money. There was always something. He took his own drink from the silver flask. Today, he was pointing out a piece of acreage to the politicians that was on the banks of the Sullivan River, less than a half mile south of Hartsfield International Airport.

Hartsfield was the busiest airport in the entire country. Unfortunately, the subject property was on the other side of the river from the airport. That was why the land was exceptionally cheap. However, if a state appropriation was proposed to build a bridge crossing the river, the price of the land would skyrocket. Upon his recommendation, his company had purchased a five-year option on six hundred and fifty acres of the land for practically nothing. With an appropriation proposed, even before confirmation the company would make a few million off speculators. If a bridge should actually be built, the profits would be enormous.

"Mr. Governor, you can see the possibilities. We both know why we're here." They were now flying directly above the optioned parcel. He gestured at the land below. With crooked politicians, he found that the direct approach worked best for him.

"Gentlemen, let's make a deal."

The conversation wasn't pleasant, but the outcome was.

That night, obviously neither the governor nor the mayor would be able to join him. That was fine, they were satisfied. A couple of their elite contributors and three members from each of their staffs would be his guests. These were the people that would actually be doing the work of pushing through the appropriation. At nine in the evening, a limousine would pick them up and deliver them to the private entrance to the VIP room at the fabulous Cheetah Club.

This Atlanta gentlemen's club was one of the world's most famous, and its most exclusive. The ownership of the nightclub was murky, but management stood behind its guarantee. Every single night at least one hundred of the world's most beautiful women would be appearing nude, and at its customers' beck and call. He entertained there regularly, and could attest that the guarantee was valid. None of his guests had ever been disappointed.

The next day he slumped in his soft leather seat on a chartered Lear jet to St. Louis. Last night's bill from the Cheetah Club was in his pocket. It came to over nineteen thousand dollars. Cheap at twice the price.

He called his wife from the plane and got the answering machine. She was angry about his missing their daughter's seventh birthday the past weekend. He wasn't getting home this weekend either. He called his east coast secretary in Baltimore and had her send flowers. He told her to keep calling his wife with apologies. He called his west coast secretary in Santa Barbara and asked her to set up his meetings with organized labor in Los Angeles for next week. He had to remember to pick up some quality cocaine for the local union bosses there. They were the greedy type.

He drank deeply from his glass of Maker's Mark on ice. He sighed. His life was a gold-plated rat race.

Poon eased gratefully back into the present. He reached again for his bottle. A few minutes later, Ted came out of room fifteen and locked the door. He was wearing a plaid flannel shirt with Levi's and work boots, the same as some construction worker might wear. Poon leaned back in his chair.

Sunny's granddad approached him.

"Hi there, Ted. Hot enough for you?" Poon asked.

"You're right about that," the man said. "Tell me, Poon, I need to get some tattoo work done, and then I need to get some more Florida clothes for me and the girl. We're short on money, so I thought maybe a Salvation Army or something like that. Do you know any good places for that kind of stuff?"

"Yeah, man, sure. You have to get out of that flannel. You'll sweat yourself into nothing but a puddle." Poon straightened in the old chair and continued. "If you go left about six or seven blocks, you'll see the FA Cafe. That corner is Pope Road. Turn left on Pope and go to the first big intersection. That's A1A. The shopping center you'll be looking at has a Betty Griffin House. It's a thrift shop. They've got great deals on used clothes.

"That sounds good."

"For the ink, turn right here on Beach Boulevard, go down to Jack's. That's a little locals' beer joint on the right at the corner of "A" Street. Right across from Jack's is the Electric Chair Tattoo Shop. Ask for Danny. He does good work fort a decent price." Poon pointed to a green and red gecko tattooed on the top of his right foot. "He only charged me thirty bucks for my friend here. I follow this lizard everywhere he goes."

Ted checked out the gecko tattoo. It looked professional. "Thanks. I'll try both those places." He moved past Poon and grasped the handle of the office door. He pulled, but it was locked. He noticed a small handwritten sign taped to the left side of the door. "Gone Fishing! Stay

As Long As You Want. Take Anything You Want." Next to this sign was an official looking demolition order.

NOTICE—NOTICE—NOTICE

This property is scheduled for demolition at 10 o'clock AM, on October 30. All personal property must be removed prior to that time. Any property remaining on this site will be confiscated or destroyed. Occupants are required to vacate this site a minimum of twenty-four hours prior to demolition. Any failure to observe the requirements of this notice will be considered an illegal act. Law enforcement will act accordingly. Demolition permits are on file at the St. John's County Clerk of the Court.

"Hey Poon. What the hell is this?" Ted was pointing at the notice.

"That, my friend, is free rent for the next few days, and then a ticket to the street." He stood and indicated the "Gone Fishing" sign. "You met Ivan. He's been managing this place for the past nine years. Since his wife ran off with a charter boat captain, he's been doing it alone. He's been one bitter motherfucker. He kept hoping she would come back. I don't know why. She was mean as hell, and ugly, too. You might have noticed he was a tad bit unfriendly."

"He's an asshole." Ted said flatly.

"Yeah, that, too. But last night, Ivan comes out to the picnic table where we were all sitting around. We think he's going to tell us to quiet down, or get the hell out of here or something. But no, Ivan puts a liter of vodka on the table and starts talking Russian to us. He's laughing and having a big old time." Poon shook his head and smiled. "We've never seen him like this before. We try to get him to speak English. He halfway does, at least enough to tell us he's leaving for the homeland. He says we can do whatever we want with this place—stay, go, trash it, take whatever we want. He tells us the investors that bought the place screwed him on his final paycheck, so fuck 'em. Then, just for fun, old Ivan picks up an empty beer bottle and throws it through the window of number six."

They glanced down at room six. There was broken glass on the sidewalk. The pieces were shining like diamonds in the sun.

"I was going to try to get him to fix our TV," Ted said.

"Just pick out another one. Kick in the doors until you find one you like, but stay away from number nine. That's mine. Number four, too, that's where Lonny has been crashing."

Ted was thinking. Is this a good thing, or a bad thing? No rent is good, and a TV that works is a plus, but what about these guys tearing the place up with their partying? Is that going to bring too much attention to the place? He'd have to let this new situation digest. In the meantime, he had things to do.

"Nine and four. Got it. See you later," he told Poon. He walked to the van.

"Nice van," the old man called as Ted got in. That's a strange one, he was thinking.

19

Poon, Donnie, and their friend Freaki Tiki used to have a hard-scrabble kind of pickup band. They would play gigs, mainly for friends, at Panama Hattie's, Jack's, Wahoo's, and RJ's Pub. They stuck with their own songs, and they weren't too good and they weren't too bad. The problem was, they couldn't stay sober and straight long enough to get through three full sets. The first one would be pretty good, the second OK, and then the third would degenerate into a mush of slurred words, forgotten lyrics, missed notes, and obvious stumbling around. Their bar tabs always ate up whatever money they earned for playing.

The bar owners quickly tired of customer complaints, and the gigs dried up. Now the only time they played together was sitting around the picnic table at the Shallow Dive. Tiki was the only smart one of the three. He found a nice responsible girl and she reined him in. She tightened his leash, hid his stash, and straightened him out. Poon hadn't seen him in weeks.

Donnie had a wife. She had more patience than sense, but she had him on notice. If he didn't clean up his act, she threatened to pack up his kids and leave him. He had a track record of working and staying at home for a few weeks, being good. Then, for no particular reason, Poon would find him passed out one morning in the hammock, or on the ground by the picnic table. Donnie would stick around drinking steadily until either his wife would come get him, or the law would.

Poon had a girlfriend, too, but she was married and just as crazy as he was. She lived in Ocala. They only got together when Josie's husband was out of town on a business trip. That only occurred every month or two, but Lord, when Josie hit town—batten down the hatches.

The two of them being together never made much sense. Josie was a nice, quiet, homebody. She was petite with plain brown hair, eye glasses, and a not-bad body. She was in her early fifties and had raised two daughters that were now married with kids of their own. During the week, she worked in Ocala as a bookkeeper for a family-owned hardware store. On the weekends, she picnicked in the backyard with her family, and went to church on Sunday morning.

Josie's husband was an optometrist. When he had to travel for conventions or ongoing training sessions, Josie would drive to Crescent Beach, rent a room with a view for the weekend, get some sun and just relax. She would sip her way through a bottle of red wine over two days, but she had never had a drink of hard liquor until she met Poon.

Welcome, disaster.

One Friday, Josie's husband was in Tallahassee for a weekend of continuing education. She packed her Volvo and drove east. For some reason, when she crossed the 210 bridge, she decided to take a room in St. Augustine Beach for a change. She thought she might go into the old town and check out some of the art galleries, or take a tour through the massive Spanish fort.

It was nearing five o'clock. Josie was tired and getting hungry, but she didn't want a full meal. She saw a little bar-b-que place on the left side of the road. She decided to stop and get a bite to eat before choosing a motel. As she parked, she could hear loud laughter and live guitar music. She carefully locked her car and made her way to a large wooden deck. It was covered with umbrellas, picnic tables, and laughing people drinking beer. There was a man sitting on a stool in front of a microphone, holding a guitar, and exchanging banter with the crowd.

Josie found a seat with two couples at one of the picnic tables. She ordered a roasted chicken sandwich and an iced tea. The man on the tiny stage started to play and sing. Her order came shortly. She bit into her sandwich and it was delicious. She sipped her iced tea. It was weak, but drinkable. As she ate, she listened to the music.

Josie had never heard any of the man's songs, but they were interesting. Lots of people on the deck were singing along with him. She asked the young lady in a tube top sitting next to her who he was. "Oh, that's Poon. He's a local," she said. "You're here early, so you're getting his clean stuff. After he has a few St. Augustine iced teas, he gets a little rowdy."

The man sang a few more songs, and then the entertainer spoke to the crowd. "What a great group we've got today! Let's have a team drink!" The members of the crowd raised their glasses. Everyone cheered and drank. There was loud applause. "One more, and then I'm taking a pause for the cause." He started singing a song about life being so good on highway A1A. Many of the patrons got up and danced. Some stood and clapped. A few sang along.

When the song was over, the man put his guitar in its stand and walked straight to Josie. "Hi there," he said, and sat down beside her. "You're new around here." He stopped a passing waitress. "Katie, can you bring us two St. Augustine iced teas, honey?"

"Sure will. Not a bad set, Poon." She hurried to the bar.

"Tell me your story," Poon immediately requested of the stranger. Josie thought he was a bit forward, but she told him a little about Ocala, her job, and her family. He was

114

very easy to talk to, and he seemed interested in her mundane life.

Katie brought their drinks, and ten minutes later, a second round. The St. Augustine iced tea that was served at this place was much better than the kind Josie was used to. She was starting to really enjoy herself.

Poon went back to the little stage and sang his way through another set. This time his outrageous songs made Josie laugh and blush at the same time. He started out risqué, quickly moved to vulgar, and then on to downright dirty. The crowd was loving it. A large family with several kids picked up their food and moved inside.

To end his set, the man called Poon stepped out of character and sang a soft sweet song about his love for his town. In it was the line, "It just might be heaven, or it just might be St. Augustine." It was obvious as he sang the ballad that he meant every word of it.

When he finished his set, Poon was ready to party. He took two more St. Augustine iced teas to Josie's table. She was feeling drunk, drunker than she ever had felt before. She liked the feeling, and she liked Poon.

That weekend fostered legends.

Josie never did get a motel room. She never did tour old town or visit the fort. She and a smitten Poon drank and partied non-stop for two full days. The following incidents occurred between Friday after Poon's last set and Sunday night.

Josie drank two full fifths of Flora de Cana rum by herself. Poon did likewise. The mild mannered accountant smoked marijuana and cheated on her husband for the first time. She and Poon were thrown out of four local bars, one of which had never thrown anyone out during its entire existence. Poon had to beg Randy, a local beach cop, not to jail Josie Saturday afternoon when she flashed the officer through the window of Poon's van. He had to park the van then, and the rest of the weekend he carried Josie around on the handlebars of his beach cruiser. Fortunately, they only crashed three times and suffered no serious injuries. Sunday at eight AM, the Beach Patrol ran the two of them off for swimming in the ocean naked at the "A" Street ramp. There were many more crazy stories, but people that knew Poon could easily fill in the blanks. The weekend was debauchery at its finest.

Poon had found his soul mate, and Josie had found her hidden self.

20

About fifteen miles before the Jacksonville city limits, Bonnie picked up a nail in her right front tire. The Corolla swerved suddenly, but she managed to get the car into the emergency lane of Interstate 10 without killing herself or anyone else. When the Toyota stopped, she put her hands together on the wheel and rested her head in their cradle, breathing deeply. "Jesus Christ, I can't die with all this shit to do!" Bonnie's profanity was like steam escaping from a pressure cooker. It calmed her.

It was almost half an hour later before a sympathetic and horny truck driver pulled over and offered to change her tire. She chatted with him while he worked, and offered him a twenty when he was finished.

"No need for that, mam. My pleasure." The man's grin revealed two, badly-rotted front teeth.

"OK, if you're sure." Bonnie gave him her best smile, a quick brush against him with her boobs, and a phony phone number. She got back into her car. She could see the trucker in her rear view mirror as she pulled off. He was standing by his eighteen wheeler, wiping his hands on a greasy rag, wondering how long he should wait before calling her.

Men were so gulible.

It was dark and Bonnie was exhausted. She decided to find a motel for the night. She wanted to get a decent night's sleep before starting an intense search the next day. After passing the "Welcome to Jacksonville" sign, she took the next exit and quickly found a Hilton Inn. Fifteen minutes later, she was slipping her key card into the door of room 106. There were two king-sized beds in the room, a huge flat screen TV, and a well-stocked mini bar. Home sweet home.

Bonnie shed her clothes and went straight for the shower. She turned it on full blast. While the water was warming, took three small bottles of Jack Daniels out of the mini bar. She emptied them all into a glass she found by the sink. She took one long swallow before stepping into the shower. Tomorrow she should find out whether this was a real lead, or just an expensive vacation.

Sam now knew that Bonnie was definitely on her way to Jacksonville. The more he thought about it, the more he worried. He knew he was just a fling for the beautiful reporter, but they had enjoyed one hell of a weekend. It left an impression on him. He lit a cigarette and gazed out of his office window, trying to concentrate.

Jack had his assistant call Bonnie. No luck. Her phone must be turned off. Any other time she would be right in his face, weaseling him for more money or special favors, but not now. Now she was off in strange territory that could hold dangers she hadn't even considered. Damn, she was a hand-full. He looked across the newsroom for Colleen, but then remembered that she was off from work this week.

New tits. What will they come up with next?

Colleen raised her arms slowly. She was very sore, but she could tell she was getting better. The places where the implants had pushed out her muscles hurt the worst. The tiny stitches under her arms were healing and nearly invisible. Her doctor said it would be a week before she could go back to work, but she knew she could handle her job in a day or two. She couldn't wait to see the reaction when she walked across the newsroom.

Donnie's wife hid the keys to his pickup and left for work before he woke up. She left a note on the refrigerator. Donnie saw it when he was searching for a breakfast beer. He didn't bother to read it. A cold, wake-me-up was more important.

Shit. There wasn't a beer left in the ice box. The garbage can was full of empty bottles. She had poured out all of his beer.

God damn women.

Donnie rode a rusting beach cruiser with no fenders into the Shallow Dive. Although the parking lot held plenty of evidence of last night's party, there weren't any people around. A couple of old cars and a bike lying in the weeds were the only vehicles. Donnie let his cruiser fall among the trash by the picnic table. He went and knocked loudly on number nine. There was no answer, but it was only noon. Poon could still be sleeping. He knocked several more times, but Poon was either missing or dead.

Donnie tried the door, but it was locked. He was hoping to get his hands on that guitar today. If Poon was dead in there, he wouldn't miss it anyway. He tried the window, but it was locked, too.

About a mile away on A1A, Poon balanced carefully as he pedaled up the road with the old guitar bungeed to his handle bars. He had wrapped it in cardboard, and that made the riding like going into a strong wind. He already had a bad shoulder from a bike wreck one night when he and Josie were bareback riding. He didn't want to go through that again. He passed the ABC and kept heading north. The noonday sun was brutal. Sweat dripped into his eyes as he pushed on. One day I'm going to oil the damn chain on this thing, he thought.

Sunny watched closely as Landon rubbed gray wax all over the top of the orange and green longboard. He was going to use it to teach her to surf. God, she was excited. Her new friend was seventeen years old and rail thin. He had a dark tan, bleach blonde hair that fell over his blue eyes, and a crooked smile. He was Sunny's first crush, and she didn't quite know how to handle it. At least her sunburn camouflaged her blushes.

Landon put the can of wax aside and stood the board on end. He smiled at Sunny. "Now we just partner up with Mother Nature." He put the board under one arm and took Sunny's hand. Together they looked out over the ocean. It was a darker green than the day before. The waves were small and choppy.

"Is that the way the sea's supposed to be?" she asked.

"The sea is always the way it's supposed to be. You're the one that has to adapt. These waves aren't the best, but you aren't either. I'm going to walk you out to where you can practice on some of this shallow chop. Remember when I showed you how to stand up fast when you feel the board catch on the wave?"

"Yeah. Sure."

"When I tell you to, do that." They walked out into the surf holding hands.

Ted found the Betty Griffin House without any trouble. It was a large, warehouse kind of an affair packed with used clothes, furniture, appliances, and kitchen items for sale. It was run by a charity. The proceeds went to help battered women. Ted decided to wander around and check things out before searching through the racks of clothes. Poon was right. Prices were terrific. A washing machine with a sign that said, "Works well," on it was $12.00. A large framed mirror was $6.00. A coffee maker in working order was only $3.00. Ted was tempted to buy the Mr. Coffee, but instead began to go through the clothes. First things first.

There was a large selection. Ted had no trouble finding three golf shirts and two pairs of shorts that fit him. He tried the shorts on in a dressing room, and almost burst out laughing. His spindly legs were ghost white. He looked like an egret. He needed to get a little sun. The price for all of the items combined was $11.00. He would have to bring Sunny back here.

On the way out of the store, Ted noticed shelves of books. Oh yeah. He loved books. They saved his life. He walked over to the shelves. He was rewarded by seeing some of the books that he had made his friends while he was in prison.

Truth was, he was much more comfortable with books than with people. He spent a few minutes just enjoying being close to so many. They were cheap. A dollar for a hardcover. Fifty cents for a paperback. He was picking out a few when a late middle-aged, somewhat attractive woman asked to slip by him. "I'm sorry," she said, "I just want to grab that Lincoln biography before someone else gets it."

"You should," Ted commented. "It's a very good one."

The woman had blondish hair pulled into a short ponytail. She was in a casual T-shirt and jeans, and she had a nice figure for her age. Her lipstick was a light red. There were tiny gold hoops in her ears. She wore red strap sandals, and smelled slightly of baked bread.

"Oh, you've read it?" she asked.

"Yes, I have. I thought the author was very informative. He stayed objective. Lincoln was such a pivotal person in our nation's history. His biography could easily have been used for propaganda, or slanted to support any number of causes."

Ted took the book off the shelf and handed it to her. He felt the hunting knife pressing against his lower back. "Enjoy it."

"Why thank you. I'm sure I will. That's an interesting theory you have. By the way, if you're a big reader, we have a nice book club that meets at the library on Wednesday evenings. There are only about ten members. You're welcome to come. Our meetings are nothing formal. We just sit around drinking coffee and talking about books."

"Oh, there's a library nearby? That's wonderful. I'm from out of town. I didn't know." Ted was thinking, this conversation seems so normal, and I'm in it.

"Sure. It's small, but it's a good one. It has books, movies, even computers. I'm going there now. My name is Katherine. Would you like to go with me? I could show you around."

"I'm Ted, Katherine. Nice to meet you. I'd love to go with you, but I have to pick up my granddaughter. Now that I know there's a library close by, I'm sure I can find it. I'm already looking forward to it. I'll keep your club meeting in mind, too. Thanks."

The lady smiled at him. Ted felt strangely uncomfortable. She was nice. "I'm going to give you my number, so if you want to go to the book club meeting, or just want some company, you can call." She took a pencil out of her purse and scribbled a number on a scrap of paper. "Well then," she handed the paper to Ted, "hope to see you around." She smiled again, gave him a silly little wave, and walked out of the store.

What just happened? Ted asked himself. He was confused. He took his bag of clothes, and without a single book, walked on out to the van. He sat there for a minute thinking. Was she hitting on me?

No, it couldn't be.

Did she like me?

21

Poon pedaled up onto the sidewalk in front of Grandpa's Music during the hottest part of the day. The little store occupied one end of a four-unit strip center. One of the units was a distributor for Datil Pepper Hot Sauce, another was a frame shop, and the last was vacant. Business had to be slow for all of them. There wasn't a car in the lot.

Poon leaned his cruiser against the block wall beside the door. He had to take a few deep breaths. His lifestyle wasn't exactly the proper preparation for a ride like the one he had just finished. He could hear banjo music coming from inside the store. He released the bungee cords that held the old guitar. He unwrapped the cardboard. He left it on the bike seat, opened the door, and was greeted by a rush of cool air and a blast of bluegrass sounds.

Just inside the door on the left there was a bulletin board where local musicians could post items for sale, job opportunities, or upcoming events. To the right, the wall was crowded with guitars hanging side by side. This line continued on around the corner so that nearly fifty guitars were displayed. Some were used, taken in trade, but most were shiny and new. In the center of the room, there was a small grouping of music stands and a display of accessories. There were large glass jars filled with picks, straps, tuners and strings. There was also a stack of T-shirts that advertised various guitar makers. The interior smelled good, like cut wood and glue and incense.

"Poon, my man! How you doing, old hoss?" The music petered out as a thin, bearded man in coveralls rose from the stool he was sitting on. He reached the hand that wasn't holding the banjo out to Poon. The man was Trey, known to all as Grandpa. He had been a friend of Poon's ever since they played the first "Flip Flop Til You Drop" charity event together. The annual bar crawl now drew a huge crowd. All the money raised benefited those with Parkinson's disease. At the end of the crawl, there was a big jam with most of the local musicians participating. The first Flip Flop was six or seven years ago. Grandpa and Poon had been swapping lies and sharing stages ever since.

"I'm good, Grandpa. Still pickin' and still kickin'." That was Grandpa's line. He laughed with Poon for beating him to it.

"Come on, you old dog, sit in a little. I've finally got Tammy to stop her worrying for a few minutes. She's letting me have a little fun. Woodsy is here, too. Tune up that guitar you're carrying. Let's put her in action, son." He went back to his stool.

Tammy was Grandpa's wife, and a damn good one, too. She was in her fifties, weighed barely a hundred pounds, and wore wire-rim glasses. Her long gray hair sprang out from her head like kudzu. Her smile was sunshiny and continual. She worked hard to keep their heads above water, both at the store and at home. The couple used any extra money they could save to go to the folk festivals they loved so much. Over the years, they had attended hundreds.

Grandpa never took Tammy for granted. He knew how hard she worked. He tried to pull his weight at the store, but he just wasn't cut out for business. He piddled around at the store, mainly demonstrating instruments and joking around with the customers. He was an entertainer at heart.

Tammy managed the bulk of the store's operations. She took care of inventory, did the ordering, set up displays, fought off bill collectors, even cleaned the place. Grandpa's value to the little shop was that he played ten different instruments, and knew nearly every musician in the southeast. They all liked and respected him, and they brought him business whenever they could. The hell with finances. He and Tammy were a great team The couple was a testament to the possibility of true love.

Woodsy looked up from the notebook where he was scribbling some lyrics. "Hey, horn dog," he called, "didn't I see you wasted at the Shallow Dive the other night? I was setting up for Ray Wylie Hubbard at the amphitheater. I could have used a few roadies. I stopped by to see if any of you guys wanted to make a few bucks. Man, you guys were trashed. I think you were the smelly dude passed out in the hammock."

"Yeah, that would have been me. I was avoiding the press. How goes it, Woodsy? Still makin' calluses?"

Woodsy was one of the best guitar players around. His voice was pretty good, but it was his guitar playing that kept him in demand. He wasn't fancy, but he could lay a rhythm line you could hang your hat on. His leads were sharp and clean, and he always showed up on time. He played with several bands around town and stayed busy. His favorite Martin D-28 was leaning against the wall beside him.

"Breaking hearts and breaking strings, man. I'm scraping by. What's that you have there? Did you get a new guitar?" The musician was only about thirty, but he had piled up a lot of gig time. His hair was chin length and shaggy, mostly hidden beneath a black pork-pie hat. He had a smile that kept the groupies coming on to him. He thoughtfully rubbed the stubble on his cheeks.

"Not really. That's why I came by. This belongs to a friend that needs money. I told her you guys would tell me honestly what it's worth." Poon handed the guitar to Grandpa.

"She must be needing money real bad," Grandpa tossed out. "I sure wouldn't be selling this Gibson unless I did."

"It's a Gibson?" both Tammy and Woodsy asked at once.

"That it is," Grandpa announced, "and not just any Gibson. This is an early, nineteen-thirties arch-top. I think I can just make out the L-7 stamp under some of the grit inside the box."

"Is that good?" Poon inquired.

"Oh, I'd say it's about fifteen hundred dollars good. That's if you want it from me right now. It could be as much as three thousand dollars good if you want to find a collector. It would take some time, but it wouldn't be that hard." He was caressing the guitar as if it were his lover. "This wood is so mellow that it wants to sing. The spruce is dark, dark yellow. The mahogany is nearly black. Perfect. If you'll let me, I'll wipe it down and put some decent strings on it. Give her a little TLC. Then we'll see how she sounds. I used to play one just like this. Your friend has a real find here, partner."

Grandpa took the Gibson into the back of the store where he made his repairs. After he removed the old strings, he wiped the guitar down with a soft cleaning cloth and a very light oil. A lot of the grime came off, and some of the scratches disappeared. He took a magnifying glass and checked the model mark inside the sound hole. Yes, it was a real Gibson L-7. He restrung it with a new set of Martin, medium-light, bronze-wound, steel strings. He was happy just to be holding the classic instrument.

For an hour or so the friends passed the Gibson around, each getting to play it for a song or two. It did want to sing. In a real musician's hands, the notes that came from it were as sweet as a dawn hibiscus. Poon was amazed. He hadn't had a clue.

Tammy almost cried during her turn. In the middle of a Joan Baez cover, she looked at Grandpa and knew that he was in love. He loved her, of course, but now he loved this Gibson, too. Tammy would do almost anything to get the guitar for this wonderful man, but they could never afford three thousand dollars. She knew Trey would insist they pay a fair price, or he wouldn't buy it.

When Poon was getting ready to leave, Grandpa went into the back room and brought out a hard-shell case that would hold the Gibson. When he began to put the guitar inside it, Poon protested. "Grandpa, I really appreciate the offer, but I don't have any money, and I don't know what my friend's going to do about this guitar. I can't let you send her guitar back to her in a nice case like this. You can't do that for nothing."

Grandpa smiled, settled the guitar in, and closed the lid on the case. "You wouldn't parade a lady around naked now, would you?"

Woodsy piped up, "That's the wrong guy to ask, Grandpa. Haven't you heard the stories?"

22

Bonnie woke up with a crick in her neck. The clock on the nightstand said 9:30. She had been asleep for ten hours. She massaged her neck as best she could, and then rolled over to sit up on the side of the bed. She yawned widely, and pulled off the Saints jersey she had been sleeping in. She got up nude and went into the bathroom. The face she saw in the mirror didn't please her. She made an ugly gesture at her reflection, and turned on the shower.

Today was important. If everything went her way, Bonnie would find the librarian. He would tell her where to find Mick. Mick would then tell her where to find the girl. The girl would tell her what they had been doing for the last week. Damn, that was optimistic. She pictured the day more realistically. Hopefully, Mick wouldn't kill the girl or her today, just for something to do.

She finished her shower, dried her hair, and put on light makeup. She put on the same pair of jeans, and then a green designer T-shirt. She slipped on a pair of white sandals, and put her high heels in her bag. She was ready.

Before leaving the Hilton, Bonnie accepted part of the free breakfast, taking a muffin and coffee. She glanced over a copy of USA Today, and then got a more detailed Jacksonville map from the desk clerk. She studied it while she finished her coffee. She had to determine her route to Talbot Street.

Here goes nothing, she thought.

Talbot was only six miles and three turns away. Bonnie pulled onto the quiet street and immediately slowed down to get a feel for the neighborhood. There was not much about it that stood out. It appeared lower to middle class, ranch houses, lots of kids, lots of blue collar pickups and vans. Many of the vehicles had magnetic signs on their sides advertising lawn care or pool service or aluminum siding. Small mom-and-pop type businesses. It was before lunchtime. Several mothers and their kids were playing in the yards. A standard brick ranch on Bonnie's right side had a faded "415" painted on the mailbox. The yard needed cutting and the screen door was sagging on its hinges. It looked vacant.

Bonnie parked the Corolla in the driveway. She got out and went to the door, but before knocking, she looked through a narrow window beside it. She could see that the house wasn't occupied. She walked around the side of it anyway, just to make sure. Through a sliding glass door in back, she could see clearly that the place had been emptied out. Newspapers and a few cardboard boxes were scattered about, but there was no visible furniture.

What now?

Bonnie started back to the car. From the front yard, she could see a woman in shorts and a halter top watching three small children in front of the house across the street. The woman was sitting in a lawn chair drinking a beer. The kids were jumping in and out of a kiddies' pool on the grass. She could hear them shrieking with delight.

Bonnie changed direction and walked across the street. She approached the woman with a big smile. She got a frown in return. "Hi there," she began, "I'm an attorney. I'm looking for Mr. Paul Mobley. I have some very good news for him. He's due to come into some money."

"I wish you had some news like that for me, honey. I could sure use it." The hefty woman took a deep swallow of her beer.

"I see his house is vacant. 415 Talbot is the only address my firm has for him. Do you know where Mr. Mobley might have moved?"

"Not a clue, but if this place gets any more like Grand Central Station, I'm damn sure going to move myself. Nearly three years Paul lives here. He keeps to himself. Never any noise, never has a visitor. He moves, and now the whole friggin' world wants to find him. It's like he was a rock star hiding from the press or something."

"I'm sorry, did someone else from the firm already inquire about Mr. Mobley?" Uh oh, Bonnie thought. Mick might have beaten her here.

"Well, let's see. First it was his niece at ten o'clock at night. A girl her age shouldn't have been out of bed, much less knocking on stranger's doors. Then it's Mister White and Mr. Black. They drop by at midnight with a 'job opportunity' for Paul. At midnight! Now it's you. Paul moved about a month ago, and I'm so glad." Bonnie felt a tingle on the back of her neck. Something big was going on. She masked her excitement.

"Actually, Mr. Mobley's niece is mentioned in the will, too. I'd like to locate her as well. Would you know where either one of them could be found? I'd be happy to pay a finder's fee."

The woman's frown vanished, and her face lit up. "Like, how much?"

"For initial information, one hundred dollars." Bonnie took a one hundred dollar bill from her purse. As soon as she showed it to the woman, she started talking.

"All I know is that Paul might still be working at New Life Printing on Barco Drive. He worked there for a year or so. I'm sure of that. The niece? She said she was staying with friends in St. Augustine Beach. She didn't say who or where or anything." The woman reached for the bill. Bonnie pulled it back.

"Did you see how the girl got here? What kind of car she was in?"

"It wasn't a car. It was an old pickup, kind of brown." Bingo! All the way from Ragley.

"Did you see who was driving it?" She gave the hundred to the woman. She stuffed it down her blouse.

"Not really. I think he was a white guy. He had on a ball cap, though, and I think he had a beard, one of those ones that just grow on your chin. The girl came to the door, but the guy driving stayed in the truck. It was dark out on the street."

"I'll tell you what," Bonnie wanted all the information she could get, "I've got another hundred for you if you tell me about the two guys that had the job opportunity for Mr. Mobley."

"Are you kidding? Sure. You must be Santa Claus or something. One was white. One was black. They both were big guys with lots of muscles. They were wearing suits. In this heat, they were wearing suits." The woman took another swig of her beer. "The white guy had this dark, shiny hair pulled back in a short ponytail. The black guy had his head shaved. You know, all skull. They were polite, but they were scary looking. I mean, it was midnight. I never took the chain off the door."

"Well, that's great information. I'm sure when I find Mr. Mobley, he will be very grateful."

Bonnie gave her the other hundred and started walking back to her car. She heard the woman mumble, "Attorney, my ass."

The kids had never stopped screaming.

Some days, getting out of bed was worth it.

Bonnie found a Starbucks a mile or so away. She parked in front of it and went in. She ordered a Columbian dark roast. When it came, she took it to a small table where she could organize notes. She was convinced that she was on the right track.

It looked like Sam's theory was panning out so far. Now, she had a more complete theory of her own. The girl was alive, and she was with Mick. They were together somewhere here in the area. Mick was able to control her somehow while he was looking for Paul, and evidently someone else was looking for Mobley, too. They were probably looking for Paul to get to Mick. Mick wasn't likely to know how close he was to being found. Shit, this was big! She downed her coffee, and called Jack in the middle of her caffeine rush.

Julie, Jack's assistant, put her straight through.

"Bonnie, goddamn it! Why haven't you called in? I've been going bat shit trying to reach you." Jack was in his usual foul mood.

"So you missed me. That's nice, Jack. Now, you calm your little ass down or I'm going to hang up on you."

"Don't you dare. . ." he started.

"Jack, I mean it."

There was silence on the line. Bonnie could hear Jack taking deep breaths, and then lighting a cigarette. He exhaled, and then said in a softer tone, "Bonnie, I've been trying to reach you to warn you that you may be dealing with some very, very bad people. I am concerned for your welfare." His voice was rising and she could sense that he was starting to stand up. "I didn't send you to Florida to get killed. You can do that here. I may even take care of it myself!" He was yelling again.

"I think I'm ahead of you, Jack. These bad people, would they be the kind that might send a couple of shooters over here?"

"That's the kind. Bonnie, I'm serious. Tony Toes, the mob boss in Galveston, might be mixed up in this thing somehow. He is nobody to mess with."

"Oh shit, I know all about Toes. I did a short piece on the Texas mob when I was still working in Atlanta. He's as crazy as Mick. He's just never slipped up."

Tony Toes ran all of the organized crime in Galveston. He had his hands in everything from gambling and prostitution, to heroin sales, armed robbery, and murder. He owned the local politicians and the cops. No one so far could get to him. He showed no mercy to those who tried.

Toes got his street name while he was still in his teens. After he made his third kill, he had a double cheese pizza delivered to his victim's family. It was topped with mushrooms, pepperoni, and all ten of the man's toes.

"So now you see why I'm concerned," Jack said. He was slightly calmer. "I think you ought to come back. I'll pay the freight. You can get back on the FEMA story. I know you've got a lot of good dirt together for that one."

"Not on your life, Jack. This Ragley story is going to be huge. I'm here and on it. Don't even think I'm leaving it to anyone else. You wouldn't, and I won't either."

"Bonnie, damn it, I can't afford to lose you. Let this one go . . . "

"No way, Jack. Listen to what I've got so far." Bonnie ran the whole thing down for him, step by step. When she finished, she told him that she thought the girl was still alive, and that she had a plan to find her. Then she hung up, and shut off her phone. She pictured Jack screaming into the phone, turning red, then purple, then smashing the phone against the desk. She had to laugh.

"OK, you smart shit," she told herself, "now you have to deliver.

23

"Want another one, Sam?"

The bartender was a pretty girl in her late twenties. She was working her way through cosmetology school, and had a new hairstyle every time the investigator saw her. Tonight, her normally blonde locks were in a twisted ponytail with colored streaks a strange shade of blue. She wore long, fake nails to match. Her name was Sandy, and she always paid a lot of attention to Sam.

"Yeah, I guess so. Switch me over to Bushmill's Irish, Sandy. I want to look over the four leaf clover." He picked a few peanuts from the bowl on the bar. The Billy Club was a drinker's dive frequented primarily by newspaper guys, ambulance chasers, cops, ex-cops, and cop groupies. The occasional hooker usually dropped by. It was early and Sam was one of only five or six patrons at the bar.

Sandy selected a bottle of Bushmill's Black and poured Sam a double. "You must be sitting on a big problem, Sam. You don't usually switch over until right before closing." It was nine thirty. "Bobby comes in to relieve me in half an hour. That's in case you want someone to talk to." She put her hand over his on the bar, and leaned forward enough to display plenty of cleavage. The offer was obvious. Sam was tempted.

"You're the sweetest, babe. You know you are, but I've got a friend that might be in big trouble, and I don't know what I can do about it. It's heavy on my mind. I don't think I would be good company tonight." He took out a cigarette. Sandy lit it for him. "That doesn't mean that another time, another place ... " He let the words hang in the air.

Sandy smiled. "You're cute, Sam, but a girl can only wait so long. You should know, a man gets only so many chances." She pinched his cheek, picked up his bowl of peanuts, and walked to the other end of the bar. She set down the bowl, glanced back at him, and began chatting with a young, off-duty detective that was well into the sauce.

Sam hadn't heard from Bonnie in three days. She hadn't returned any of his calls to her house or to her office. She hadn't responded to his messages, and that damn Colleen was still refusing to give him Bonnie's private number. If she was telling the truth, Bonnie hadn't called her either. He felt helpless. He had to do something.

Sam crushed out his cigarette and put two twenties on the bar. He gave a wave to Sandy as he was leaving, but she ignored him.

Tough times call for tough choices. Sam went back to his office. He rented a thousand square feet in a modest, three-story office building near the city center. He let himself in the building, and took the stairs to the upper floor. He unlocked his office and turned on the lights. The place was not impressive. There was a wooden receptionist desk with a computer and multi-line phone on it. Three metal, army surplus desks were lined against the right wall, with a wooden chair in front of each one. The desks had stacks of files scattered on top of them. There were a few Crime Stopper posters tacked on the walls. A worn couch and a bank of dented file cabinets completed the decor. Behind the reception area, there was a door leading to Sam's office. He opened it, and turned on his lights.

Welcome back to nowhere.

Sam didn't sit at his antique oak desk. Instead, he walked to the tall file cabinet closest to the window. He opened the middle drawer and shuffled through a few files before selecting one. He closed the drawer, and took the file on Anthony Cicarella back to his desk. He sat down in his swivel chair.

Ok, Toes, let's see what you might be up to.

It was past midnight when Sam closed the file. He was bushed. He got up, turned off his lights, locked up, and went home. Tomorrow would come soon enough.

His apartment was in a decent complex with a courtyard pool. It was only a couple of miles from the office. Sam parked the Cadillac in his numbered space. He walked through the courtyard, ignoring two gay guys that were skinny-dipping in the pool. He unlocked the door to his first floor, two bedroom apartment and went in, going straight to the refrigerator. He took out a Bud, popped the top, and took it into the bedroom. The place was a mess, but what did it matter? He wasn't planning on company.

Sam picked up his phone. He dialed Bonnie's number . . . the damn answering machine again. He hung up without leaving a message. He laid down on the bed. He was in the same clothes and in the same position when he woke up the next morning,

But he knew what he was going to do.

A thousand miles away, Bonnie was in Jacksonville looking for Barco Drive. She found it after getting caught by a one-way street and having to circle back. The phone book said New Life Printing was at 2008 Barco. The building there was a stand-alone concrete block square. It had a metal roof showing orange rust, and a parking lot with two older cars and a lot of pot holes. There was a large wooden sign over the door that pictured a pair of praying hands. Beneath them, in gold painted letters, were the words, "NEW LIFE." Bonnie pulled in and parked the little rental. She checked her face in the rear view mirror, and then stepped out of the car.

The front door of the shop was glass. Bonnie looked in. She could see a brunette woman, mid-forties, going through some papers at a pine counter. When she tried the door, it was locked. She knocked, and the woman looked up. She walked around the counter and came to the door. She gave Bonnie the once over and, apparently satisfied, unlocked it.

"Sorry about that. It's the neighborhood, you know."

"Sure. I understand," Bonnie said, "Gets worse every day. Say, I'm hoping that you can help me. I'm an attorney looking for Paul Mobley. I have some very good news for him. He's come into some money."

The woman gave Bonnie a strange look. "Paul? I'm afraid he's not here right now. Can I take a message?"

At least Mobley was still working here. "I'm afraid not. The matter is private, but you can tell Mr. Mobley it has to do with a will." Bonnie tried for an intriguing smile.

"Gee, who died?" the brunette asked.

"I'm so sorry. I've already said more than I should. Can you tell me when I can see Mr. Mobley?" Bonnie now used her sincere look.

The woman picked up a pencil and tapped it on the counter. "Paul comes and goes. He's not really on a fixed schedule. He works on special projects."

I bet he does, Bonnie thought. "Well, do you have an address for him, or a phone number?"

"You know, I think I better check with my boss before I give out any of that stuff. You have a card or something?"

"Of course." Bonnie pulled a card case from her purse. She handed the woman one from the assortment of business cards she always carried. This one identified her as an attorney. It had the telephone number of her private phone. If the woman decided to check up on her, Colleen would answer it in the appropriate manner. Bonnie had cards identifying her as a private investigator, a building inspector, a theatrical agent, even a doctor. They came in handy.

The woman took the card, looked it over, and put it on the counter.

"You do a lot of business here?" Bonnie asked.

"The Lord's work is never done," the woman replied. "Now, if you're finished, I need to get back to work." She opened the door pointedly.

"Sure. Thanks very much." Bonnie wondered just what work of the Lord was going on behind the closed steel door to the back of the shop.

She got into her car and drove to a Wendy's a few blocks away. She went inside and ordered a large coffee. She took a sip on the way to an empty booth, and decided it wasn't drinkable. At least the dollar fifty bought her a place to sit. Bonnie needed to think, but first she had to call Colleen.

The call went through. Colleen answered on the second ring. "Bonnie?"

"Yeah, Colleen, it's me. I need your help."

"I'll help you with anything you want, Bonnie, but damn, boss, where have you been? Everyone has been worried sick. Jack's going to have a stroke, and Sam is wearing me out with his calls."

"Listen. Don't talk, just listen. I'm fine, and I'm on the edge of something big. Very big. Every time this phone rings for the next week you have to answer, 'Brock and Finman, Attorneys at Law.' Every time without fail. Whoever calls will ask for Candace Brock. She is always out of the office, *always*. Ask to take a message. Try to get a number. Then you call me right away and let me know someone called. Can you do that, Colleen? It's critically important."

"OK. Brock and Finman. Candace Brock. Out of the office. I've got it."

"Great, Colleen. Do this right. If you screw up, I could lose my chance at a blockbuster."

"I will Bonnie. You can count on me. Are you coming back soon?"

"Doesn't look like it. You've got to hold things together back there."

"OK. Will do . . . Bonnie, I can't wait to show you my new boobs. They're terrific!"

I forgot all about that, Bonnie thought. "I'm sure they are, hon. Can't wait to see them. You take good care of them, or find some nice man that will. Got to run now. Bye, sweetie."

24

Ted had no trouble finding the Electric Chair Tattoo Shop. It was less than a half mile from the Shallow Dive.

The funky little shop was a block from the beach on the corner of "A" Street and Beach Boulevard. Jack's Bar-B-Que, a surf shop called The Pit, and Mango Mango's restaurant occupied the three adjacent corners at the busy intersection. There was a huge, metal-flake green, boat of a Cadillac parked beside the building. A stylized sign with the name of the shop covered the visible part of the wall above it.

Ted parked the van and went into the shop. It was late afternoon, a quiet time for that kind of business. Most of the people that want ink show up after dark, drunk or stoned, like vampires. Ironic, Ted thought. So many people want to put me in the electric chair, and here I am going on my own.

The inside of the shop was extreme. The walls were painted in bright primary colors. There were enlarged photos of garish tattoos hung throughout the place. Moveable screens covered with examples of wild tattoos and display art separated the shop into three or four work stations. A young girl was sitting on a leather couch. She had stars tattooed around her right eye and a ring through her nose. She looked up from the magazine she was reading, and then stood and greeted Ted.

"Hi there. What can we do for you today?" In spite of her bizarre body decorations, the girl was very pretty. Ted remembered times before he went to prison when a girl with a tattoo was automatically considered a slut. Now, half the girls he saw on the beach had ink. Times do change.

"I need to get some work done, a cover up." A man walked out from behind one of the screens. He was in his early thirties, clean shaven, and wore a black ball cap backwards. Both of his arms were sleeved with wild tattoos. He had round plugs in his ear lobes. He was wiping his hands on a paper towel.

"I've got this, Amy," he told the girl. She smiled at Ted, and then moved back to the couch. The man turned to his customer. "Welcome. My name's Danny. This is my shop. I do most of the work here. Where is the tat you want worked on?" he asked.

"Here, on my forearm." Ted rolled up the sleeve of his flannel shirt.

"That's nice work, mister. It's been there for years. You sure you want to get rid of it?"

"I'm sure. Real sure." Ted remembered Sunny's comment. "Who wants to advertise a broken heart?"

"Well, OK, as long as you're sure. What did you have in mind? You know the possibilities are limited when I try to go over someone else's work."

"I'm not too particular. This tat just carries bad memories with it. I think a change would be good for me. I was thinking maybe a rising sun with some clouds over it. Maybe a morning scene. You know, new horizons and all that."

"Well, I can come up with something close to that. The red heart could become the sun. I'll have to jazz it up, though, to get the stab wound to blend in. Then with some new lines and shading, I could make the dagger's handle into a storm cloud."

"Storm clouds, huh? I was thinking about something calm, but storm clouds might make more sense. That's sounds OK. Whatever you think."

Danny led Ted behind a screen. He indicated a padded stool with arm rests. Ted sat down, and Danny pulled another stool close to him. The artist pulled on rubber gloves and set several small containers of colored inks on a counter.

"I'm going to sketch something like what we're talking about right on your arm. That way, you can see what it will look like before we go for real." Danny used colored markers to roughly draw a flaming sun and billowing storm clouds over the heart and dagger. Ted thought it looked pretty good. He gave his OK, and Danny started with the ink. The buzz of the needle sounded like a dentist's drill, but the pain was a lot less.

The cover art took about an hour. Ted was pleased. The new tattoo looked good. The sun rose into angry clouds. There were a few lightning bolts scattered among them. You couldn't see the original tat at all. Danny wrapped the fresh work with a plastic bandage material. "You're all set," he said.

That's one more thing I can quit worrying about, Ted thought. He paid Danny, shook his hand, and walked away from the Electric Chair. He got in the van and drove back to the Shallow Dive. When he pulled in, Poon and Donnie were sitting at the picnic table arguing. There was a half-empty bottle of rum, and a plastic liter of tonic between them. A cheap Styrofoam cooler swung slowly in the torn hammock.

Ted walked over to the table. Donnie had his back to the parking lot and didn't notice him approaching.

"You're stupid, man! I tell you that guitar is worth money." Donnie was banging his fist on the table. "Give it to me. I'll get us some fast cash for it."

"It might be worth something. Might not. I don't care if it is, amigo. It belongs to Sunny. She can do what she wants with it. I'm not ripping off a little girl." Poon took a long drink from a red plastic cup sitting in front of him. When he put down the cup, Ted was standing behind Donnie.

"Is that my guitar you're talking about?" he asked the men, his gravelly voice chilling.

Donnie was surprised to see Ted looming over his shoulder. He looked at the table top sheepishly, and then raised his cup to take a drink. Ted slapped the cup out of his hand. He grabbed Donnie by the neck. He found a pressure point and Donnie folded like a tent, whining the whole way to the ground.

"I asked you a question, asshole."

"Whoa, amigo," Poon stood and pleaded, "no need for this rough stuff. Donnie was just kidding around. Your guitar is right there in my room. Just take it easy. I'll get it for you." He waited expectantly.

Ted eased the pressure on Donnie's neck. "Yeah, why don't you do that? Then we'll have a little talk. Maybe we'll have a drink together."

Poon walked over to number nine. He went in and got the guitar. He brought it out to Ted in the new case. Donnie sat back at the table, rubbing his neck with one hand. He chugged his drink with the other.

"Here you go," Poon said. "I even found a case for it. It's a good one, too." He stayed standing, not sure what to expect from his new neighbor.

Ted took the case and put it on the picnic table. When he opened it, he could tell someone had done some nice work on the guitar. It was cleaned up, and the strings had a shine to them. They looked new. Opening the case set free the sweet smell of oil and old wood. He didn't bother taking the instrument out of the case. He couldn't play it. All it was to him was possible cash. The fact that someone had put some work into it meant for sure the guitar was worth something to someone.

"So let's hear it. What's it worth?" Ted asked. Before Poon could respond, Sunny rode up on the handle bars of Landon's beach cruiser. Both the teens were laughing as they stopped near the men. Sunny hopped off. Her hair was wet, and she was bright pink.

"Thanks for the ride, Landon. I'll see you tomorrow, and I'll do even better!" Sunny gushed.

"OK, then, about noon at the pier. Nice job today, Puddles." Landon laughed again, and then rode off. Sunny watched him go. He was wonderful, and he called her "Puddles."

Poon was the first to speak. "Hi Sunny. Good times today?"

"Guys, it was awesome! Landon taught me some surfing moves on the beach. Then he took me out into the ocean. I caught a wave on my third try! It wasn't a big one, but it was just too cool. I loved it! I want to be a surf chick. The beach, the sun, the waves . . . "

"And Landon," Ted added. Sunny blushed beneath her sunburn, but she didn't deny it.

Poon started to speak. "Sunny. . ."

"Sunny," Ted interrupted, "get in the room. I've got to talk to these guys. I'll be there in a minute."

"Sure, granddad. What a great day!" She skipped across the parking lot and went into room fifteen. In a few minutes, they could hear her singing to herself in the room.

Ted closed the guitar case and addressed the men. "Now, back to business. What's this old guitar worth? And you better be damn straight with me."

"Fifteen hundred dollars," Poon replied. Donnie and Ted were both shocked.

"You're serious?" Ted patted the case. "Someone will pay that kind of money for this?"

"That's right. I can get it for you today if you want the deal."

"Damn right I want the deal, but if you're bull-shittin' me, you're gonna regret it."

"Poon, who you going to sell it to?" This from Donnie. "And maybe we should get some kind of finder's fee or something."

Ted rested his hand lightly on Donnie's neck. "What was that, peckerhead? Why do you care what happens to my guitar?"

Donnie leaned away from Ted's touch. "I don't, Ted, not a bit. I was just curious. Do what you want with it."

"I plan to. Here, Poon, take this thing and sell it. I expect the money this afternoon, in cash. You can keep fifty bucks for your trouble." He pushed the case in Poon's direction. Ted turned and walked across the lot to number fifteen.

"Did you see that?" Donnie whined, "That maniac almost broke my neck!"

"Quit complaining. You deserved it."

"Fifty bucks? That's all he's giving us on a fifteen hundred dollar deal. That's bull shit."

"There's no 'us' on this, Donnie."

"Ahh, come on."

"No way. You tried to steal it and it didn't work. It's your loss."

Poon finished his drink, picked up the case, and began to wrap it in cardboard he picked up from the ground. When he had it protected, he attached it with bungee cords to the handle bars of his cruiser. He left Donnie pouting and drinking even faster at the picnic table.

Grandpa was going to be happy, but these long bike rides were killing him.

25

Sam pulled his silver Cadillac to the curb outside Antonio's. It was four in the afternoon. The street was busy, but the two parking spaces directly in front of the restaurant were kept empty. A dark haired man opened Sam's car. He had bulging arms that were squeezed into a tight fitting suit. The PI stepped out.

"Sam?"

"Yeah."

"Over here." He motioned Sam under the awning that shielded the entrance.

"Arms up." The man patted him down in a way that let Sam know that he knew what he was doing. He took Sam's wallet from his pocket and checked the ID. He took Sam's phone and put it in his own pocket. He handed the wallet back to him. The man opened the restaurant door, and stood aside so Sam could enter. It was a Monday, and the place was closed for business. Honest business, anyway.

The Italian restaurant was small, twelve tables and four booths. There were landscape paintings on the walls and red checked table cloths. Chianti bottles held candles on the tables. Rolled napkins designated seating. A small bar with ten stools was on the left side of the room.

Tony Toes was sitting alone in the last booth at the back of the room. There were two very large men at a table close by. Another sat on a stool at the bar. He was big, too. All the men wore shiny fitted suits.

"Sam, how good to see you. Come. Sit." The gangster gestured to Sam with a chubby hand. Tony Toes spoke in a voice as soft as a whisper. It came from a round olive face with a pencil thin moustache, and several chins. He was at least sixty or sixty-five years old, but his hair was full and black.

"Mr. Cicarella, always a pleasure. It's an honor to see you." Sam sat across from the man. He didn't offer his hand. No one ever touched Tony Toes. "I hope you are well."

"Ahh, Sam, I get old like the olive tree. I'm bent so much by the wind, I get crooked." He chuckled. "You want coffee? A homemade wine maybe?"

"No thank you, Mr. Cicarella. I don't want to take too much of your time. I came to see you to ask a favor."

"In the past, we have always been able to help each other, Sam. What is it you need?" Tony was referring to a couple of jobs Sam had done for him. They were surveillance stuff, and a few skip traces. Sam wasn't above taking some of the mob's money. As far as he knew, no civilians were hurt by his actions.

"I ask this favor realizing that I may be out of bounds, so I ask with serious purpose."

"Go on." Tony Toes looked pensive. The wrinkles on his forehead deepened.

"As I'm sure you know, last week a convicted killer escaped from prison while being transported. He hasn't been recaptured yet. His name is Michael Parsons, but I believe you know him as Mick."

"Ah, yes. I read about it in the papers. Michael was not right in the head. He did terrible things. He was doing life without parole." Tony shifted in his seat and the friendliness left his eyes. He sipped some coffee from a tiny cup in front of him.

"Yes, sir, he did. But my problem is this. I have a friend, a special female friend, that is trying to find Mick. She's somewhere in Florida right now. I think she may be

150

close to locating him. I want to be sure she isn't doing anything that might interfere with any of your interests."

"That is very thoughtful of you, Sam, but what could your friend do that would interfere with me?" The eyes were dead now.

"Probably not a thing, Mr. Cicarella, but I want to be sure."

"This friend works for you?"

"No. She is a reporter for a newspaper."

"Then she is good?"

"Yes, she's very good."

"About this favor you ask of me. Well, Sam, if this woman finds Michael, you have her call me. No, better you call me. I would perhaps like to say hello to Michael. It's been a long time since I have seen him." He nodded to the man sitting at the bar. He stood and came to the table.

"Give Sam a card."

The man handed Sam a business card with nothing but a phone number printed on it. Then he went back to the bar.

"You hear anything, anything at all, you call that number."

"The woman, Mr. Cicarella?"

"I'm sure she won't inconvenience me, Sam, but if she does in some way, I will let you know. As a favor, I will try and see that she returns to her home safely."

"That is all I ask, sir. This woman is special to me. I thank you very much, Mr. Cicarella."

Tony dismissed Sam with a nod. The investigator got up and walked out of the restaurant. The same huge man met him outside the door. He handed Sam his cell phone, and opened the car door for him. He got in, thankful that the meeting was over.

Tony finished his coffee and motioned to one of the men at the table. The man came and sat in the booth across from his boss. He leaned forward so he could hear Tony's whispers.

"I want you to get word to Richie and Tank. There's a broad chasing Mick. She's a reporter. Sam says she's good. Tell them to watch for her, spot her if she's around. If she gets anything before they do, I want to know about it. If they find Mick first, or through her, the contract still stands. The first thing, though, they have to get the book. They can scare the woman, but no hit on her unless that's what it takes to get the book. I want that god damned book." The man got up from the booth. He walked out of the restaurant.

Tony went back to sipping his coffee.

Back at the office, Sam was rotating in his swivel chair. He felt good about his meeting with Tony Toes, but their discussion didn't remove Bonnie from danger. Tony was an honorable man to a point, but the point was only when honor was to his advantage. He was seldom a hundred percent truthful.

And Mick was still out there.

His inner office door opened and his secretary walked in. Angie was a looker, a bombshell type that Sam had once spent a lot of evenings with. Her platinum hair was pulled back to show off a pair of diamond earrings. A matching diamond tennis bracelet graced her narrow wrist. She wore a custom, light wool suit. The rings on her fingers held several thousand dollars' worth of diamonds. Angie was able to dress well because her income was supplemented by her bookie boyfriend, but she was proud that she held a real job. She worked hard for what Sam paid her, and she had a weird loyalty. She was one of the few that let water stay over the bridge as far as their affair was concerned.

"You've got a stack of messages. I passed some of them off to the boys, but there are a few here you'll have to handle." She put the slips on his desk and walked out of his office. He couldn't help appreciating the swing of her ass. He sorted through a few memories, but soon returned to his immediate problems.

Sam picked up the pink slips and sorted through them. Nothing from Bonnie, and nothing from Colleen. Not even a call from Jack. This waiting was going to drive him crazy. He tossed the slips back on the desk and decided to head for home. He wanted to try to think, or not to think, or to think.

26

Poon was sweating and gasping for breath when he got back to the Shallow Dive. He had delivered the Gibson to Grandpa. He got a hug from him, and a nice kiss from Tammy. The problem was, they didn't have the fifteen hundred in cash. They gave him a check instead.

He was sure the check was good, but he wasn't excited about betting his future on it. He had to get back on his cruiser and pedal to the Bank of America branch down in the Publix shopping center. He let his cruiser drop to the ground, and carefully eased his weary body into the community hammock. He took a big swallow from his plastic bottle full of rum. He had to rest a bit, and then gather his energy before he made the trip.

He must have drifted off. Out of nowhere the hammock flipped over, throwing Poon on the ground. "So where's the money?" Ted was a black silhouette against the afternoon sun. He looked bigger than life looking down on Poon that way. His voice was like roofing nails in a slow blender.

"Whoa, amigo. Be cool. I've got your money. I just have to cash a check."

"I told you cash."

"Yeah, and you'll get cash. I just have to go to the bank. Not many of my friends have that kind of cash just lying around."

"Well then, what the hell are you doing here sleeping in this hammock? You get off your ass and go get me the money."

Poon rolled out of the hammock and picked up his cruiser. "No problem, amigo. I'll be back in half an hour." He mounted his bike and rode off. He was thinking, man, I'm doing this guy a favor, and all he does is cuss me out and threaten me. What's this world coming to?

Ted went back to room number fifteen. Sunny was lying on her bed watching their new TV. It was a color set. With only a few days until demolition, everything was up for grabs. Jake picked it out for them from one of the vacant rooms while he was hauling furniture out of the place in a borrowed pickup. Most of the vacant rooms were already stripped. The last day, it would be the wire and copper plumbing pipes.

Ted had some planning to do.

"Fun today?" he asked, as he entered the room.

"Oh granddad, you can't believe it. The ocean is so great. It's a whole new world for me."

"I'm not your granddad. You don't have to call me that when we're alone." He sat on his bed. "So, what did you do?"

"Landon gave me some instructions. Then I just did it. I surfed! The waves were small, but I could ride them. I mean, I really could ride them. Landon said I was a natural. He's such a great teacher. I'm meeting him tomorrow for another lesson."

"It sounds like you like this kid, the great teacher bit and all."

"Well, yeah. He's nice to me, and he's cute. Don't you think he's cute? I think he's gorgeous!"

"What do I know about cute? To me, he's just a skinny kid that wants to get in your pants. You watch what you're doing. We've got to get out of here in a day or two."

"We're running again, huh? Why can't we stay? This is a friendly place. I like it. It's a place where you could make a real home."

155

"It's a place that can get you caught and killed, too. Sure it's nice, but the longer we stay here, the bigger the chance that we'll be spotted. Or maybe you'll slip up and say the wrong thing to the wrong person. Just because we aren't headlines any more, that doesn't mean the feds aren't busting balls to find us. Murderers. We're murderers! Think about that for a few minutes. They want our asses on the hottest seat in town. Being a sweet kid doesn't mean shit to the law."

"How much longer do you think we can stay?"

"I'm going back to Jacksonville tomorrow and finding that librarian. You do your surf shit or whatever else you want, but keep your stuff packed. When I get back, we may need to get out of here in a hurry." Ted pulled the hunting knife from his back waistband. He put the knife on the bedside table. "We made some money today."

"How did we do that?" Sunny asked.

"The old guitar. Turns out it was some kind of special antique instrument. I sold it for five hundred dollars. Poon's getting the money for us now."

"You're saying my grandfather's guitar was worth five hundred dollars? I don't believe it." She was thinking, Ted said the money was for us.

"Us?"

"Believe it or not, the money's on its way." Ted went into the bathroom. Sunny was stunned. She flipped through the TV channels for a while, but she couldn't pay attention to the crap displayed on the screen. She and Ted. They had some money. Whether Landon knew it or not, she had a boyfriend. It was Florida and sunshine and ocean. Life was great! She was never going to let Ragley into her thoughts again.

Poon got back to the Shallow Dive about four thirty. He dropped his cruiser in the sand and fell into the hammock. His heart was racing. He wasn't sure what to do. He took deep breaths, and a big, long swallow of his Flora de Cana. The roll of bills was in his shirt pocket. He was getting his body back under control when Ted came out of room fifteen.

Ted walked straight to the hammock. "Got it?"

Poon took the roll of bills from his shirt pocket and handed it to Ted. "You're a hard guy to do a favor for."

Ted counted the money. When he finished, he handed Poon two twenties and a ten. "You did good. Thanks."

"Nearly killed me," Poon commented.

"It would have for sure if you had fucked with me. I think you're OK. I'm not too sure about those assholes you hang around with, but I think you're all right."

"That's good to know. And thanks for the fifty."

"Don't mention it, and I *mean* don't mention it. Not to anyone. Not even Sunny. She and I are leaving in a day or two. I want all of you guys to get a good case of amnesia when we're gone."

"That we can do. You want to give me a reason?"

"Not on your life, and it *is* on your life. You get it?"

"Yeah. I get it."

Ted put the money in his pocket and went back to number fifteen. Sunny was sleeping when he opened the door. The sun had sapped all her energy. She was a bright pink. She looked so relaxed that he envied her. When he closed the door, she opened her eyes and looked at him.

"Everything OK?" You could hear the sleep in her voice. She rubbed her eyes.

"All is well," he told her, "and we've got some cash. That old guitar saved somebody's life." Ted pulled a hundred dollar bill off the roll of cash and tossed it on the bed by the girl. She reached for it happily.

"This is cool, but shouldn't I get half?" she asked.

Ted gave her a mean look. "You get what I give you. Be damn glad it's anything at all."

He went into the bathroom, but Sunny kept talking. "So what now?" she asked. She was holding the bill up to the light. She had never seen a hundred dollar bill before.

"Soon as I finish pissin', I'm getting some rest. You stay here tomorrow while I go to Jacksonville. Go to the beach. Do your surf thing. Just don't be talking out of school. And remember, your boyfriend is a teenage kid. He's probably horny as a goat. Keep your pants on and your mouth shut."

"You know, granddad, I really like this guy."

"Yeah. I like maple syrup, too, but if I guzzle it, it makes me sick. You take it slow. Stay out of trouble."

She replied in a soft voice, "It's not like I'm a virgin. I know what sex is about."

"I doubt you do, little girl. Not the kind that's any good for you. Now shut up. I want to get a good night's sleep." Ted adjusted the air conditioner and crawled into bed.

"Who was Ben Franklin?" she asked, as she examined the bill.

"He was a guy a hell of a lot smarter than the fools running things today."

"He looks like he'd be a good grandfather."

"Well, he sure knew how to fly a kite."

"Good night," Sunny whispered, "granddad."

"Yeah, whatever," Ted replied.

27

Colleen had tons of fun picking out new clothes to fit her great new body. She bought lacy bras and low cut tops, all the time thinking about the first time she would walk across the newsroom.

She wasn't quite as sore three days after her operation, so she practiced walking naked in front of the full length mirror on the back of her closet door. Oh, it was terrific! There was just the right jiggle. Her doctor was a god. She knew Sam wouldn't be able to resist a chance at her new puppies. She hefted them each one more time, and then sat back on the bed. Sam's number was on speed dial.

Here we go.

The call was picked up by some kind of answering machine. Colleen knew Angie, Sam's secretary, so she waited for the beep and then left her message. "Hi, Angie. Hi, Sam. Sorry I missed you. Call me and I'll bring you up to date on Bonnie's adventure."

Colleen hung up. She was disappointed that she hadn't reached Sam directly, but glad that she had a good reason to call.

Meanwhile in Jacksonville, Bonnie was parked up the street from the New Life Print Shop. She was concentrating on the front door. Three cars behind her, Richie and Tank sat in their white Lexus rental. Bonnie was a reporter, OK, but how good was she? The boss said she was very good, but she wasn't checking for a tail. Maybe she wasn't so hot shit when she had to work out in the field. Women shouldn't be close to this business. Give them a vacuum cleaner and a couple of kids. That's enough.

Richie called in. The voice that answered the call sounded strange, but it always did. Conversations on this phone were short and sweet.

"We got eyes on her. No luck on the missing package."

"OK." The line went dead.

Just sitting on your ass wasn't Richie's thing. He liked to get in . . . bang! bang! . . and get out. Tank had more patience. He had been in the hit business too long to get in a hurry. He was nibbling on a ham sandwich he brought with him for the day. He was a big guy, over two fifty, with a scar over his right eye and a gold incisor. His arms threatened to burst out of his tailored suit.

"We're not supposed to do the woman," Tank said.

"We're not supposed to still be here, either, but here the fuck we are. A one day job is now more like a week."

"So we put it on our expense account. The boss won't care. He just wants the job done." Tank folded the paper towel that held his sandwich. "I've got another sandwich if you want one."

"No thanks. I just want to get this shit done and go home. This heat is killing me."

"Man, it's just as hot back in Galveston. Maybe hotter."

"Yeah, but that's my heat. This Florida heat is different. It makes me sweat more." Richie wiped his forehead with a handkerchief.

"Hey, here we go." He was looking at a blue Dodge Charger that pulled into the parking lot. Sure enough, Paul Mobley stepped out of the car, looked all around, and then went into the print shop. Tank checked the picture they had to be sure. Yeah, it was him.

In front of them, Bonnie opened her car door and headed for the building. She had checked her picture, too, but it was an old one taken right after Mobley's trial. She was going to have to look him in the eye to be positive.

"So how do we play this?" Richie asked. "We can't finish this guy, or we won't get to this book, or to Mick either."

Tank looked serious. He took his pistol out of his shoulder holster. "So, we follow the broad. If she's as good as the boss says, she'll take us to Mick. Then we very strongly encourage him to give up the book." Richie knew what that meant. "We get the book. We clip Mick clean, dump the woman tied up somewhere, and head back to Texas. Vacation time then. Drinks all around." The big man smiled. "Can you dig it?" He checked his bullet count.

"So do we go in, or wait out here? It's so damn hot."

"Let's see where she's going with this. She found Mobley. Maybe she can find Mick, too."

The same woman was standing at the counter when Bonnie entered the shop. The door was unlocked this time. "Hi again," Bonnie said. "I'm still looking for Paul Mobley."

"Oh yeah, I remember you. You're the attorney. I'm sorry, Paul hasn't been in this week. I don't know when I'll see him." The woman busied herself shuffling papers.

"That's strange," Bonnie said. "I just saw him walk his skinny ass through that door. Let's cut the crap, sister. Paul Mobley is somewhere in this building, and I want to talk to him. I'm not a cop, but I can get one if I need one. I don't care what you do behind that steel door, but some of my friends might. So what's it going to be?"

"First, lady, what's this about? You know I don't buy the 'mystery will' fantasy, and Paul doesn't either."

"Nice of you to discuss it with him. Let's try this one. How do you like saving his life?"

The woman dropped the papers on the counter. Scowling, she said, "I'll see if he'll speak to you. Wait here, *counselor*." The woman took a key from a chain around her neck and walked to the steel door. She hit a buzzer, then unlocked the door with her key. She disappeared into the back of the building.

Bonnie stood at the counter waiting. She stared at the giant praying hands painted on the wall. I hope that prayer is for me, she thought.

After six or seven minutes, she was walking towards the steel door when the buzzer sounded again. The door opened. An older, weary-looking Paul Mobley emerged from the back room. His face was gray and wrinkled. His glasses were much thicker than in the old photo Colleen had found in the archives. He had a pistol in his hand and a frightened look on his face. He pointed the handgun at Bonnie. "Who are you? What do you want?" His hand was shaking. He gave off the smell of printer's ink and fear.

"Look, Paul, my name doesn't matter. What I want does. I want Mick Parsons and the girl he's got with him." She paused to let this sink in, then she went on. "I don't think you'll use that gun. You're a counterfeiter, not a violent man, not a killer. You're an artist blessed with talent. You're sensitive. But you and I have to talk. You can keep the gun pointed at me if you want, just don't let it go off accidently."

Mobley leaned against the counter as if he was weakened by Bonnie's speech. She kept at him. "I'm a reporter and all I want is a story. I have reason to believe that Mick either already has, or will be, contacting you. That's why I'm here. You're the only contact he had for

162

years, and with your talent, you can do something for him that few people can. You can give him a new identity. I know he headed in this direction after his escape. You're the only reason I can come up with for him to do that. Help me, and I'll do all I can for you. You have to realize that once he has his new ID, Mick will kill you. He will eliminate the only person that will know who he has become."

"Mick wouldn't do that," Mobley protested.

"His total body count is estimated at about thirty-eight. There are probably more. Why would you be any different? Mick is a certified psychopath. He has no trace of conscience or feeling of any kind for others. He will use you to provide what he needs, and then he'll get rid of you."

Mobley looked physically bent under the weight of the reporter's argument. His hand holding the gun fell to his side. "What can I do? I'm screwed. He hasn't gotten to me yet, but I know he will." Mobley hung his head. "I've got something else he wants just as much as an ID."

"What's that?"

Mobley raised his eyes. Fear flashed through them. He was looking over Bonnie's shoulder at Mick Parsons in the flesh. The killer was coming through the door. His hair was different. He wore a goatee beard and glasses, but it was Mick, and he had a gun in his hand.

"Hi, Paul. Who's your friend?" Mick asked calmly. "Somebody else I've got to kill?"

28

Outside, Tank and Richie were discussing their options. Richie wanted to go into the print shop and abduct Mobley and the woman. He thought they could then take them somewhere private, and force whatever information they needed out of them. Tank was for waiting to see if Mobley came out with the woman. He wanted to follow them to see if they would lead them to Mick.

"Come on, man. We bust in, chloroform the two of them, load 'em in the car and haul ass. What's the problem?"

"There's a few of them, Richie. Man, you got to start thinking." Tank was getting fed up with this cowboy. "First, there's a customer in there. That means that we'd have to do something with him as well as the other two. Second, we can't kill the woman or Mobley, even by accident, unless we get this damn book. If we do, Toes will be serving us on his next delivery pizza. Third, we don't know where in the building they are. What if we bust in and they're way in the back somewhere? And how many people are in there? You planning to chloroform a whole herd of company employees?"

Richie didn't have an answer for that.

"Then dipshit, think about this. What if Mick hasn't contacted Mobley at all? Then he won't have dick to tell us no matter what we do to him, and any chance of a connection is broken. Pick up that other sandwich and calm down."

"But damn, Tank, it's so fuckin' hot. I just want to get this over with." He reached into the backseat and grabbed a paper bag. "You put mustard on this?"

Inside the shop, Mick had taken Paul's gun, and then patted him down. He made Bonnie lean on the counter and he frisked her. Bonnie felt his hand linger slightly in certain areas. She thought that maybe if she wasn't killed right here, that sense of touch might be helpful. She wished she had taken more time with her make-up.

Mobley was now stuttering. The fear was leaking through his pores. "I done everything, Mick. When I read about your escape, I put together a driver's license, credit cards, even a passport. It's all ready except for whatever name and picture you want to use. I've got the book, too. All the stuff is in a safe place."

"That's good to know, Paul. You're a friend indeed." Mick gave him a salute. "This is what we're gonna do. We're walking out of here like we're going for a stroll in the park. My van is a little 'warm.' We'll take Paul's car. I watched him drive up in that blue Dodge. You two will sit in the front. Paul will drive and I'll sit in the back. I'm sure you both will make sure the drive is comfortable and safe. We don't want anyone to get hurt. Paul will take us to his secret place where I'll collect my things. I'll tie you both up loosely so you can get free pretty easily. Then I'll leave and go about my business." Mick stepped back and lowered the gun. "Any questions?"

"Yeah, I have one. Where's the girl?" Bonnie asked.

"She's safe, staying with friends. She's enjoying the nice weather." Mick smiled. "Now, to show you how intent I am on getting things accomplished ... " He suddenly gripped Paul by the testicles and squeezed hard enough to drop him moaning to the floor. In almost the same motion, with his other hand he seized Bonnie's thumb. He bent it in a way that sent a terrible stab of pain straight into her brain. She fell to the floor by Paul.

Mick stood over them. He looked at the reporter. "You know, you are very, very pretty. I've always liked redheads. I hope we can get along." He spit on the floor beside her. "OK. Now up and at 'em." He grabbed both Paul and Bonnie and lifted them to their feet. All those years of push-ups and jogging in place had made him exceptionally strong for his size. He hustled the pair to the door, and took a careful look outside through the glass.

"Got your keys, Paul?" The man was still bent over in pain, but he nodded. "Good. Let's go then." Mick opened the door.

Richie was scraping the mustard off Tank's ham sandwich when his partner hit his elbow. "What the hell, man, you just ruined my suit! Look at this shit!" He quickly tried to wipe a gob of mustard off his pant's leg.

"Shut up! Start the car. Something's happening," Tank said. "The three of them just came out and got into Mobley's car."

"Three of them?"

"Yeah, damn it. That's Mobley, the woman, and the customer, but I don't think that was just any customer. I think that fucker might be Mick. Gimme that picture." Richie handed it over. "Yeah. Yeah! Older. Different hair. Glasses and a faggy beard, but that's Mick. Follow that Dodge. If you lose it, I'll kill you myself and save Toes the trouble." Richie floored the Lexus and squeezed it into traffic. The Dodge was four cars ahead of them.

Mick sat in the back seat with his gun held in his lap. His years of confinement were so ingrained in him that a simple drive was a great pleasure. The freedom of movement excited him. He alternated between watching the passing scenery, and keeping watch on his fellow passengers.

Mobley and Bonnie were silent. They both were wondering what the next few hours would bring. The greatest story of her life, and Bonnie was afraid she wouldn't live to write it. She began glancing in the car's side mirror to see what their captor was doing. The angle was wrong to watch Mick, but there was a white, expensive looking car a few lengths behind them that caught her interest. It looked like the driver was white and the passenger was black.

"How far to my stuff, Paul?" Mick asked. "I'm getting antsy."

"About twenty minutes. It's stashed on a small cabin cruiser I keep docked on the Trout River."

"Excellent. Is it damn well hidden on board?"

"Yeah, for sure. I built a couple of false compartments in the boat with hidden latches. It would take a bloodhound to find them. The boat is tied up at a dock I lease in a residential neighborhood. If anyone but me shows up there, someone will call the law."

Way to go, Paul, Bonnie was thinking. Don't give him anything.

"That's good planning. I guess I can use some of the anchor rope to tie you two up. So how did you hide the latches?"

"We'll be there before long. I'll show them to you."

Mick frowned. "What about the book? Did you get everything into it?"

Mobley turned right. Bonnie watched the white car make the same turn. Her eyes were on the mirror, but her mind was wondering about this mysterious book.

"Every word. It's your autobiography and your ticket to a new life. Every name and every date is there just like you planned. Cicarella will pay you whatever you ask."

So that's it, she realized. Blackmail.

Mick relaxed, and settled back into the rear seat. Such a nice day for a drive.

Richie's hands were sweating on the wheel. He had never been a great driver. He usually had a wheel man deliver him to his target, and then get him the fuck away. Keeping on this tail was important. He couldn't screw up.

Beside him, Tank was keeping his eyes glued to the Dodge. He wished he was driving, but there was no way to switch places now. He slipped a couple of pills out of his shirt pocket and swallowed them dry. Now he was feeling like Richie. He just wanted this job over.

Ahead of them, the Dodge was starting over the Trout River Bridge. One of the cars screening them turned off before the bridge, leaving just one car between the Lexus and the Dodge.

"Better drop back a little, Richie. Mick spots us, we'll never get him."

"I'll drop back some, but if we lose them, we won't ever get him either. I wish to hell you were driving."

"Not as bad as I do," Tank muttered.

29

As the Dodge passed over the river, Mick's mind wandered. He remembered a kickball game in a vacant lot down by the railroad tracks in Galveston. He was enjoying the extra freedom he got when the shrimp boat his father worked on was out in the gulf. It was a sweltering August day. The strong smells of crude oil, gasoline and cow manure drifted over the weedy field from a passing freight train. The grinding of steel wheels was loud enough to cover the shouts of the nine or ten boys playing. The two sets of railroad tracks not in use gave off rippling shimmers of heat. The boys continually wiped sweat from their foreheads with grimy bandanas.

The game was going fine. Mick was only eight at the time, but he was naturally athletic and had no problem matching skills with the ten year olds that made up the majority of the group. The boys had been playing a couple of hours when a group of eleven and twelve year olds came walking up. There were four of them. The group was led by a curly headed, buck-toothed boy named Junior.

Mick smelled trouble coming. At least every week or two, Junior chose someone at random to pick on. The last few weeks, it had been Mick. He had been knocked off his bike. He had been pushed into the drainage ditch at the end of his street. His football was snatched and thrown up on a candy store roof. Mick was strong, but no match for the bigger bully.

Junior wasted no time making his intentions known. He pointed at Mick, and the group had its designated target. They advanced in a line, picking up rocks as they came. Mick stood there helpless, but he refused to run.

When the bigger boys were close enough, Junior gave the signal and the rocks flew. Mick tried to cover up with his arms, but he took several hits. The worst found its way between his hands to strike him above his right eye. The blood flooded down.

Humiliated and in pain, Mick screamed in rage. "I'm telling! I'm telling my mom and she'll take care of you. You're jerks! All of you!"

"Oh shut up, little baby. You're not going to do nothin', and your mom won't neither."

"She will, too. I'm going home to tell!"

"Who cares? You're a little baby and your mom is just a drunk. Everybody on the street knows that."

"She is not! You shut up." Mick wiped the blood out of his eye. "I'm going home. I'm telling her right now. You'll see." He turned. To the amusement of the bullies, he started running. He could still hear their yells as he turned the corner and raced up his block. "Drunk mother! Drunk mother! Drunk mother!" The terrible chant was followed by clapping and cruel laughter.

When he got to the little two-bedroom house the family rented, he took the front steps in a leap. He threw open the door and rushed in. There, lying on the couch in her housecoat, was his mother. There was a burned-out cigarette between her fingers and an empty wine bottle on the floor beside her. He ran to her and shook her shoulder. The blood on his hands smeared on the housecoat. She smelled sour and terrible.

He shook her again. "Mom, mom! Junior and his mean friends hit me with rocks and cut my head. Wake up. . . .Mom?"

His mother rolled onto her side. She halfway opened her bloodshot eyes and mumbled, "Go 'way. I'm sleeping."

She pushed out weakly with her hand. "Go 'way." She closed her eyes again, and rolled back over.

Mick kneeled beside her for a minute. The truth was washing over him like boiling water. He stumbled to his feet, blindly kicking the wine bottle. He took a long, bewildered look at her, and then he ran back out of the house.

That night, Mick took a baseball bat and beat Junior's German shepherd puppy into a gory mess of pulp. There was nothing left of the animal but teeth and fur. He stood there over the carcass, screaming defiantly, swinging the bat and daring Junior or anyone else to come near him. He was still standing beside the dog's corpse when the police came and arrested him.

That was the first time.

When the shrimp boat returned after six days, Mick was released from juvenile hall to his father. The grizzly bearded man used his belt on him until he got tired of swinging it. The welts were raised a quarter of an inch on Mick's back.

The third night after he was home, Mick snuck out and set Junior's house on fire. No one was hurt, but the family's bungalow was destroyed. Mick smiled even now at the memory.

After that, it was in and out of the reform school system. When he was out, he lived on the streets. His parents were glad of it.

Finally, he turned eighteen and was sent to a real jail. He had been shooting cats around the neighborhood with a stolen twenty-two rifle. He learned to shoot live targets with that gun.

The skill paid off for him later.

30

Mobley took the off-ramp and turned right just over the bridge. He began following a winding road that traced the curves of the river. The houses on both sides were upscale, but the ones on the river bank were a notch above. Two story mini-mansions sprawled across wide, perfectly groomed lawns. Oaks and cypress trees were plentiful. Boathouses and docks were the norm. They were exclamation marks to the river's exceptional scenery.

Bonnie took a quick, careful glance in the side mirror. Sure enough, the white car was further back, but still behind them.

Mick was totally relaxed. He was on his way to real freedom. A passport and lots of money would insure that he could live the kind of life that he dreamed about. He pictured himself at the wheel of one of the beautiful boats tied up to the docks along the river. As he watched, a blood red, speeding ski boat began to race past them on the river. The driver and the gorgeous woman that stood beside him, both waved at them at the same time. The man pushed his boat even harder, throwing a tall, white, rooster tail into the air behind them. The boat shot ahead.

"I'm going to get a boat like that," Mick commented. His words, the first in a long time, surprised the front seat passengers. He slid over a bit so he could see Bonnie in the rear view mirror. He imagined the redhead in a gold bikini, standing beside him as he powered them across Lago Peten Itza, the scenic lake in Guatemala where the last Mayans held out against the Spanish. He planned to live there. He was going to live the good life on the tiny island of Flores. It was a special spot of beauty, a refuge from all worry. At least that's the way the encyclopedia described it. He felt himself getting hard.

"Yeah, Mick," Mobley said, "I think you should get a nice car, too. Maybe a fancy European job."

"Maybe, or maybe a four wheel drive."

"Think you'll need one?" This came from the redhead.

"What do you care?" Mick asked. He sensed that she was smart. Her job was to figure things out with the smallest of clues. By now, she must have figured out this was her last ride.

She also was very fine looking. He suddenly decided that he would give her his prison virginity. He would taste her. He would then ride this woman the way he had dreamed.

After that, she was history.

Five hundred yards back, the two men in the Lexus felt naked. With no cars between them, they were completely exposed. If Mick looked behind the Dodge, he couldn't miss them.

"Remember," Tank commanded, "we can't waste anyone until we find out where the damn book is. We've got to get that. Once we do, the woman stays alive, but for Mick and Mobley, it's lights out. I'll take the grenades. We'll use them if we need to." He held a gas grenade in each hand. "We might have to take them somewhere private. We'll work them over until one of them gives up the location of the book. Are you ready? Locked and loaded?"

"Yeah, but I don't like this." Richie's knuckles were white on the steering wheel.

Tank smiled. "If it was easy, everyone would do it."

While Mick was fantasizing about his life to come, Bonnie was desperately trying to think of a way to get out of her situation alive. She saw her captor watching her in the rear view mirror. God! Could she smile? She had to.

"I love boating. I wish I could live near the water," Bonnie said. "What could be more fun?" She managed a weak smile. From the back seat, Mick smiled back.

He noticed the sweat dripping down Mobley's forehead. The man was wiping his eyes every few minutes. He was nervous, but he was driving OK, staying within the speed limit, and obeying all the road signs. "We're almost there," the man said. "It's at the dock behind that big, two story stucco ahead." You could hear the fear in his voice. "I'll have to pull in the driveway. It goes past the garage and all the way down to the dock."

"What about people in the house?" Mick inquired. "Will I have to kill anybody?"

Just us, Bonnie thought, after you get what you want.

"No. I'll honk as we go by the house. If anyone is home, they'll recognize my car." Mobley turned into the driveway. As he did, he noticed a white Lexus following close behind them. He didn't have a clue who it might be, but anyone showing up now was better than being alone with a smiling, confident psychopath.

Mobley honked the horn three times as they drew alongside the house. He slowed the car, but there was no indication anyone was home. He continued down the driveway as it curved between several large oak trees. There were carefully trimmed shrubs scattered about, and through the vegetation they could see a gray wooden dock about fifty feet long. It ended with a nice, slatted-wood boathouse with a dark green, baked steel roof.

"That's it. We're here." Mobley pulled up in a parking area by three wooden steps that led onto the dock. As he got out of the car, he saw a foot and a half of white Lexus hood protruding at the corner of the house.

"The boat's in the boathouse. I've got a key."

"Lead on, Paul. I can hardly wait." Mick got out of the car. He put the pistol in his back pocket.

"Yeah. This is exciting. I've never met a real criminal before," Bonnie smiled. She maneuvered herself so that she was just enough in front of Mick for her walk to get his attention. With her body blocking the action, she casually undid one more button on her blouse.

"Nothing better than a life of crime," Mick said with a laugh.

The trio walked the length of the dock. The winding river was beautiful. The slow-moving water was a light brown. They could see minnows flashing by the pilings. There were oaks and pines on both banks, and birds overhead. A slight breeze held the odors of cut grass and outdoor cooking. When they reached the boathouse, there was an entrance door with a hasp and a padlock. Mobley unlocked the padlock and pulled open the door.

The inside of the boathouse was darker than the dock outside, but their eyes adjusted quickly. There was the boat. It was a Chris Craft, 34-foot cabin cruiser. It was an older one, but Mobley had maintained it well. The name, "FREEDOM," was written in golden script across the boat's mahogany transom.

"Not bad, Paul. Not bad at all. Now, let's get to these special compartments and grab my things."

"They're in two places, Mick. I kept the IDs and the book separate." Mobley stepped on board and into the cockpit. He offered a hand to Bonnie. She took it and got on deck. Mick followed. Bonnie moved into the cockpit. She sat on one of its two chairs.

Mick was looking around, checking the boat out. "Why don't you just show me the compartments so I can get the stuff?"

"No can do, Mick. Just to be on the safe side, I booby trapped them. If you want, you can watch me open the first one. Then you can do the second one yourself."

"OK, but let's get to it."

Mobley nodded. He stepped up onto the side of the boat. He made his way past the pilot house to the front deck. He motioned for Mick, and he followed.

"Now look, but don't touch." Mobley went to the bow and knelt down. He took one of the stainless steel cleats that were spaced along the edge of the deck, and twisted it. He lifted it up and there were two wires, one black and one red, attached to the bottom of it. He carefully detached each of the wires. "There you go. Now it's safe to open the first compartment." He pulled open the deck hatch over the anchor locker. The interior looked solid. The anchor was lying on top of coils of rope. Mobley removed the anchor and set it on the deck. Mick leaned over to watch him. Mobley reached up along the deck seam and pressed a spot Mick never would have found. A six inch section of the locker wall fell onto the rope. Mobley reached into the exposed cavity and pulled out a plastic baggie. He handed it to Mick. "Here's your new identity, Mr. John Doe."

Mick opened the bag. He found a Florida driver's license, a library card, a gym membership, a social security card, two credit card applications and a passport. They all looked real to him.

"I just have to put in the name and the dates that you want," Mobley said, "and get a couple of pictures for the license and the passport. That will make you all set, a new man."

Mick hadn't thought about pictures. Damn. These papers were his ticket to freedom. He was going to need Paul a little bit longer. "You have to have special equipment for that?"

"No, not really. I've got to have a good computer with a laser printer and a laminating machine. I've got them at the shop."

"OK, then." He'd have to think about this. Those papers had to be perfect. "Now Paul, where's the book?"

"It's hidden down below in the cabin. I wanted to make damn sure no one could get near it."

Mick stuck his new papers inside his shirt. The men made their way around the cabin and back to the cockpit. Bonnie was still in the chair, her red hair a bit mussed, her legs crossed, her blouse spilling ivory cleavage.

Oh yeah, Mick thought. I can hardly wait.

Mobley stepped past Bonnie and turned the knob on the cabin door. "Shit, man, it's locked. Don't worry. I've got the spare key on a separate ring in the glove compartment of the Dodge."

"Well, go get it, Paul. Hurry the hell up. I've waited years for this. I don't want to wait much longer." Paul stepped up on the dock and left the boathouse.

Mick turned to Bonnie. "So, you say you like excitement?"

Tank and Richie were checking out the Dodge. Richie was leaning in the driver's side door. Tank stood beside him looking over his shoulder. They both heard the boathouse door open. They ducked behind the car.

Mobley hurried down the dock, head low, obviously distressed. He came quickly down the three steps. As he rounded the front of the car, Tank and Richie stood up. Their guns had silencers, and they looked like cannons pointed at his head.

31

Sunny staggered out of the shallows near the pier. She laid the longboard Landon rented for her beside the straw mat where he was snoozing. She was completely exhausted. It was close to four o'clock. They had been surfing almost continuously since nine in the morning.

Landon was face down, warming in the sun. He leaned up on his side to look at her. "Hey Puddles, had enough?" he grinned. He had made Sunny do it all today. She showed up at the pier at nine like he asked. The waves were good, so after they stretched and put on sunscreen, they each paddled longboards out past the pier.

A longboard is a good way for beginning surfers to learn. They are more stable and a little bit easier to ride than short boards, but they are also heavy. It takes real effort to get them out through incoming waves. Tiny little Sunny did well. She fell a lot, but she rode a few good waves, too, and she never complained about the work it took her to get outside on the board.

About eleven thirty, Landon put her on a skimboard. He had a thin, plywood, varnished disc with a skull and crossbones painted on it. She tried to throw, and then jump on the flat disc at the very edge of the water. He had to laugh as she kept falling on her butt. When she finally managed to skim a few yards, she raised her hands and laughed in victory. He called for a break.

They asked Pete and Al, a couple of local hot-doggers, to watch their boards while they went across the street to the F.A. Cafe. As they approached the restaurant, they began to smell some tasty cooking. They stepped onto the deck, and sat at an outside picnic table with an umbrella. They checked out the menu. Cindy, the woman that owned the place with her husband, knew all the surfers. Her son often surfed by the pier. She greeted Landon warmly and introduced herself to Sunny. The place was lively, and the food was good.

After two nice plates of shrimp and fries, they went back to the beach for a short rest under the pier. Landon spread their mat in a shady spot near a piling. Sunny lay down on her back and closed her eyes. Her mentor squatted down beside her. She looked really cute lying there in her new bikini. Sunny was developing nicely. She would fill any bikini and look great in a year or two.

"What are you doing?" Sunny asked from behind her closed eyes.

"Just watching you. You did good today, Puddles. You deserve a break."

"I'll do even better after I rest for a few minutes."

And she did. They swapped their longboards at the rental shop for shorter, more maneuverable ones. They waxed them down while pelicans danced in the air currents above them. Then they headed for the ocean. That late afternoon, Sunny got her first taste of what surfing was really about. She got outside much easier on the lighter board, but wave after wave, she would try to stand and then wipe out immediately. Landon was doing his own thing with his buddies. He was little help. Sunny was getting frustrated.

The wind was from the north. The waves had grown during the day. Her teacher was having a blast, catching wave after wave, and cutting and spinning, matching Pete and Al move for move. The three of them were putting on a show. A small crowd had gathered on the beach to watch them perform.

Sunny paddled away from the boys so she wouldn't embarrass Landon. She sat on her board a few hundred yards south of the pier. That's where it happened. A large, three wave set rose up behind her. Suddenly, she knew. She didn't hope. She just knew.

Sunny let the first two swells roll under her. She began to paddle as the third one approached. She felt the wave rise up and then, amazingly, she was standing. She wasn't sure how she did it, but she did it! The wind rushed past her. The froth surrounded her. The power carried her. It was such a glorious feeling that she shouted out loud. Not words, just yelps of pure joy.

That first wave carried Sunny all the way to shore. For the rest of daylight, the ocean was her friend. She rode wave after wave until her arms were so sore she couldn't paddle out one more time. Hooray!

Now she was standing on the beach, looking down at a boy she really liked, completely pleased with life.

"Why do you call me Puddles?" she asked.

Landon shielded his eyes from the sun. "Because, just look at you. When you come out of the water, you never grab a towel and dry off like a normal person. You stand in one spot and let the wind and the sun take the water off of you. Look around your feet." He pointed. "Puddles!"

Sunny looked down, and he was right. She kneeled in the sand beside him, looked straight into his blue eyes, and touched his cheek. "You know, you're very nice to me." She stood back up, surprised at her own action. "I better be getting back to the motel now. The sun is almost down."

"Yeah, I guess it's time. Want a ride?"

"Sure!"

They returned their boards to the rental shop. Then, with Sunny on the handlebars, Landon aimed his cruiser for the Shallow Dive.

They were giggling together, sharing wave replays, when they rode into the parking lot. Landon stopped the bike, and Sunny hopped off.

"Hey, Sunny!" Poon was calling her from the picnic table. Donnie and Woodsy were there with him, drinking out of red plastic cups, sharing a bottle of rum. There was a liter of coke on the table, too. Sunny and Landon walked over.

"Hey, guys. What's up?" Sunny sat at the table across from Poon. Landon stayed standing behind her. He idly picked peeling skin from Sunny's shoulders.

"Well, little girl, Grandpa—that's the name of the guy that bought your 'yard sale' guitar—stopped by this afternoon. He's dying to put that old Gibson to the test. We went down to Panama Hattie's and talked to Kirk. He's a friend of mine that runs the place. He's going to let me, Grandpa, and a few friends set up for a 'tips-only, a few free-drinks' type gig, up on the deck at eight o'clock tonight. Woodsy here is free, so he's coming. We left a note at Freaki Tiki's place to let him know. It should be fun. You two ought to come."

"Ahh, Poon, you know I'm too young to get into a bar," Sunny complained.

"Right, but this is a restaurant. You're welcome there as long as you stay away from demon rum." He took a long pull on his drink. The guy he called Woodsy added, "Grandpa's real good, and his wife can sing." He wore a pork pie hat. He was kind of cute, in a scraggly way.

Landon spoke over Sunny's shoulder. "I've heard Poon and Woodsy play on the beach. They're fun. Let's go, Puddles, it will be great."

"I have to check with granddad. He might not like it."

Donnie was very drunk. He didn't say anything at first. He just kept nodding his head, and drinking from his plastic cup. Sunny could smell him from across the table. He finally said, slurring, "That big bag of shit doesn't like much of anything. He's a real prick."

Sunny stood up angrily. She knocked the drink out of his hand. Landon caught her wrist before she could slap his face. "You shut your drunken mouth, you idiot!" She was fuming. "Don't you dare talk about him that way!"

Landon wrapped his arms around her tightly. "Whoa, Puddles. Slow down! He doesn't mean anything." He led her, struggling, away from the table. "He's just drunk."

She shouted over her shoulder, "Yeah, he's drunk, and he's an asshole!" Poon hadn't moved or said a word, but he was laughing inside. He knew that one day someone would call Donnie on the carpet. He just didn't think it would be today, or be a little girl.

Just before the couple went into number fifteen, Poon hollered, "Eight o'clock! Should be fun."

Woodsy laughed out loud.

32

Mobley was staring at two guns pointed right at his face. He was shaking so badly that his knees threatened to buckle. "Who are you guys?" he whimpered. "What do you want?"

"Where's the book?" Tank demanded.

"What book? I don't know wh. . ."

Richie didn't wait for the man to finish his lie. He took a step forward and swung his pistol so that the barrel came slashing across Mobley's forehead. The skin burst like a cocoon releasing a butterfly of blood. The librarian fell to the ground, crying with pain. His hands went to cover the wound.

"Please! No, don't do this!"

"The book." Tank said calmly.

"But I don't . . . "

Tank nodded. His partner shot Mobley in the right leg below the knee. The man's whole body jerked, and he screamed. Tank wanted the man to know they were serious.

Richie just liked shooting people.

Tank towered over the moaning man. "We've got plenty of bullets, and you've got plenty of handy places to shoot them. You might as well make it easy on yourself."

"OK. OK! Just no more, please!" Between crying and groaning, Mobley squeezed out, "It's on the boat."

"Where on the boat?"

"It's hidden in the ceiling. There's a latch above a false smoke alarm." Blood was all over the man now. It was starting to coat the grass around him.

"Does Mick have any copies?"

"No. No, he hasn't even seen it. I was just getting ready to give it to him." Mobley was growing pale.

"You're sure about that? It's above the smoke detector? I don't want to have to come back and ask you again."

"Oh god, please! No more. I'm sure." His words were slowing, less frantic. "Just no more." Mobley rolled onto his side.

He's going into shock, Tank thought. "You believe him, Richie?"

"Yeah. He doesn't have the balls to lie, not under the circumstances."

"I agree." Tank nodded. Richie shot him a final time.

"Look at that, Tank." Richie laughed. "I gave him a third eye . . . dead center."

Back in the boathouse, Bonnie was playing a game for her life. "Sure, I like excitement. That's why I became a reporter. You're the reason I'm here. I think you're fascinating. I wanted to meet you."

"Reporter, huh? That can be dangerous work." Mick reached out and cupped her right breast. He watched her eyes as he worked it slowly with his thumb through her thin blouse. My god, Bonnie thought, as she felt her nipple harden. What is wrong with me? This psycho is turning me on.

Mick slipped his left arm behind her back and pulled her to him. He moved his hand from her breast to her thigh and began to caress it gently. The kiss came. It wasn't the rough, aggressive attack she expected. It was tentative and shy. Bonnie found herself putting her tongue in the mouth of a serial killer.

Then they heard it. It was the scream of a wounded animal, a cry of desperation. Mick broke away. He jumped from the boat onto the dock. "Stay right where you are!" he commanded. He moved to the boathouse door.

Mick eased the door open no more than an inch. Still, that was enough to allow him to see two huge men standing by the Dodge holding guns. The guns were equipped with silencers, so they weren't cops. They had to be hit men sent by Toes. He pulled the door closed and went back to Bonnie.

"Listen to me. Listen good. There are a couple of men out there that are looking for me. They don't want to lock me up. They want to shut me up. They're going to kill me, and since you're around, you'll get it, too. I'm going to do my best to stop them. I hope that's exciting enough for you."

Mick needed them, and his old black-op skills came back to him rapidly. He stilled himself, and then looked around the boat and the boathouse. There was only one way in unless the men were swimmers.

Bonnie was standing next to the boat's cabin wall, trying to make herself small. She shrank back when Mick grabbed for her hair, but he only snatched away her hair clip. He opened it and bent the clasp. In less than thirty seconds he had picked the lock, and the cabin door was open. He told Bonnie, "Get in there and stay on the floor." She moved into the cabin.

Mick took a position on the dock with his back against the wall. He was just inside the boathouse door. He waited with his hunting knife in one hand and the gun in the other. He didn't have to wait long. He heard soft footsteps approaching. Then he saw the door knob begin to turn. The door opened slowly, and some kind of awful creature looked in. Mick didn't hesitate. He ran his knife straight into the creature's ear. As he did, he realized that it was a man in a gas mask. Richie fell and died without a murmur. As his body collapsed, a green hand grenade rolled onto the dock. Mick stepped forward and kicked the grenade as hard as he could.

The move was partially successful. The grenade bounced down the dock and into the river, barely beyond the end of the boathouse. It went off underwater with a muffled thump. When it did, a small fountain of water sprayed a few feet upward.

Mick jerked the mask off the fallen corpse and put it on. He pulled the body through the doorway, rolled it into the water, and slammed the boathouse door. He turned in time to see white smoke bubbling out of the river. Some of it was dispersing harmlessly into the outside air, but about half of it was drifting into the boathouse.

Mick jumped from the dock over the boat's stern and into the cockpit. He jerked open the cabin door, threw himself inside, and slammed it shut. Leaping over Bonnie, he immediately began searching the walls and ceiling for any openings where gas might enter. He closed one hatch to the upper wheelhouse and another starboard side porthole, but those were the only two openings he found. Satisfied, he took the mask off and took a tentative breath. The air in the cabin was hot and muggy, but so far, it was gas free.

"Mick! What in hell is going on?" Bonnie was petrified.

"Not now! Stay on the floor and put that mask on." Mick's reactions were kicking in. He was thinking like an assassin again. Two well-armed men against Mick and the woman, and they were trapped. Why hadn't the men tried to kill him? They could have used a real grenade. They could have set the boathouse on fire. There were lots of ways to get the job done.

They wanted him alive. They were here to get Mick, but Toes was playing some kind of perverted game for his personal amusement. Whatever the game was, it required that Mick be alive to participate.

Mick thought about the attack that would certainly come. The second man outside would know he had a limited time to check things out. The gas was only good for a short time. Walking in from the daylight, his vision would be poor until his eyes could adjust. He would be wearing his own gas mask and that would limit his sight.

Since the boathouse was enclosed, the man had no way of knowing that Mick had killed his partner, but he would wonder why he hadn't gotten some word from him. He would be suspicious, but he would probably assume Mick and Bonnie were unconscious and his partner was busy tying them up.

Mick pulled the mask off Bonnie's head, snatching out some of her red hair in the process. He put it on, and as quickly as he could, slipped out of the cabin door, slamming it behind him. The gas was like a thick fog. He didn't know how much had gotten into the cabin, but he couldn't worry about that now. Mick felt his way around the cockpit until he found the ladder to the upper wheelhouse. He climbed it blind. At the top, he laid down prone and motionless, facing the stern, directly above the cabin door. He rested his hand that was holding the pistol in front of him.

Tank was waiting at the dock stairs. It had been almost ten minutes since Richie gassed the place. That damn fool should have Mick and the woman tied up by

188

now. These young kids could shoot 'em up, but they were dumb as shit. He waited a few more minutes, and then decided he had better give Richie a hand. Mick and the woman might wake up early. That would create a problem.

Tank pulled on his mask and walked the dock to the boathouse door. He checked his gun a last time, and then he entered. The interior of the boathouse was thick with gas. He could barely see. He called for Richie, but he could hardly hear himself with the mask on. He slowly made out the back end of a cabin cruiser. He couldn't see any movement. Richie, the damn amateur, probably put his mask on wrong and gassed himself.

Pushing his feet ahead one at a time, Tank managed to move up the dock to the side of the boat. He stood there a minute as the outline of the cabin and the cockpit emerged through the fog. The gas was starting to dissipate. He had to hurry. He stepped over the rail, caught the cuff of his suit pants on a cleat, and fell headlong into the cockpit. He landed on his face and cut his lip badly in the fall.

The cut lip was the least of his problems. As he stood back up, his six four frame put the top of his head eight inches from Mick's gun. He never heard the sound when Mick put a bullet through his skull and blew his brains straight into his neck.

Mick climbed down the ladder, stepped over the body, and jumped up onto the dock. He opened the boathouse entrance door. He could feel the cross breeze quickly pulling the gas out the open end of the structure. Mick kept his mask on and made his way back on board and to the boat's cabin. Stepping over the huge black man, he slipped through the door, closing it quickly behind him. Bonnie was slumped against the wall, unconscious. Enough gas must have gotten inside the cabin to knock her out.

Mick left his mask on and sat down to wait for the air to clear.

While he was waiting, he thought about Flores and the Lago Peten Itza. He pictured his little storybook island in the middle of that beautiful lake. Man, he was so close. There was still the book and Toes to take care of, but there was now a real possibility that life could be good again.

He wondered just how much excitement this redheaded reporter could take.

33

Jack was going crazy. The newsroom was nothing but chaos. Over the weekend there was a city commission member exposed as having a gay affair. A local shrimp boat was caught with nine tons of marijuana. An eighteen wheeler jack-knifed, hitting a van on Interstate 45 and killing six people. Then there were the normal fires, murders, and the crash of a private plane. Two of his best reporters were out sick.

They better die.

Another reporter was on vacation and on her honeymoon. His assistant was trying to reach all of them now. How dare they!

And where in hell was Bonnie?

"Julie!" Jack screamed. "Get Colleen on the phone." He opened his desk drawer and took out one of his bottles of Maalox. It was only half full, so he chugged it down. He threw the empty at the wastebasket, missing it by a good two feet. He reached back into the open drawer and took out a half pint of Jim Beam. He chugged that as well, but he did manage to hit the trashcan this time.

Julie came hurrying but the news wasn't good. "I can't reach Colleen, Jack. She must have her phone turned off." She put a thick stack of papers in front of him. "These sheets are all copy that you have to approve." Julie scurried away before Jack could throw something at her.

At that exact moment, Colleen was pulling into the building's parking garage. She took the space with Bonnie's name on it. She always did that when her boss was out of town. She sat in the car for a few minutes. She checked her makeup, adjusted the scoop of her nicest, low-cut blouse, and then hefted her new, braless breasts for luck. She ran her fingers lightly through her blonde locks, picked up her purse, and she was ready.

Colleen took the elevator from the garage that opened directly into the newsroom. As it reached her floor, she crossed herself, even though she wasn't Catholic. Careful of her posture, she put on her practiced smile, and walked into madness.

As the elevator opened, three people pushed Colleen back trying to get in. She forced her way through them and out into the newsroom. She found herself in a swirling mass of desperate humanity. There was yelling and cursing, and not one person seemed to notice her as she threaded her way towards her area. Fifty employees worked in the newsroom, and it looked like every one of them had been shooting speed. Colleen wished she had shot some herself.

As she neared her desk, she did get one nice, long low whistle. That cheered her up until she turned, and realized that it came from a Lesbian sports reporter that had been sniffing around her all year.

Well, so what? She arched her back, and turned slightly so she presented a better angle. She gave up her vacation and paid five grand for these breasts. By god, somebody was going to appreciate them.

As soon as Colleen sat down at her desk, Julie came rushing up. "Colleen! Where the hell have you been? Jack is going nuts looking for you. Get over to the editor's desk right away."

"Hi Julie, did you notice ... " but Julie was already gone.

Jack's self-medicating did little to ease his anxiety. He had a phone at each ear and a stack of papers in his hands.

"Listen to me, you little twit. If you want your job, if you ever want any newspaper job for the rest of your miserable life, you'll tell your selfish groom to jack off for a week, and get your ass back here!" He slammed that phone down, and it began to ring immediately. Now he had the other phone at his ear. "No, sir, no problem. No, sir. I wasn't speaking to you, sir. Yes, sir . . . yes, sir! Of course, sir. You have a nice day."

The whole time she was listening to this one sided conversation, Colleen was standing a safe five feet from Jack's desk. She watched as steam seemed to start pouring out of his ears. He began rising from his chair as he carefully hung up one phone. His face had gone from red to purple in seconds. She stepped back another foot. He ignored the other ringing phone, grimaced, and let loose with a muffled scream.

Some of the blood must have left his brain with the scream. "Colleen! Get over here and sit down." He was so angry he was sputtering. He gestured at a space in front of his desk.

Colleen hesitated. "But Jack, there's no chair."

"Well, shit, get over here anyway. I want to know where Bonnie is, and what the hell she's doing. I want to know now!"

"Jack, I haven't spoken to Bonnie since Sunday. When she called, she was in a hotel in Jacksonville, Florida. All she would tell me was that she was working on something really big, that I should take care of things here, and then she hung up. I've tried to reach her every few hours since, but she isn't answering her phone."

"I must have been on drugs when I hired that woman! She is the most stubborn, irresponsible, frustrating . . . "

"But Jack," Colleen felt she had to defend her boss, "she's the best you've got."

"Don't you think I know that? Don't you think I hate it that she's so damn good that I can't fire her? That's what's so frustrating." He pulled open his desk drawer and took out his last bottle of Maalox. He twisted off the cap and downed half of it. Finally, he sat down.

"All right. I want you to keep trying to reach her every hour. Let me know right away if you hear anything." Julia slinked up and dropped another stack of copy in front of him. She scurried away. "Give Julia the number of Sam Jeffers and have her get hold of him, then tell one of the cub reporters to go get me a couple of half pints of Jim Beam. Now get the hell out of here." Colleen gratefully turned to go.

"Oh, wait. One more thing, Colleen."

God, what now, she thought. He might throw something.

"I like the new tits." He gave her a thumbs up.

"Why thanks, Jack." Colleen smiled. "You say the sweetest things."

Ten minutes later, Julie had Sam Jeffers on the phone. She transferred the call to her boss's line.

"Jack. Sam here. What can I do for you?"

"You can find our favorite redhead so I can kick her ass. That's what you can do."

"What's up? What's Bonnie done now?"

"It's not what she's done," Jack said, "God knows what that might be. It's what she hasn't done that worries me. She hasn't called in. I'm here in the dark. Have you talked to her at all since Sunday?"

"Sure haven't. Colleen wouldn't give me her number, and she hasn't called me. I thought she would stay in touch with you." Sam lit a cigarette.

"Well, she hasn't."

"You worried about her?"

"Of course not. Bonnie's as tough as nails. Still, damn it, I'd like to know what's going on with her. Isn't she supposed to work for me?"

"I don't think I would ask her that, Jack. So, why call me?"

"If you want to rip me off for a few day's billings, get over here and see me."

"Plus expenses, Jack. I always get expenses. That means getting there, too. Don't forget that." Hot damn! Sam was thinking. "No offence, but this is business."

"You're a blood sucker, you know that? A regular fucking vampire . . . . OK. Plus *reasonable* expenses. Now get your ass here as soon as you can."

"Bye, Jack." But the phone was already dead.

Good thing Jack didn't know that Sam already had booked a trip to Jacksonville. Now the newspaper could pay the freight for the trip he was going to take anyway.

"Angie! Cancel my plane ticket to Jacksonville and get me on the next flight to New Orleans. Until I tell you to stop, all my expenses go straight to the Times-Picayune account."

Sam smiled. He felt better already.

34

Landon was still holding Sunny as they stood one step inside the door of room number fifteen. She had calmed down. Now it was more an embrace than a restraint. Landon knew she was young, but she was so sweet and so enthusiastic. She was appreciative about everything he did for her, too. Gee whiz.

The old AC unit rattled away, but the room was still hot and muggy. The musty curtains were drawn and the only light came from the bedside lamp. An empty bourbon bottle on the dresser added its fragrance to the room's atmosphere.

The couple broke apart. Landon sat on the far bed. He didn't want to stay long, and he sure didn't want to be there when Sunny's granddad came home. He patted the bed beside him, but Sunny ignored the gesture. She began to pace. There wasn't a lot of room, so it was mostly a few steps and then turn, but she kept at it. As she paced, she began to talk. She never looked at Landon, but he could tell that whatever she was going to say was important to her.

She started with an apology. "Landon, I acted so silly out there. I'm sorry. I know what a dick Donnie is. What he says shouldn't matter to me one bit. I acted like a kid."

"Don't. . ."

"Wait," she interrupted, "I've got to talk now, and I want you to just listen. Please, just listen." She was speaking more forcefully now. She suddenly stopped her pacing. She stepped close to Landon and kissed him long and hard on the mouth. He was stunned.

"What was that all. . ." Sunny stepped back and put her fingers over his lips.

"Landon, you might think I'm a little girl, but I'm not. I haven't been a little girl for a long, long time. When I wanted to be one, I couldn't. Now it's too late." She unconsciously rubbed her wrist. "You and everyone living here take life for granted. You see the ocean, the palms, the pelicans every day. You surf in the sunshine. You play your music and get high. You laugh. You never worry about tomorrow. The air you breathe, the food you eat, the life you play around in, they are every one better than what I thought was possible." Sunny bent and kissed Landon again. This time it was a gentle, lingering kiss.

"And now there's you. I've wanted to kiss you since the first time I saw you. I know you think I'm too young. I really wish I was, but that's the way it goes. Did you like kissing me? Tell the truth. I know I surprised you."

"Puddles, those were the best, the sweetest kisses I've ever had. They were amazing." He hung his head shyly, and then lay back on the bed.

"Me, too." Sunny blushed. "But here's the deal. I don't know how long we're going to be around here. As long as we are, if you like me, really like me, you can kiss me anytime." She grinned when she said this, "except maybe when granddad is around."

"You're not leaving, are you? Not really?" He was lost. Things were changing fast.

"I don't know. I don't want to, but granddad makes the decisions."

Sunny looked at the ceiling. This had to be said, too. She faced him head on. "And Landon, I mean this, I like you. I like you a whole lot, but you can only kiss me. I won't sleep with you. Not yet, anyway. Maybe never. I made a promise to myself that I'll never sleep with another man unless I love him completely. I have to know for certain that he loves me, too. I'm going to keep that promise, Landon, or I'm going to die trying."

"Another man?"

"You heard me. If my rule is going to bother you, then we can forget the kissing." Her eyes welled up. "We can forget everything." Her shoulders began to shake, and Sunny turned away from him. She went into the bathroom, and shut the door.

Landon sat on the edge of the bed with his chin cradled in his hands. What had just happened? He was bewildered. He stood up and went to the bathroom door. "I'm going to go outside, Puddles. I'll be there waiting for you when you're ready to come out."

Landon walked outside and closed the room door behind him. Poon and the drinkers were gone. It was after seven. They probably went on down to Panama Hattie's to get set up for their gig. He walked over to the picnic table and sat down. Someone was passed out in the hammock. It was Donnie, of course. Landon looked up at the evening clouds and listened to his snoring.

Landon was right. Grandpa picked up Poon about six forty-five and they drove in Grandpa's van over to Tiki's house on "F" Street. It was a nice, gray Cape Cod with a metal roof and a three story, wooden observation tower stuck on one side. When they drove up, Freaki Tiki was shirtless and sweaty, busily pushing a lawn mower across his yard. There were two large piles of cut brush near the driveway. An old boat sat on a trailer on the far side of his lot. The cut grass smelled fresh and clean. The noise of similar activities could be heard throughout the neighborhood.

Tiki was the only one of the local musicians that had a house. Most of them lived in cheap apartments or shacked up wherever they could. Lawn maintenance wasn't a passion with any of them. It wasn't for Tiki either, but he had the house, a steady girlfriend, and a real job. He was trying to be responsible.

The men got out as Tiki finished cutting the last row of grass and weeds. Poon was laughing. "Looking good, amigo. Real domestic. Makes me want to have my own house."

Tiki pushed his long brown hair back over his shoulders. He wiped his face and chest with a blue bandana. "Better they get a cage for you, dickhead."

Grandpa spoke up. "Aw, Tiki, go easy on old Poon. He's going to be homeless soon."

"Yeah? I'd say he is already. What do you really mean? Are they finally gonna level the Shallow Dive?"

"That they are, amigo," Poon replied. "We're in the final days. We'll have to have a for-sure party before the old girl goes." Poon hung his head.

"You get our note, Tik?" Grandpa asked. "You gonna jam with us tonight?"

"Man, I'd really like to. I haven't been out in a while. I'll check with Kate and see what she says. Shit. I just mowed this jungle of a yard. That should be worth something."

"Want us to ask her for you? We wouldn't want you to get in trouble." Poon loved ribbing Tiki about his domestic situation.

"Screw you old guys. You're just jealous. Want to come in and have a cold one?"

"Naw," Grandpa said, "we don't want to get into the middle of anything. We've got to get on down to Panama's and set up. I've got a real nice Gibson I want to test drive."

"I'll try and make it, Grandpa. For you, even if Poon is gonna play. I might be a little late, but I'll see you guys there." He was smiling.

That was good. Both men liked playing with Tiki. They loaded back in the van. They had to pick up Woodsy on Second Street and head for the gig.

Kirk managed Panama Hattie's. The friendly bar and restaurant had been a fixture on the beach scene for twenty years. It was a two story, ramshackle, clapboard building located directly across from the pier. It was painted gray with white shutters, and the forty or so bi-annual coats of paint on its outside were believed to be the glue that kept it standing. The creaky upper deck offered a great view of the ocean and the public volleyball courts. The manager's close watch on the signature seafood, and the strength of the cocktails brought in the customers. The place was popular with locals and tourists alike.

Kirk was five foot ten, in his mid-thirties, pale from all the working hours it took to run a beach bar. He was burdened with a beard so heavy that he had to shave twice a day. Kirk's upper teeth were white and perfect, but when he laughed his bottom teeth were exposed. They looked like a jumbled group of dominoes. He had the typical belly of a food service manager, and a proven record of business success. His employees liked him, but knew that to work at his place, they had to toe the line.

It was six o'clock and Kirk was having a meeting with his bar staff on the upper level of the restaurant. There was one stocky guy for the heavy lifting and three hot girls to keep the customers happy. All of the staff wore matching yellow and blue Hawaiian shirts. The girls left theirs unbuttoned and tied them tightly up under their ample breasts.

"Listen up, people. We're probably going to have a good crowd here tonight. I'm letting Grandpa and Woodsy play up here for free drinks and tips. They'll be starting about eight o'clock."

The staff all nodded and smiled with pleasure. The duo's music meant there would be lots of locals showing up and drinking heavily. They tipped well. Plus, no cover charge meant more money for tips.

"Don't get too excited, guys. There's always a catch." Kirk enjoyed the puzzled look on his bartenders' faces. "Poon and Tiki are coming, too." Their faces fell and there were mumbled curses. "Now wait," he held up his hands, palms out, "Grandpa promised to keep Poon under control, and Tiki hasn't even been in a bar in weeks. Customers enjoy their music. With the help of you guys, we'll have a killer night with no problems."

"What do you want us to do?" Lindsey, his head bartender, asked. She was terrific looking. Like the other girls, she had an attention-drawing body. Her blonde hair was up today, revealing the tattoo of a black widow spider on the back of her neck.

"Good question. First, take all the rums and put them under the bar, especially the Flora de Cana. Poon is to get beers only, and watch the count on those. If he or Tiki give any of you any trouble, tell Grandpa or come get me. I'll shut them down."

The employees looked around at each other. They appeared satisfied with that arrangement.

"OK. It's after six. Let's get ready. They'll be setting up about seven thirty for the eight o'clock show. Go get 'em, guys! Let's have a great night, and make plenty of money."

35

Mick looked out the side window of the cabin cruiser. He couldn't see any gas in the air, but he couldn't be sure there wasn't any left. There was no smell, but the stuff was odorless. He had used plenty of it in Viet Nam. Most types of it would knock out an average sized adult for roughly fifteen minutes. Nearly that much time had passed since the grenade went off.

Sunlight was streaming clearly through the boathouse door again. That was good. Mick waited until Bonnie began to stir. She was his canary in the mine shaft. He figured when she woke up completely, it would be safe for him to take the mask off. Mick checked out the books arranged by height on the cabin's wall shelf. He got a somewhat distorted view through the plastic windshields of the gas mask, but he could make out a few of the titles; *The Sun Also Rises, The Art of War, The Complete Works of William Shakespeare, In Cold Blood.* Good for Paul. He still kept the books he loved close by.

Mick adjusted the mask straps around his ears. He could feel hot, beading sweat on his forehead and upper lip. The rubber mask was very uncomfortable, but necessary. He had to be sure before taking it off that he wouldn't be put to sleep.

Mick tried to think of a plan to get the two of them out of there safely. The mystery men must have followed them in a car, so the vehicle would be somewhere close by. The Dodge was parked at the beginning of the dock, but it might have been disabled. He was sure Paul was dead, but he still had to check in case he was just tied up or handcuffed. Paul knew exactly where the book was hidden.

If he was toast, Mick would have to find the book on his own. He would also have to figure a way around any booby traps.

Bonnie began to moan softly. She shifted her body to stretch her legs. Mick reached down and took off her sandals. Her feet were tiny. Her toes were polished a light pink color that matched her lipstick. He held one foot in his lap and rubbed its sole. She was coming around.

"Where am I?" Bonnie asked in a squeaky voice. "You're taking a boat rid—" Mick began, but he realized he was speaking through the gas mask. Bonnie wouldn't understand him. He pulled it off and started again. "You're on Mobley's boat. We're in a boathouse. We had some visitors and they brought us a gas grenade. Some of the gas seeped into the cabin and knocked you out."

"Christ, my head hurts. I remember that first guy coming through the door. Are they gone?"

"Yeah. You could say that. I lost my hunting knife in that first guy's ear, and the other one is lying outside the cabin door. I don't think he's sleeping."

"You killed them? My God!"

"I guess I could have made them cocktails, but they didn't look too sociable to me."

"Ha, ha, ha. Damn, my head aches." She rubbed her temples. "Mick, you really do kill people. I mean, without a thought."

"Not true. I thought about the scream we heard. I thought about the gas that was filling up this boathouse. I thought about the two huge guys with guns that were coming after me and would have killed us both. Aren't you glad I thought?" He reached down and pulled Bonnie to her feet. "Now, you can do some thinking, too. How do we get away from here? I'm going up to the Dodge to check out the situation."

Mick shoved the cabin door hard enough to push Tank's leg out of the way. He exited the cabin, jumped to the dock, and left the boathouse. Bonnie grimaced at the sight of the body. She turned around so the grizzly scene was behind her. She sat on a padded seat and ran her hands through her hair. She slipped her sandals back on and sighed.

What a day.

Mick made his way up the dock. When he neared the Dodge, he could see that the driver's door on the far side of the car was open. He walked around the front of the car and found Mobley lying there, blood soaking into the ground around him. His open mouth testified to a painful death. A black circle was slightly above and between his eyes. Mick admired the work. The gunman was a damn good shot.

Paul wasn't going to help him with the booby trap.

A quick look around the yard revealed the white Lexus in the driveway up by the house. Mick checked it out. There were no keys in it. Mick decided that it had been visible to neighbors too long for it to provide a safe escape. It was blocking the garage. If anyone came back to the house, they would want Mobley to get it moved. Mick opened the door of the luxury car. It smelled of new leather and fast food. He put the car in neutral, and walking along beside it, he steered as gravity rolled it down the drive. He jumped into the car and stopped it before it could hit the Dodge.

Mick got back out and squatted next to Mobley's body. He took the wallet from the man's pocket and put it in his own. He took a quick look into the Dodge and found a ring of keys in the glove box. He closed the car door, and dragged the corpse around to the side away from the house. Mick thought about wiping both cars down to get rid of prints, but it was far too late to be worrying about things like that. When the people that owned the house came home, they would recognize Paul's car. If they couldn't see the body, they might think he was just fooling around on the boat. He would put Mobley in the river. That would give him a few hours. The important thing now was to get that done, and get them gone.

A dead body is dead weight. Mick struggled to get the corpse up the steps, and then far enough out on the dock for the river's current to take it when he pushed it in. He was finally satisfied with its position, and he rolled it under the rail. There was a splash, and so long, Paul.

Bonnie was calm and collected when Mick got back to the boat. "Hi, honey," she said with a tentative grin. "How was your day?" It looked like the redhead had washed her face and straightened her clothing. He didn't bother to answer, but he did appreciate her cool.

The big black's body was taking up most of the cockpit. Mick rifled the man's pockets. He found eighteen hundred dollars in a money clip, and the keys to the Lexus, Mick took the watch off of Tank's massive wrist, and then pulled the body into a sitting position. He found the silenced nine millimeter Browning underneath him.

"How about a hand here?" he asked Bonnie. "I need to take out the trash."

Bonnie stepped into the cockpit gingerly. There was blood all over the floor, and one of the two chairs was smashed. They were both overturned. Mick took the body under the arms and Bonnie took the feet. Together they managed to raise it to the gunnels. A final shove rolled it over. The black, bloody, well dressed corpse splashed into the space between the boat and the boathouse wall. Mick tossed the Lexus keys after it.

Bonnie was hurriedly washing the blood off of her hands in the galley. Mick said, "Thanks, you're pretty strong for a woman. Tell me something, you ever drive a boat?"

She dried her hands with a towel hanging by the sink. She was thinking fast. What kind of answer would kill her, and what kind might save her?

"There's no car?" she asked.

"Not that we can use, but you didn't answer my question." Mick was not terribly patient.

"Well, I keep a boat on Lake Pontchartrain, but it's smaller, just an outboard. I don't get to use it very often."

Mick pulled Mobley's key ring from his pocket. "Take these and see if one works this boat's ignition." He tossed the ring to her. He then took a steel gaff from its slot on the side of the hull. The fishing tool was menacing. It was five feet long and ended in a shiny, barbed steel hook three inches across. Mick hefted the weapon, and found a comfortable grip.

"No! No, don't do it!" Bonnie was shrinking back against the galley wall, her hands crossed in front of her face in fear.

"Oh, calm down, woman. I just need to do some fishing. Where's that hard core attitude of yours that likes excitement?" Mick was chuckling. He leaned over the back of the boat near the dock. He was humming as he probed the water with the gaff. Before long he mumbled, "There you are." He jerked the gaff hook through the water. "I got one!" he called out.

Bonnie had identified and inserted the right key into the boat's ignition. She made sure the gears were in neutral, and then she turned it. The motor came to life, and quickly settled into a pleasant, rumbling idle.

Mick was reaching far out over the transom. She thought of rushing him and pushing him overboard. Before she could will herself to move, he leaned heavily backward, and Richie's body rose out of the water. The gaff hook was firmly lodged in his neck.

"Give me a hand here!"

Bonnie went into the cockpit. She got a decent grip on the coat of the corpse. Together they brought the body to the level of the transom. Mick took a length of line and looped it over the head. He tied it off on a cleat, and then they both let go and stepped back. Their trophy was secure.

"You got the boat going. Nice work. The question is, can you drive it?"

"I guess so. Well enough. There's plenty of gas."

Mick started going over the body. He was collecting items and dropping them behind him. A sodden wallet, a nice watch, a pinky ring. When he finished, he said, "Too bad his gun sank." He untied the line holding Richie's body and watched the corpse slide back beneath the water's surface.

"So lady, the engine's running. I'm going to untie us. Then we can go, right?"

"We can try. Make sure to bring the lines on board."

"Aye, aye, Captain." Mick saluted.

35

The Delta flight to New Orleans was right on time. Sam boarded wearing a freshly pressed, tan, western suit. He had on a nice pair of brown, Lucchese, horsehide boots. He held a small carry-on bag. Anything he might need along the way, he would buy and put on the expense sheet. Angie would bill it to Jack. He would have to get a gun when he arrived in New Orleans, or maybe he would wait until he got to Florida. Trying to carry one on a plane was just a pain in the ass.

The plane took off after the crew dispensed with the usual crap that the company wanted you to think could save your life. Sam was seated in first class. He was in an aisle seat so he could stretch out a little. The plane wasn't full, and the window seat was empty. After the plane reached altitude, a cute little blonde flight attendant came by to offer refreshments. Sam chose two miniature bottles of Jameson's Irish, and a large cup of ice. He passed on the snacks. It was only a one hour flight, and he didn't want to ruin a good buzz.

Sam leafed through the in-flight magazine. Before he had completed the article telling him how to improve his golf game by twenty percent, the Captain announced they were beginning their decent. Sam had never played golf in his life, but the pictures were nice.

The landing wasn't smooth, but after the initial jolt the plane straightened its taxi run, and they made it safely to the gate. Sam was one of the first people off the plane. He got out of the security area quickly, too. Just outside the glass doors, he was greeted by a beautiful young woman in a low cut blouse. She looked vaguely familiar.

"Hi, Sam! How was your flight? Welcome to New Orleans." The attractive woman gave him a tight hug. He could swear she pressed her breasts against him suggestively. Sam knew when to fake it. "It was fine, just fine. How have you been?"

"Oh, you know," the woman responded, "with Bonnie gone, I've got to run the whole show."

Bingo! She was Colleen. Colleen with the new boobs.

"But I was glad when Jack asked me to pick you up. We haven't had the pleasure of your company since last year." She smiled, took his elbow and held it against her. He could feel the jiggle as they walked. "Jack is so nuts lately. I hope you can help him with whatever it is that's making him crazy."

"Well, I'll do all I can." Sam said modestly.

"I told him you might want to freshen up, but he insisted I get you straight to the paper. We can be there in twenty minutes." She steered him towards the escalator that led to the garage. "While you're here in town, Sam, anything you need, anything at all, you just let me know." She smiled provocatively, and slipped a card in his jacket pocket.

"That's so sweet of you, Colleen." Sam gave her his "just-wait-until-I-get-you-naked" look. "I'm sure I'm going to need your help at some point. You look terrific, by the way. You haven't changed a bit."

Colleen looked up at him with a puzzled expression.

"I'm kidding!" He leaned into her and whispered, "They *are* magnificent!" Colleen giggled. She gave his elbow a squeeze.

Oh yeah. She was glad to see him. He was as tall and as rugged looking as she remembered. Bonnie said he was fantastic in bed, and the boss had plenty of men to compare him with. Colleen wanted the first time with her new boobs to be perfect. She also wanted to find out if that "diamond hard" reference was true.

They could hear Jack screaming as soon as they got off the elevator. People scattered like chaff in the wind as he moved across the newsroom. They were just ripples rolling away from Jack's splash of life.

"I don't give a shit if a point nine earthquake hits Washington, D.C. I don't care if your entire family is on fire! I don't care if anacondas have invaded the break room and are squeezing the guts out of half the help. We are putting out a newspaper, people, a damn good newspaper. It has my name on it, and by god, we're putting the fucker out on time!"

Sam held his arm across Colleen to hold her back. "Let him get to his desk. I want something between us when I talk to him." They watched Jack's back as he stormed through the newsroom. As he moved out of sight, people began returning to their desks. They came from all directions like water seeking the lowest point. In minutes, the newsroom was back to its normal chaos.

"OK. Now we go," Sam said. They made their way through the maze of partitions and desks until they got to Julie's. She looked up, and broke into a huge smile.

"Thank god you're here! He will see you right now." She gestured to the side of her partition.

"If I worked for Jack," Colleen whispered, "I'd have that made out of concrete."

The editor was facing away from them, talking on the phone. "Just do it!" He slammed the phone down and turned.

"Hello, Jack," Sam began.

"You hear from her?" the editor demanded.

"No, I . . . "

"Colleen. You heard from her?"

"No, Jack."

"Goddamn it! Why did I ever hire that nightmare of a woman? What did I do to deserve this shit?"

"Jack," Sam risked it, "I can stand here and listen to you cuss at every rock on the face of the earth, or you can tell me why I'm here, and I'll get to work. It's your dime."

Money was the one thing that could make Jack focus in a hurry. He scowled, but took his seat behind his desk. "Sit down, both of you."

"That's a nice offer, Jack, but there aren't any chairs."

"Well, stand up then. Goddamn it, we've got to get busy. My number one reporter has been completely out of touch for four days now. My top reporter! I want you to find her. You know everything I know, probably more. She never tells me a frigging thing, and I want her found!"

"Well, that seems plain enough. Any instructions?"

"Julie has a plane ticket for you. You're leaving at eight in the morning on a Delta flight for Jacksonville. There will be a rental car reserved there for you. The tickets and a Hertz reservation are in an envelope at Julie's desk. Also, in that envelope is a name and phone number for a friend of mine at the Jacksonville Times-Union. He owes me a favor, and he'll help you any way he can. Other than that, earn your damned money."

"All understood, Jack, but when I get there, I'm going to need a gun."

"That's one reason you're getting the phone number. This guy owes me big time. He won't mind bending a few rules. Just tell him what you need." Jack pointed his finger at Colleen. "You get Sam over to the Marriott. Get him checked in. Pick him up in the morning. If he misses that plane, don't even think of showing your face, or any other parts of you, around this place again. Now get out of here, the both of you."

Jack was jerking open his desk drawer as the pair turned and made their escape. They hardly slowed as Sam took the envelope from Julie's outstretched hand. He blew her a kiss and aimed Colleen at the elevator.

The Times-Picayune kept a suite at the downtown Marriott that was used for entertainment and bribery. It was on the fourteenth floor and overlooked both the Mississippi River and a tiny slice of the French Quarter. The suite consisted of two full bedrooms, two very large baths—the master's had a Jacuzzi—a huge living room with a bar and, best of all, a nicely landscaped balcony that looked over the city. Sam was pleased. He handed the bellhop a five and then turned around several times, basking in his surroundings.

"Don't you just love it?" Colleen said. "Bonnie has used it a few times, but this is my first." She walked to him from the bar. There were two very brown drinks in her hands. She gave one to Sam. "Jameson's, isn't it? I hope I remembered right."

Sam nodded. "Right the very first time."

Colleen smiled. She said, "Here's to first times," and touched her glass to his. She took a big swallow. Sam did likewise. The sun was going down as the pair walked out on the balcony. They leaned on the railing together. The noise of the traffic below was so far beneath them that they could barely hear it. Lights were coming on like fireflies across the city.

"I'll have to pick you up at six to make your eight o'clock flight, Sam." The investigator nodded, and took a swallow of his whiskey. He looked up and down the beautiful girl, being obvious about it. She smiled under his inspection, and moved so that she was tight against him. "I know I'm not Bonnie . . . "

"Hush, now. I don't want Bonnie. I want this brand new you." Sam bent and kissed her deeply. Her arms went around his neck and her body pressed into him. "Now, no more talking. There are two bedrooms here. I want to try them both." He took her hand and led her into the first of them.

Five minutes later they were both naked. Colleen still wore her stiletto heels. Sam lifted her onto the bed and propped her back up with pillows. "Are they tender, sweet one?" he asked.

"Just a little bit, but I want you to have them. I want you to be the first man to have them." She leaned her head back on the pillow. Sam got onto the bed with one leg on either side of her. He braced himself with his hands and kissed her breasts with passion. The kissing went on and on. He raised his head and kissed her mouth. When their lips broke apart, Colleen was panting, "Oh, Sam!" but she was now speaking only to the top of his head. His face was again lost in the glory of her new breasts. He was kissing the nipples one after the other, his hands serving them into his mouth. He began to lick circles around them, and to nip them with his teeth. He went on and on until he was licking each whole breast in turn. He sucked as much of them as possible into his hungry mouth.

Colleen was nearly delirious. She had worried before the operation that the implants in her breasts would keep them from being as sensitive as before. Sam was quickly proving that theory wrong. She held his shoulders, her legs spread wide, her heart beating like a bongo drum. She wanted him, needed him inside her, but still he worshipped at the temple of her new breasts. God, it felt good! She was becoming so wet that when she finally did manage to pull Sam into her, his cock slid past the lips of her vagina like they were made of hot, melting ice.

Colleen came in seconds, but Sam was just getting started. He pumped her like a playground seesaw. He stabbed her with his penis as if to defend from an attack. He probed her as if she were a newly discovered species. A second, a third, a fourth orgasm. She thought she would faint, but now Sam was nearly there. In a last savage thrust, he burst inside her. She came and screamed at the same time.

It was minutes before either could move. "Damn," Sam finally gasped, "I need to quit smoking."

"Damn is right," Colleen agreed with a sigh. "I need to start."

36

Mick had no trouble untying the knots on the boat lines. When they were undone, he gave Bonnie the high sign. For an instant, he was unaware that his foot was inside a tangled coil of the anchor rope that Mobley had pulled out of the anchor locker. Bonnie knew instinctively that she could gun the boat's engine, throw it in gear, and Mick would be caught in the loose line. Maybe he would be pulled overboard. He would have a hard time swimming attached to the double-fluke anchor.

But she didn't do it. She couldn't bring herself to attempt the drowning of her captor, even if he might kill her further down the line. Instead, she kept the engine in neutral. Mick noticed the loop around his foot. He carefully stepped out of it. Then he made his way around the side of the cabin, and jumped back into the cockpit.

"The ropes are all off. The boat is loose and so are we. Let's go, Captain."

Bonnie left the engine in neutral to idle. She climbed up the ladder to the upper pilot station. She wanted to steer and control the boat from there. After releasing the stops on the upper controls, she eased forward on the throttle. The cruiser moved slowly out of the boathouse, the motor gurgling pleasantly. As soon as she was clear, Bonnie turned and called down to Mick. "So now what? Which way do we go?"

"The current will take the bodies downstream. Let's go upstream and see what we can find."

Mick was carefully examining the interior of the cruiser. Mobley was going to unlock the gangway door, so the book's hiding place had to be somewhere inside the cabin.

"Is there anything in particular that we're looking for?" Bonnie was watching the river bank.

"Yeah, I just don't know what it is yet." Mick continued touching and tapping the walls and floor. If it wasn't for the hidden booby trap, he would tear the place apart. He swayed with the motion of the boat, searching as carefully as he could.

Bonnie was handling the boat well. Mick checked their progress along the river through a porthole. Satisfied, he went back to his hunt. He wasn't having much luck until his attention was drawn to the tiny stove in the galley. He was thinking of making some coffee to help keep him awake, but there was a smoke detector directly over the stove. He was afraid that he would set it off some blaring type of alarm. Then he paused. How could anything be cooked with a sensitive smoke alarm above the stove?

It couldn't.

Mick turned a plastic milk crate over and stood on it. He took a close look at the smoke detector. There was no light on it to show that it was activated. The plastic device was only mounted to the ceiling by two small screws. It could be a fake. This could be what he was looking for.

Mick took a kitchen knife and slowly removed the two screws. He twisted the detector slightly, and it dropped a few inches into his hand. There they were. No battery, just a red wire and a black wire. At the edge of the exposed hole in the ceiling, Mick could see a length of woven stainless steel cable with a loop at the end. He didn't want to stop and think about what he was going to do. With one quick jerk, he pulled both the red and the black wires free.

Nothing happened.

Mick sighed deeply. He reached above the now harmless detector and pulled the stainless cable. With a thump, a piece of tile fell from the backsplash behind the tiny sink. Where the tile had been, Mick could see a velvet, Crown Royal drawstring bag. He pulled it out of its hole and jerked it open.

There was the book.

It was only about four inches across. The cover said "Diary," but there, right in his hands, was his history with Toes, and his ticket to financial freedom.

Bonnie turned the boat to starboard and gave it some gas. She quickly increased their speed to nearly full throttle. She figured the cruiser was doing about fifteen land miles an hour as they powered up the river. In five or six minutes, they passed under the Trout River Bridge, the same bridge they had crossed by car barely more than an hour earlier. Mick climbed up the ladder and stood beside her as she guided the cruiser. She handled the boat well. The scene was similar to his fantasy, except he was supposed to be the captain and she—beautiful, red haired Bonnie, in her golden bikini—was supposed to be standing next to him. It didn't matter. His time would come. He was very pleased with the way things were developing.

Two hours later, a bronze Honda minivan turned into the driveway of the stucco house. The driver pulled the vehicle into the garage. Its driver's door opened, and a rather haggard looking, brunette housewife wearing shorts and a green T-shirt stepped out. She opened a rear door, and out spilled three shouting children.

"Kids!" she pleaded. "Get in the house and go into the kitchen. I'll make you a snack, but only if you can behave yourselves."

The children, a girl age four, and two boys, six and seven, ran screaming into the house. Their mother slowly followed. She was suffering a throbbing headache. When she reached the kitchen, her youngest was beating on the dining table with a large carving knife.

"Amy! Give that to me." The mom reached for the knife. As the child tried to pull it away, the woman mistakenly grabbed it by the blade. "Oh, Amy," she complained. A thin line of blood emerged on her palm. The little girl began to cry.

The two boys were wrestling on the window seat below the bay window. As the housewife stood at the sink washing the blood from her palm, she glared at them. She noticed through the window that Paul's car was at the dock. Sometimes he would take her and the kids for a short ride on the river. It usually calmed them down a little. This time, though, it looked like he had friends down at the boat. There was a beautiful white Lexus parked behind his Dodge. He was most likely taking a group for a boat ride, or just enjoying cocktails on the boat. She could use a stiff drink herself.

Mick was loving their ride on the river. He liked the steady rumble of the engine, the splashing at the bow as they cut through the water, the white wake that followed them in the shape of a curling ostrich plume. There were billowing cumulus clouds up above. Trees leaned over the river bank. It felt so free to be up high on the boat, above all the little things that nagged at him.

A dark green speedboat was coming in their direction from up the river. "What should I do?" Bonnie asked, turning to Mick.

"Keep on piloting the boat the way you are. When that other boat gets closer, I want you to smile and wave. A big wave. Anyone out on this river today should be happy. If you're not, it will look strange and draw attention."

The speedboat was nearing them on the starboard side. Bonnie and Mick smiled and waved down at it energetically. Mick slipped his arm over Bonnie's shoulder. They were just another happy couple out for an afternoon on the river.

The speedboat was driven by a blonde, teenage girl in a shiny bikini. Two of her friends in similar bathing suits sat beside her. They were drinking from cans of beer. They waved back as they swept past, leaving a wide wake and the fading sound of laughter.

"I was like that when I was a girl," Bonnie said. "I don't know how, why, or even when, I got to be so serious."

"I was never like that." Mick said. "At least, not that I can remember. I hope I can get like that sometime before I die." He gazed out at the winding river ahead. "I do know someone like that. She is full of curiosity and enthusiasm. Life is an adventure for her."

Bonnie looked at Mick. "The girl, Brenda Rose?"

"She'd hit you hard for calling her that. She's left that name behind."

"Tell me the truth, Mick. Have you hurt that little girl?"

"Look! There on the left." He pointed ahead. "Take the boat up that way. We'll have a better chance to hide it getting away from this main channel." There was a small sign at the opening of a smaller channel on the left bank: "Ribault Creek."

Bonnie turned the cruiser and reduced the gas. The boat settled down from its plane, and slowly moved out of the Trout and up into the smaller stream. "I'm going down on the deck," Mick said. "I need to gather up some things. You watch for a place to leave the boat. It has to be a place with some cover, and enough cars around for me to steal one." He hurried down the ladder.

Inside the cabin in a storage locker, Mick found a canvas bag of nautical flags. He dumped the flags on the floor, and put the two guns, the jewelry, and the watches inside. He sat on the portside bench and went through the wet wallets. He stuffed the damp bills in his pocket, and then took the driver's licenses out and set them on the tiny galley counter. Just as he thought. He didn't recognize the names, but both men were from Galveston.

Tony Toes. He sent them. That son of a bitch.

Mick sat very still for a minute. Why was Toes after him? He hadn't threatened the mobster. Of course, he did plan to blackmail Toes to get enough money to retire. But he hadn't done it yet. How did Toes know about the book? How could he know that over the years, one memorized sentence at a time, Paul had transported Mick's confessions and revelations onto paper?

Mick felt so stupid. He could have slapped himself. He had answered his own question. Mobley! The quiet, mild mannered librarian had decided to do the deal on his own. No doubt, when Paul heard that Mick had escaped, he knew Mick would be coming for the book. Once the psycho killer had it, his accomplice would no longer be useful. Mick wouldn't leave anyone with information on him alive, so what's Mobley to do? He makes his own pitch to Tony Toes for a lot less money than Mick would. He does it as if he is trying to be helpful. Mobley would go to the lawyer, Zimmer. They had been meeting for years. Mick could clearly imagine Mobley's side of the conversation.

"Please tell Mr. Cicarella that I wish to prevent possible trouble for him. Mick Parsons has sent a book to me that could be very damaging to your client and his Galveston operations. I haven't mentioned it before now, because I did not expect Mick to ever get out of prison. I didn't think he would ever be in a position to use it against Mr. Cicarella. I have guarded it. Now that he's out, however, I want your employer to have this book so he can destroy it and rest easy. I would only ask that he recognize my friendship and reward me with a small token of appreciation. Say, half a mill?"

Zimmer would pity the amateur. No one with any sense would ever attempt to screw with Tony Toes. Who was he kidding? Toes would chew this guy up like a buzz saw. First he would find, imprison, and torture Mobley until he got the book. Then he would wait for Mick to appear and take the both of them out. End of Mobley. End of Mick. End of story. That had to be the way it was supposed to go down.

Mick took the canvas bag and went back up the ladder. The redhead looked good at the boat's controls.

37

It was only seven-thirty and Panama's upper deck was already filling up with a noisy crowd. Kirk stood by the back wall and watched the people coming in. His staff was performing well. The female bartenders looked great. They were scurrying around behind the bar, keeping the customers happy with drinks and chatter. His lone male bartender was busy bringing booze and supplies as they were needed from downstairs. It was going to be a very busy night.

Over in the corner, Grandpa was arranging various amps and other pieces of equipment on the small stage. Poon was stretching cables and taping them to the floor so no one would trip over them. He looked sober. Woodsy was centering the monitors and adjusting microphone stands. Everything seemed to be going smoothly.

When the musicians were satisfied that the stage lights, equipment and instruments were all ready to go, they walked over to where Kirk stood at the bar.

"All set, Grandpa?" Kirk asked.

"Yeah. Should be fine. We're hoping a few more guys will show up to play, but we can manage if they don't."

"How 'bout one of those free drinks over here, amigo?" This from Poon.

Kirk looked away. "Poon, I'm going to save both of us some trouble tonight. I've told all the bartenders that you aren't to get anything to drink but beer. Get pissed off if you want. Walk out if you want. But that's the way it's going to be."

Poon scowled. He started to protest, but Grandpa held him back with a gesture. "Kirk, whatever you say is fine, but don't you think a free gig is worth a *whole bottle* of Flora de Cana? That is, as long as Poon picks it up after we play our last song? I bet he would agree not to open it until he's back at the Shallow Dive."

Kirk smiled. Grandpa was a diplomat. "Sure. I guess so. I'll have Lindsey put a fifth behind the bar for you, Poon. You can get it after your last set," Kirk promised. "But keep the top on until you're long gone." Poon relaxed, and grinned a little.

"Well, I don't much like it. I'm a grown man playin' by kids' rules. But OK, I'll go for it if I can have a beer right now. That suits you, then it's a deal." The men shook on it.

"Lindsey!" Kirk yelled. "Get this gentleman a beer."

Lindsey looked perplexed. "You mean Poon?"

Back at the Shallow Dive, Landon was still sitting at the picnic table listening to Donnie snore. He heard a door opening, and saw Sunny coming out of her room. She walked slowly towards him.

"I didn't think you'd still be here," she said.

"I told you I would," Landon said. "I would have waited all night."

"That's nice to hear." Sunny sat beside him and clutched his hand. She leaned her head on his shoulder. "That Donnie sounds like an old John Deere tractor in need of a muffler."

"Oh yeah? What do you know about tractors?"

"I know I never want to see another one. Landon, you know I don't know a thing about you except that you surf. Do you go to school? Do you work? Where do you live?"

"Aw, my life is pretty boring. I'd rather talk about you."

224

"That's not going to happen. At least not until you tell me about yourself."

The young man stared into the darkness. His foot was tapping a steady rhythm underneath the picnic table. He took a quick look at Sunny. Then he looked away.

"OK, here goes. I don't go to school. I dropped out of high school last year when I was sixteen. I was surfing a lot, and I had this crazy idea that I could get good enough to get a sponsor. I thought I could drop out and just practice all the time. Don't laugh, but I really thought I might be able to go professional. That would be the perfect life for me. Just surfing all the time, traveling to all these cool places, and meeting cool people from all over the world."

"What happened?" Sunny asked.

"Reality happened. It slapped me in the face. I entered a tournament in Daytona. It was the first time I competed against surfers that weren't local. I'm a hot dogger here. I'm one of the best. Even then, I thought I was something special. Damn, Sunny," he took a deep breath, "the tournament was horrible. I was outclassed from the very first wave. I mean the new guys were not just great, they were awesome! I finished my first fifteen minute ride, and then skipped my other ones. I was too embarrassed to even compete with those guys. I had to get out of there. My friends were all still interested in the competition, so I left my board with them and hitchhiked home. I never competed again." He turned to see her reaction. Sunny sat still. She stayed silent.

"After that, I started getting high more often. I wasn't surfing much, but I still refused to go back to school. My parents got disgusted with me. They said I had to go back to school, or live on my own." Landon let go of Sunny and clenched his hands on top of the table. "Aw, Puddles, you don't want to hear this."

"I do! Landon, I really do." She put her hands over his.

"I let my pride get the best of me. I took my stuff and moved out. I didn't have any money or any place to go, so I started sleeping under the pier. Pretty stupid, huh?" He went on. "One of my surf buddies got me a part time job bussing tables at the Beachcomber Restaurant. It's a cool little seafood place down on 'A' Street by the water. I didn't make much money, but it was a fun place to work. I didn't need much. Actually, life didn't look too bad right then."

"OK. I understand. What happened next?" Sunny asked.

"Randy."

"Who's Randy?"

"Randy is one of our local cops. He's a real good guy, but it's up to him to enforce the law. Randy found me sleeping under the pier early one morning. He woke me up and flat out laid into me. No more crashing on the beach. He put me in his patrol car and pumped me for information about my situation. I was scared, but I was straight with him."

"Did he arrest you?"

"No, nothing like that. Randy just wanted to make sure I was safe. He drove me to my parents' house and left me in the car while he went in to talk to them." Landon unclenched his hands. He slipped one arm around Sunny. He pulled her closer to him. "He came out and got back into the car. 'You were right,' he told me. 'They're done with you. Tell you what. I'm taking you to a house over on "D" Street. It's a crash pad for street kids. You'll have to pay a little rent and live pretty basic. You don't tell your parents or the other kids how you got there.' I figured it couldn't be more basic than underneath the pier." Sunny put her head on his shoulder. "It turned out to be a great thing for me. I still live there, me and eleven others. It's a three-bedroom house, and we have extra cots set up in the garage. We share the rent and we charge other kids what they can scrape up if they need to spend a night or two. I still bus tables two nights a week at the Beachcomber. I've picked up some construction work, too. I'm getting by OK." Landon smiled at her. "I've still got time to surf, and now, you've come into the picture."

"Are you glad?" Sunny asked shyly.

"What do you think, Puddles?" He kissed her gently.

Donnie continued to snore.

It was a few minutes after eight. Grandpa made a final adjustment to his microphone. Then he said hello to the crowd. "Evening, guys and gals. Sure is nice to see you all out there itchin' to help us have a good time. Sing along if you feel like it. Stomp your feet if you want." He hit a few chords. "Kirk has some great adult beverages for you folks at the bar. The more you drink, the better we sound. I think you know Woodsy and Poon. I'm Grandpa, and here we go."

The trio broke into a rousing bluegrass number about an illegal moonshine still on a wooded mountain. Grandpa took the lead on the Gibson. He loved his new axe. Woodsy was playing bass on this tune, and Poon was playing rhythm on a nice Martin Grandpa loaned him. His own, six-string Taylor was back in hock down at Ancient City Pawn. It had been in and out so often that the men who worked there kept a place in the display window for it. They were good guys, and Poon was confident they would never sell it out from under him.

The trio got a nice round of applause when they finished the song. Grandpa beamed at his friends. Tammy joined them for the second song. She added some beautiful harmony to the three contrasting voices. For the next hour and a half, the friends happily played a mixed selection of songs, everything from classic rock to blues to country and folk. Woodsy's friend Jay came up and played banjo. Tiki and their friend Jeff arrived to add their voices and guitars to the last four or five songs. At about nine thirty, the group announced a break. Amid lots of cheers and clapping, they made for the bar. The musicians and the audience were having a blast.

Sunny and Landon were still sitting at the picnic table back at the Shallow Dive. A cream colored crescent moon was shining through a wisp of clouds. The beam from the lighthouse swung around every sixty seconds. The scene was very romantic.

"We can go back to the room if you want," Sunny said shyly, "but just for kissing."

"Thanks, but no thanks. I wouldn't want to be in there when your grandfather gets back. He looks at me with daggers in his eyes as it is."

"You know," Sunny said thoughtfully, "he went up to Jacksonville today, but I thought he would be back by now. I'm getting a little worried about him."

"You shouldn't be. That old man is as tough as nails. What you should do is walk up to Panama's with me and listen to Grandpa and the guys play. They should be really cooking by now."

"But what about my granddad?"

"We can leave him a note. Come on. It will be fun."

228

Sunny thought for a minute. Ted was probably OK. She knew he was looking for that man, the printer. He probably had to chase down some other leads. He might even have to spend the night in Jacksonville. As long as she left a note for him, it should be all right to listen to some music for a while. It would be fun, and it was almost like a real date. It would be her first.

"Tell you what. You wait right here. I'll go write a note for granddad and change my clothes. I can be ready to leave in ten minutes." She gave him a quick kiss, and skipped off to her room. Landon just sat there in a daze. He was smitten. This younger girl was knocking him out!

In room fifteen, Sunny scribbled a note on a paper bag. She propped it on Ted's bed. "Gone to Panama Hattie's. Back soon, Sunny Catherine Cantrell." She exchanged her shorts for her new sundress. It fit her nicely, but revealed that her shoulders were still peeling a little. She wiped some lotion on them, and then quickly brushed her short, dark hair. Her blonde roots were beginning to show. She would have to dye her hair again soon. Ted's hair must need it, too. Sunny looked at herself in the mirror. She smiled at her reflection. She was going on a date! Life was good.

Landon watched Sunny approach from across the parking lot. She had a real dress on. She looked so pretty in the moonlight. He found it hard to believe she was only sixteen. She looked more like a woman than a girl.

"Hi, again. You ready to go?" she asked.

She smelled faintly of soap and coconut lotion. Her eyes glistened in the moonlight. "You bet." Landon stood up smiling, and they started walking across the parking lot.

"Wait just a minute," Sunny said. She hurried back to the picnic area. Grabbing one edge of the old hammock, she jerked it hard, flipping Donnie flat on the ground. She ran back to Landon laughing. "OK. Now we can go."

They turned up Beach Boulevard arm in arm.

38

The sun was going down. It wasn't long before dark. Mick stood next to Bonnie. They both scanned the sides of the creek for a place to ditch the boat. Up ahead, Bonnie spotted a sign at the canal entrance. It read, "Wish and Fish, Your RV Park and Fish Camp." A thin, shiny slick of oil drifted from the opening. "What about there?" she asked.

"No good for dumping the boat, but a great place to pick up a car. Keep going, but let's try not to go too far. I'd like to be able to get back here on foot."

They were in luck. As the light was fading, less than a quarter mile upstream they saw a small wood-framed house on the left bank. It had a dock that ended in a "T" made by two boathouses. They couldn't see any cars parked at the house, and there weren't any lights on inside it. The lawn was ragged and needed tending. There was a bass boat covered with a blue tarp tied up in the boathouse facing them. As they passed the dock, they could see that the far boathouse was empty. "This is it," Mick said. Bonnie nodded, and let off the throttle. She let the boat's momentum take them past the boathouse. Then she turned sharply so that they were facing its open end. Now the cruiser moved with the current. Bonnie maneuvered the boat inside the shelter as pretty as you please.

Mick climbed down the ladder, went forward and took the bow line. He grabbed a dock piling and stopped the boat's motion. He jumped onto the dock and secured the line to a large cleat. Bonnie killed the engine. Mick took another line from the dock and tied off the boat at the stern.

"Nice work, Captain. You did yourself proud." He offered her a hand to get off the boat. Bonnie ignored it and stepped onto the dock unaided.

"Look, redhead, like it or not, you're stuck with me for a while. Of course, if I'm too much trouble for you to bother with, I can end your part of this trip any time."

Bonnie realized that she had screwed up. Ignoring Mick's hand had been a big mistake. She had offended a deranged mass murderer. Unless Mick either liked her or needed her, she would end up fish food. She had to keep her cool, and be very careful.

"My name is Bonnie, Bonnie Fitzgerald," she said. "Do you mind if I call you Mick?"

He looked at her coldly. He didn't answer the question. "Let's go, Bonnie Fitzgerald."

They exited the boathouse and walked up the dock. Mick went to the house and peered in a window. The place appeared to be either a vacation home, or one just used on weekends. It was clearly vacant. So far, so good, but then it got even better. On the other side of the house, there was a small, self-contained RV. It was an older model Voyager, about twenty-five or twenty-six feet, and it looked to be in drivable condition.

The yard was streaked with shadows in the dim light of dusk. Bonnie stood next to a large oak dripping with Spanish moss while Mick jimmied the door of the RV. He got inside easily. He took a quick look at the interior. It was typical, with a fold-out couch and a fold-down table, a tiny bathroom, and a bed in the back. There were plaid curtains on the windows, and a dull brown shag carpet on the floor. Mick noticed a small metal toolbox on the floor by the table. He checked its contents. Then he took it back up front and sat it by the driver's captain's chair.

"Come on. Get in," he called, leaning to unlock the passenger door. Bonnie complied. Mick took a pair of needle nose pliers from the toolbox, and got on his knees between the seats. He reached up under the dashboard and grasped a tangle of wires. He pulled them down far enough to examine them. He found the two he wanted, and used the pliers to strip an inch or so off of the insulation on each of them. He touched the two bare spots together. The RV's motor whined, and then caught.

Mick hadn't expected the battery to have any life in it. He chuckled as he let the engine idle. It had been forty years since he had hotwired a vehicle. He turned to Bonnie. "Just like riding a bicycle. You never forget." He put the Voyager in gear, and they eased away from the house.

Mick turned left when they got to the road. The old vehicle swayed with every turn. They passed the Wish and Fish, and a mile further, turned right onto the ramp for Interstate 95. There was a map pocket on the dash. Bonnie began to sort through it.

"What are you doing?" Mick asked.

"I'm looking for a Florida map. Don't you want to pick a place to go?"

"I know where I'm going. You do, too."

"The girl?" Bonnie asked. Mick just stared at her.

"You know, all these shitty things you do, the people you hurt, the murders. The chaos you leave behind you, they're going . . . "

"Shut up! You had better shut up, Bonnie Fitzgerald." His face was turning crimson. His lips tightened across his teeth.

She swallowed her words, and turned to look out the window. Mick was driving in the right lane, five miles under the speed limit. The old RV was straining some, but the oil pressure was good, and there was a half tank of gas. They made it south through Jacksonville in half an hour. When the interstate traffic began to thin out, Mick's shoulders seemed to relax.

"You know the oldest city in the United States?" Mick asked.

"Umm, Jamestown? Maybe Plymouth Rock?"

"Naw, but lots of people guess it's one of those two."

"Then what is it?" Bonnie wondered.

"You're gonna find out pretty soon." He adjusted his hands on the steering wheel, and settled further into the big chair. He began to hum, "When the Saints Go Marching In."

Sunny and Landon turned from the top of the outside stairway at Panama's onto the upper deck. There was a big, noisy crowd seated at round tables and standing in groups. There was a line of customers along the bar.

Landon led Sunny to a small gazebo. From this point, they could see distant whitecaps on the Atlantic. They could smell the ocean from the railing. The music was coming from inside, but they could hear it clearly. Landon said, "That's Grandpa and his wife singing this one." It was a fast tempo, lost-love, folk song.

"Oh, Landon. This is so cool!" Sunny had never been in a place like this before. It was almost too much. "Take me to where the band is. I want to see the guys play."

"Yes, ma'am. That I can do." Landon took her hand. He led her through the crowd to the bar area. The booze was flowing. The couple pressed against a post at the corner of the bar. From there, they could see the stage and watch their friends performing. Sunny stood in front of Landon. He wrapped his arms around her shoulders, and she held his forearms to her. The song finished and the rowdy crowd cheered happily.

Grandpa announced that Poon and Freaki Tiki were going to sing one. He counted down and hit a loud chord that got things started. The song was a Jimmy Buffet tune about a volcano blowing up and a poor man that had nowhere to go. A lot of the audience members knew the song. They loudly sang along. A few of the patrons jumped up and began to dance. Everyone was having a great time.

After a few more, well-received songs, it was time for another break. The musicians would be back in fifteen minutes. They were having fun, and they would play as long as Kirk would let them. The group came to the bar near where Sunny and Landon were standing to order their free drinks. Poon was grumbling about Kirk's "beer only" policy. Just wait until we knock off, he was thinking.

Lindsey brought drinks for everyone. Poon introduced Sunny to Freaki Tiki and then to Grandpa. "This is the guy that bought your guitar, honey."

"You are the perfect picture of wonderful youth," the old musician said gallantly. "Come and join us at the band's table. I want to tell you how much I appreciate your parting with that old Gibson." The jammers made their way to a back table where Tammy was nursing a gin and tonic and guarding their places. They all found chairs except Landon. He stayed standing behind Sunny as she sat between Grandpa and Tammy. Grandpa's wife introduced herself, and the two females began to chat like old friends.

Woodsy, Jeff, and Freaki Tiki were trying to put together the lyrics to "House of the Rising Sun." Jay was hitting on a very drunk, very cute brunette sitting at the table beside them. Poon was guzzling his beer so he could get another one before they had to play again. They all looked up at a sudden commotion coming from back by the stairs.

Oh, shit. The standing crowd was parting like the red sea. Donnie was stumbling and staggering toward the musicians. He was using one hand to sweep people out of his way. His other held a tall glass of some dark brown liquid. He was almost to his objective when a four-person table jumped in front of him. He fell right into it. There was a crash. Food, silverware, glass and people hit the floor Donnie let out a solid thunder of curses. People were yelling and cussing. Kirk was pushing his way through the crowd to the scene of the crime.

Poon was laughing so hard he thought he might cry. "They were so sure it would be me!" he shouted to no one in particular.

Kirk wasn't laughing. He grabbed Donnie by the shirt collar. He hauled him partway up and without even slowing down, dragged him towards the stairs. Donnie slid backwards along the floor without protest. A thin stream of vomit dripped from his chin to his chest. The crowd filled back in behind them. That was the last of Donnie the jammers saw.

Grandpa wasn't fazed. "Well, boys, back to business." The musicians gulped their last swallows, and left the table for the stage. While they were getting ready to play, Tammy spoke to Sunny. "Sweetheart, you just don't know how happy you've made my old man. He loves that guitar as much as he loves me. He had one just like it when he was a boy. He's looked for one we could afford ever since." Sunny liked this woman. She felt a little guilty.

"Gee, Tammy, I'm just sorry you had to pay so much money for it. It was my grandfather's idea to sell it."

236

"Honey, that man up there has always been good to me. We've been together it seems like forever. I would do just about anything to make him happy." Tammy was beaming. "I'm so glad we could swing it. Unless Grandpa wants to start sleeping with it instead of me, that's the best fifteen hundred dollars we've ever spent."

It was noisy in the bar. Sunny wasn't sure she heard the woman right. Did she say fifteen hundred?

"Fifteen hundred dollars is a lot of money," Sunny ventured. She watched Tammy's reaction closely, but there was none. The woman had a beautiful smile on her face.

"Yeah, it is, but we appreciate you letting us have it for that. We couldn't have gone any higher, and Grandpa couldn't be any happier."

That fucking Ted!

Why did he lie? What was the point? He had her totally under his control. Why not just tell her the truth, and then still only give her a hundred dollars? Shit. He didn't have to give her a dime. He lied because he enjoyed it. It's just what he does. That worthless fucker!

39

"Sam? Sam, you've got to get up and get dressed. If you miss this plane, Jack will have my ass." Colleen was awake, but still lying next to him. She was only wearing his dress shirt. The wake-up call from the desk came just three hours after they finally went to sleep.

Colleen answered the call with a groan. It was five fifty-five. They really had to get moving. She reached across Sam, spooning herself against him. "Sam . . . Sam! Come on, it's my ass!"

"Is there any of it left, baby?" he managed to say. "You know I did my best for an old guy." Sam groaned a little, and then rolled over enough to grab his cigarettes from the nightstand. He shook out a Marlboro and lit it with his old zippo lighter. He took a long drag. Colleen kissed him quickly before he could exhale.

"You were great, old man, but now we have to hurry." Colleen got up and pulled the covers off of Sam. The look of his pasty skin was not flattering. He rolled face-down to minimize the view of his pot belly, and his generally pitiful condition. Too many cigarettes, too much booze, too many years of overdoing both.

"All right. Just go away and let me get cleaned up." He was speaking into the mattress, but Colleen figured out what he was saying.

"You have just about enough time to vacuum yourself. Really, Sam. For me? Come on, I can't afford to lose this job."

"How old are you?" Sam was peeking at her sheepishly. She was so very pretty and so very young.

"Goddamn it, Sam. I am twenty-four years old. I lost my virginity at fourteen. You have nothing to feel guilty about. You did nothing to seduce me. I have sex because I enjoy sex. Your age doesn't matter one bit to me unless you have a heart attack and die in the saddle. Even then, only if it's my saddle. Now get up!"

Sam did as he was told. He took his shaving kit into the master bathroom while Colleen went to prep in the other one. She was knocking on his door in less than ten minutes. He was still shaving. Damn, he'd never met a woman before that could get dressed that fast.

Sam cut himself in two spots on his chin. He stuck toilet paper to the cuts to stop the bleeding. Then he finished up as quickly as he could. He ran a comb through his hair, and stepped out of the bathroom, still damp from his two minute shower. Colleen was standing there in a fitted suit and suede pumps, makeup perfect, her blonde hair up, looking completely prepared for a serious day at the office. She was truly beautiful, and the new tits just gilded the lily. She had his pants in one hand and a fresh shirt in the other. Ten minutes later, they left the hotel.

They made it to the airport with a couple of minutes to spare. Sam walked straight to the gate and boarded his flight. As the Delta jet flew east, he sat in the cramped, economy seat Jack had stuck him in, and sipped a Bloody Mary. Colleen had provided him with quite a night. Ahh, he would savor the memory.

Back in Galveston, Angie was getting upset. She was getting some strange calls for Sam at the office. The other investigators thought she was silly to worry, but she still did. Sam hadn't called in since he left the city. She decided to try to reach him once again, and this time he answered. Sam was standing at the Hertz counter trying to swap the

Fiesta Jack had reserved for him for a car he could actually sit in. A fucking Fiesta!

"Yeah? This is Jeffers." He was hoping it might be Colleen checking to make sure he arrived all right. Or even better, Bonnie.

"Sam, it's Angie. I've been trying to reach you since yesterday."

"Well, now you've reached me. What's up, angel?"

"It may be nothing, but there is a strange man that keeps calling for you, and he won't leave his name. He sounds creepy, Sam. I've got five messages here and they all say the same thing."

"What's that?" Angie could really drag things out.

"He says, 'Tell Sam to call the number on the Goddamn card.' That's it, word for word, the same words, five times. He asks for you. When I tell him I can't get you, he just says that and hangs up."

"Umm. OK, sweetheart, if the guy calls again, tell him you're still trying to reach me. Do not tell him I got his message. Understand?"

"OK, Sam. I hope you aren't doing anything crazy." She was sweet to worry.

"I wouldn't think of it. Bye, sweetheart." This wasn't good. No one wants a message like that one from Tony Toes.

Sam turned back to the Hertz counter. He got the papers for a Lincoln, and grabbed a map of Jacksonville. He walked out to the street, and took a quick look at the road map while he was waiting for the car to be brought to him.

He used his cell phone to call Jack's friend at the Times-Union. He worked his way past the receptionist and a man answered the designated extension on the second ring.

"Frank? This is Sam Jeffers. I was sent here by Jack over in New Orleans."

"Yeah, right. This is Frank. I've been expecting your call. You couldn't have come at a better time."

"Oh yeah? How's that?"

"The shit is hitting the fan around here. All hell is breaking loose."

"Give me the dirt."

"For starters, about nine o'clock this morning, a floater was pulled out of the Trout River. The body was spotted by a bass fisherman not far from the Trout River Bridge. Prints make it to be a mid-level button man from your neck of the woods by the name of Richard Castilano, AKA Little Richie."

Sam began to frown. Richie was the head of one of Tony's loan sharking crews. This might be the reason for the phone calls.

"Of course the murder brings in the big guns." Frank coughed. "A canvas of the area turns up a housewife that thinks a guy that rents her boathouse spent the night, but it turns out that he didn't. Cops look at his car, and there's blood all around it. There's blood on the dock, too, and no one in the boathouse. The guy's boat is gone, too. But this guy isn't Castilano. It's some guy that works in a print shop."

"Keep going. I'll try to follow." Sam fired up a Marlboro.

"There's another car parked there, too, a fancy Lexus. The cops run the prints on both cars, and bingo! Richie's show up as well as a Gerome Johnson and a Paul Mobley. Gerome is also from your great state of Texas, and Mobley was an ex-con that did time there, too. He's the missing printer."

"I'm still listening." Gerome Johnson was Tank, one of Tony's own bodyguards. Holy shit. Toes was making this personal.

"There is one other set of prints that they find, and you're not going to believe this . . . "

"Michael Jason Parsons."

Frank was caught off guard. "How'd you know?"

"Intuition. Look, Frank, did Jack tell you I might need something?" I am sure going to need it now, he thought.

"Yeah. He filled me in. I've got a room for you at the Red Roof Inn on Becker, right off 95. When you check in, there will be a package waiting for you at the desk."

"You're a good man, Frank. Can I check with you every so often for updates?"

"Sure, any time, but you be careful out there. There's some very bad players in this game."

"Right. I hear you." Sam hung up, took the keys to a silver Lincoln from a car jockey, got in the nice-sized car, and headed for the Red Roof Inn.

Damn that Jack . . . a Red Roof Inn.

40

"Excuse me, Mr. Cicarella. We have word on the situation in Florida."

Tony was eating a plate of lasagna, sitting alone at his usual booth in Antonio's. There was a bowl of flowers in the center of the table, and a glass of Chianti at his elbow. He had a large linen napkin tucked into his collar to protect his custom made, Italian silk suit.

The stocky, dark haired soldier delivering the message was smart enough to step back respectfully. He waited for Tony to acknowledge him. His hands were held loosely at his sides, and he looked steadily at the wall beyond the booth.

Tony took a final bite of lasagna, and wiped his plate with a piece of crusty bread. He pulled the napkin from his shirt and used it to wipe his hands. He tossed the napkin on the table and took a sip of the Chianti. He then smoothed his tie and leaned back. He was ready for business.

"OK, let's take a walk," he commanded.

The soldier stood aside. Tony climbed out of the booth and stepped into the lead. He nodded to the three men at the bar, and they fell in behind him. Outside, Tony told his man that watched the door to stay there. He led the rest of the men up the street in a small parade. When he reached the corner, he looked around carefully, then gestured for the messenger to approach.

"So?" he said, leaning close to the man.

"The last call we got from Tank, he and Richie had Mobley with them at some dock on a river. Mick was trapped in a boathouse. There was a redheaded woman with him. They got the location of the book out of Mobley. They were getting ready to go in."

"So, what's the rest of it? You don't look so happy." Tony patted the soldier's shoulder.

"We couldn't reach them after that. This morning, our people in Jacksonville called. Richie turned up dead. Some fisherman found him floating in the river. He's got a knife planted in his brain. There's no word on Tank, but the cops have identified both of them. They left prints in a car parked by the dock. Tank hasn't called in. You gotta. . ."

"I don't gotta do nothing!" Tony was turning a nasty color. Tank was one of his best men. He grabbed the soldier's lapel. "You stay on this. I mean it. I want to know everything there is to know. It's that fucking Mick!"

"Yes sir, Mr. Cicarella." The soldier shrank back.

"And I want Henry here. Right away. Get him here fast!"

"Yes sir. I'm on it. Right away." The soldier hurried off. Tony gathered the others around him.

"When Henry gets here, you guys do whatever he says. Anything. This shit is going to end!" There was an unholy menace in Tony's coldly uttered command.

"So, it's St. Augustine," Bonnie said. They were still on Interstate 95, going south at a steady sixty-eight miles an hour.

"Huh?" Mick had been concentrating on his driving. The old Voyager took some getting used to. When big trucks passed him, the wind made the RV swerve. He had to react quickly to counteract the motion.

"The oldest city, remember? You asked me." She was looking at a sign advertising the Ripley's Believe It or Not, just eleven miles. It was located in St. Augustine, the nation's oldest city.

"Right you are. It was founded in fifteen sixty-five, over a hundred and fifty years before the United States was born. Lots of history in the town. The first village run by blacks was here, too, but they called them niggers then."

"Were they slaves?"

"Not a one. There were slaves in the main town, but the ones that made this black settlement, Fort Mose, they were either run-a-ways, or free. They hired out as soldiers and did all kinds of other jobs in the main town."

"You know a lot of stuff, Mick. How did you get so smart?"

"I'm not smart." He glanced at her. "I just know a lot of things." He suddenly grabbed her wrist. "Don't you ever mock me, Bonnie Fitzgerald. I *like* knowing things."

"I'm not mocking you, Mick. I like knowing things too."

He released her. Bonnie lightly rubbed her wrist. She had to be more careful. "So, how did you pick up all this stuff?" The more he talks, she thought, the better my chances. "Did you do well in school?"

"Ha, ha. That's funny. The only schools I ever went to were in the streets . . . the streets, the Army, and prison. I had to make my own school in my head."

"Did it work?"

"Well enough," he said. He sat up straight and adjusted his hands on the wheel. The gauges all looked good. This old camper might be the perfect way to get on the run again.

"I taught myself to read. I mean, I could read a little before prison, but I taught myself to read real well inside the walls. Books were the only friends I had. I loved books.

I still love books." Mick looked very thoughtful. "Books might be the only thing in my life that I have ever loved."

Bonnie didn't comment. What do you say to that?

In about ten minutes, they took the off ramp at State Highway 207. Mick turned east on the two-lane, and after a few miles, they saw another sign, "Beaches, State Highway 312," with an arrow to the right.

There was a large stucco building at the right corner of the intersection. It had a clay tile roof and a big parking lot full of cars. It was after ten o'clock at night, but all the lights were blazing in the building. The landscaped sign outside said, "The St. Augustine Record." It had to be the local newspaper. Bonnie felt pangs of regret hit her in the stomach. Just a week ago, she was bitching about being stuck in the newsroom. Now she would give anything to be back in the middle of one.

"Won't be long now," Mick said. He was starting to drive over a long, tall bridge. As they ascended, the view of the fairy tale town on the left was breath taking. The lights on its buildings and spires formed a kaleidoscope of beauty. "That's old St. Augustine over there," Mick said. "Not bad, huh?" A lighthouse somewhere in front of them added its signature illumination. The reflections in the water far below them were magical. A lone fishing boat moved along the channel below the bridge. Its red and green running lights blinked as it weaved its way down the waterway. Bonnie could smell the ocean, but she didn't know where it was.

"Is this where we're going?" she asked.

"Close enough," Mick said. "We'll be there in a few minutes."

A plain, tan, Ford station wagon pulled up in front of Antonio's. The huge man that watched the street stepped up and opened the door for the driver. A thin man, a hundred and sixty pounds, five ten, wearing glasses, got out of the car and walked to the door. He had a crew cut and wore a short-sleeved white shirt and khaki pants. He stepped inside and paused there, waiting to be patted down.

When the search was completed, the man crossed Antonio's and walked directly to the back booth where Toes was waiting. The man took a seat opposite him without saying a word. Tony Toes was willing to talk in the restaurant. The boys had gone over it with a bug detector less than an hour before just for this meeting.

"Henry. How good to see you. I hope you have been well."

"I'm still alive. That's well enough for me."

"Yeah, I understand. Life can be hard sometimes." Tony leaned forward. "Henry, I want to speak to you frankly, and time is passing. I have a serious job for you. It's someone you know."

"It's Mick, isn't it?" The smaller man took off his glasses. He cleaned them with the edge of the table cloth. "I saw in the paper that he escaped. That can't be good for you." He held the glasses to the light, and then slipped them back on. Tony nodded. Henry was a thinker.

"You know the story with Mick," the smaller man said. "This isn't a typical hit, Tony. I'm going to need more money, a lot more money." No one else ever called Anthony Cicarella Tony to his face. Only Henry could get away with it.

"I'll double your usual, Henry. That's a hundred large. You can use any of my men you need. I just want the job done, and done right."

Henry just sat there, fiddling with his glasses, taking them on and off.

"There's one other thing," Tony continued, "Mick has a book that I don't want getting around. You have to either get it back for me, or make sure it's destroyed."

Henry was silent. Tony wasn't a patient man. He wasn't used to waiting for anything. "So what do you think, for Christ's sake?"

"A couple of things, Tony." Henry set his glasses on the table. He looked at the mob boss with dead eyes. "First, let me assure you, if I take the contract, I won't use any of your boys to help me. Mick is the only person I have ever worked with, and I'm the only person he's ever worked with. We have a mutual respect." He picked up the glasses again.

"Secondly, now that this mysterious book is in the picture, I want a hundred and fifty thousand for the job. Also, I want to know, what if I hit Mick and there is no book? What then?"

"Without the book, it's a straight hit. Fifty thousand, but I want that book."

Henry thought for a minute. "With Mick, I'll do him straight for seventy-five."

Toes clinched a fist, but slowly nodded his agreement.

"Third and last, if I clip him and get it all just right, I want our friends to know about it, everyone in our world." Henry set his glasses on the table. "It's always been between Mick and me. Who is best? When he got sent up, I thought we could never settle it. Now we can."

Henry put his glasses on again. "You got any Perrier?"

41

The Voyager was stopped at a red light at the intersection of A1A and 312. The lighthouse beam swept methodically overhead. Bonnie was staring at the "Welcome to St. Augustine Beach" sign across the road. It was painted a cheerful turquoise with lettering in gold. She was very tired and not very cheerful. This town might be her final resting place.

Out of nowhere, Mick asked her, "What do you drink?"

"Do you care?"

Careful, you idiot! She forced herself to smile. She answered more engagingly. "If you're buying, Jack Daniels with maybe a little ginger ale."

"I'm buying. I made some money yesterday selling a guitar. I took close to three thousand off those two jokers at the boathouse today. I'm rolling in it." He laughed, and turned into the entrance to the ABC store. "I like this being free. It suits me fine."

Mick parked the RV at the edge of the lot and left it running. As he got out of the driver's seat, he noticed a bulge under the floor mat. "Well, look at this." Mick picked up a ring of keys. "The nice people that own this RV left us our own set of keys." He took one and tried it in the ignition. It fit. He grinned and turned off the engine. He pocketed the key ring.

"Let's go. I'm taking a gun. I can keep an eye on you, and you can help me shop."

Mick got out of the RV. He walked around it and opened Bonnie's door. He offered her his hand. This time she took it. "Thanks," she managed, as she stepped out.

There was a lone cashier and a couple of customers in the liquor store. The pair took a cart and wandered around, looking at the brightly colored bottles and displays. Mick was still amused by the variety of alcoholic drinks available. They found the Jack Daniels and took two bottles. Bonnie chose a bottle of Seagram's Ginger Ale from the cooler. Mick picked up a six pack of Sam Adams beer. As Bonnie was adding a package of red plastic cups, he noticed the rum section. "One more thing," he said. He found a square bottle of the rum that Poon drank. He added it to their selections. The cashier took a hundred dollar bill from Mick without comment. After collecting their change, they carried their purchases to the RV.

"You ever eat at one of those?" Mick was pointing at the McDonald's across the parking lot. "They make some great stuff."

"I'm not really hungry now," Bonnie said, picturing the greasy meat and fried potatoes.

"Well, maybe later." Mick started the RV, and they drove less than a mile, made a gradual right turn, and then drove slowly alongside the ocean. The white caps on the waves seemed to glow in the dark. The sound of the crashing surf was clear and beautiful. They passed a motel and a restaurant, and then they pulled into a large municipal parking lot. There was a group of energetic teenagers playing volleyball under the lights. The silhouettes of an open-air pavilion and a long pier were in front of them. Lights on the pier drew a line out into the sea, and a crescent moon shone through wispy clouds above.

"Honey, we're home," Mick joked. He turned off the RV.

"This is nice, but you can't live here. Not in a parking lot."

"Well, I could now. Now that I've got this rolling palace."

"But you didn't have this yesterday," Bonnie said.

"No, I know. I just wanted you to see it here. All those years I was locked up, I used to dream of places like this. I'd dream of living on a white sandy beach next to a noisy ocean. I dreamed of a life that would be pleasant and warm, clean, full of sweet smells. I read about lots of places like this. This is the kind of place where regular people make that kind of life for themselves. You know, just a normal life.

"What do you know about a normal life, Mick? Did you ever have one?" Bonnie was writing the story in her head. It would be a prize winner if she lived to get it on paper.

"I couldn't," he replied softly. "It wasn't my life that wasn't normal. It was me. I never fit what you'd call normal." An injured look flashed across his face, and then it was gone. "I was always different. Different and alone. But look at me now!" he beamed, slapping the dash. "I've got a home—even if it is a rolling one—I've got plenty of money and a couple of guns, and I'm vacationing in Florida with a family and a beautiful woman. Isn't that pretty normal?"

"Well, all except the 'guns' part," Bonnie replied. "And what about family? I didn't think you had any family."

"You haven't met Sunny yet."

After Donnie's screw up at Panama's, the musicians played another half hour and then quit. The crowd clapped and cheered for an encore, but the guys were beat, and they put their instruments away. "Leave 'em begging for more," Grandpa said. He was a happy man. His Gibson performed as sweetly as he had hoped. He and Woodsy began to break down the equipment. Poon and Tiki went to the bar.

Landon noticed Sunny's mood had changed. She was quiet, and she didn't have her usual enthusiasm. "Hey, Puddles, how about a smile?" He touched her hand. She turned to him, but a quick grin was all she could manage. Then she looked away again. Something was wrong.

"Are you all right?" Landon asked. "Is there anything I can do?"

"I want to go, Landon. Will you walk me back to the Shallow Dive?"

"You know I will, Puddles. Are you still worried about your grandfather? I'm sure he's all right."

"Oh yeah? Well I couldn't care less." She said her goodbyes, kissed Tammy on the cheek, and got up and started for the stairs. Landon had to hurry to keep up with her.

Mick drove the RV into the Shallow Dive parking lot. The place looked even shabbier in the headlights. The palm trees and hibiscus were brown and dying. Trash was scattered about the property. The dirt patch around the picnic table, and the torn, twisted hammock hanging between two dead palms, made the place look abandoned. Broken glass on the walkway flashed as the lights swept by.

"Home, sweet home," Mick stated. "Now, look. We're going to spend the night here. We're going to have some drinks and you and me can get better acquainted. There are people here that know me. They think my name is Ted, so if we run into any of them, you better remember that. Sunny may be here or she may not. She's got herself a boyfriend now, so who knows."

"Tell me, Mick, is Sunny really Brenda Rose?"

"Yeah, but don't let her hear you call her that."

They got out of the Voyager. Mick locked it and led the way to room number fifteen. He unlocked the door. He stood aside and Bonnie went in. She had no idea what to expect.

The place was a dump. It smelled of mold and stale cigarette smoke. A rattling air conditioner wasn't doing much to fight the heat and humidity. Both the beds were unmade, and clothes littered the floor.

"I like what you've done with the place," Bonnie said.

"It beats an eight by ten foot cell."

"Yeah. I guess it does. A little."

"The county is tearing the place down in a few days."

"It looks like they've already started."

Mick bristled. "Are you some fancy kind of interior decorator? Maybe you should stick to reporting."

"You're right," Bonnie admitted. "I was out of line. Let's have a drink."

Mick took a bottle of Jack Daniels from their bag and set it on the nightstand. He opened the package of cups. He put two beside the bottle. "Sorry. No ice."

"No matter."

Mick opened the bottle and poured three fingers in each cup. He handed one to Bonnie. "Here's to us," he said, and downed the whiskey.

Landon and Sunny were walking into the parking lot. Sunny had remained silent the whole way home.

254

Landon wasn't used to being a boyfriend, and this girl was driving him nuts. He wanted to comfort her, but he didn't know how.

There were two cars and an old RV in the lot. "I guess your granddad's not home. I don't see the van."

"Good. I hope I never see him again," Sunny's voice was hard as nails.

Landon was puzzled. His girlfriend—girlfriend?—was stressing out, and he didn't know why. "Puddles, come on. Tell me what's bothering you."

"I just want to go to bed. It's got nothing to do with you." She stopped long enough to give him a quick kiss. Then she walked on. There was a light on in fifteen. That was odd.

As they got close to the door, they could hear voices. One of them was Ted's. The other was female. Sunny didn't even knock. She burst into the room with Landon close behind her, completely forgetting about Ted's lightning fast instincts. The two found themselves staring down the barrel of a gun.

"Brenda Rose!" a strange woman sitting on the bed called out.

"Shut up!" Mick commanded. The four of them were frozen in the moment. None of them knew what would happen next.

Defying Mick, Bonnie was the first to speak. "Mick! Mick, please, put down the gun." He glanced at her, but he didn't comply. He addressed the teens.

"Sunny, what in the hell are you doing busting in here like that?" he asked. "And bringing Landon, too. I might have killed you both." He slowly lowered the pistol. "I want you to meet someone." He said it so casually. "This is Bonnie." He gestured with the gun. "She's a reporter from New Orleans."

Landon was stunned. What had he got himself mixed up in? He'd never seen a pistol that close in his life, and he never wanted to again. He could be killed. So far, having this girlfriend was a whole lot of hassle. It was a roller coaster ride with an expensive ticket. It might be time to get off.

"Now, sit down, you two. Let's have a little chat." Mick took a drink of his whiskey. "Landon, you're probably more in the dark than anybody else in here."

"I can tell him what a snake you are, and a cheat and a thief." Sunny spit out the words.

"What's gotten into you, little girl? I thought we had agreed to get along."

"Oh, we get along all right. We get along just as long as I do everything you want, exactly the way you want it. We get along as long as you can lie to me, and cheat me, and I stay stupid."

Mick was puzzled. "What are you talking about? I'm the boss, Sunny, and that's the way it is. You don't like it? Tough shit. You've got no say, but what about this other stuff? Lying? Cheating?"

"That's right, Ted." The name resonated through the room. "Did you have fun spending our guitar money today? Our five hundred dollars? You want my share, my one hundred dollars back? You're a liar and a jerk." Sunny stomped past Landon, out the door, and into the parking lot.

Mick was taken by surprise. He made no move to stop her. The drinks had him feeling mellow, but now this. Landon and Bonnie were baffled. What the hell was going on? A five hundred dollar guitar? Lies and cheating? And just who was Ted?

Bonnie spoke first. "That was Brenda Rose Martin," she said to Landon. "Abducted and missing for ten days. At least she's alive."

"No," Landon protested. "that was Sunny Cantrell, my girlfriend."

"You two shut up. I need to think." Mick sat on the bed by Bonnie. He kept the gun in his hand, but pointed at the floor. He could see trouble coming. Maybe it was time to put these three in the RV and waste them. Cut their throats and roll on down the road.

There was a good chance no one would miss the RV before the weekend. He could steal a new set of plates for it. The bodies wouldn't be a problem. There would be plenty of ditches between here and Fort Pierce. He had picked that town off the map he found in the RV. It was a random choice. The place was small enough to learn his way around quickly, but big enough to hide in until he could get his papers finalized, and get out of the country.

"I've got to go check on Sunny," Landon said. He began to stand, but Mick grabbed his shoulder and pinched. He winced, and sat back down.

"Come on, Mick, he's just a kid."

Landon was thinking through his pain. Who is Mick? Who is this woman? Man, I've got to get out of this madhouse.

"We were all kids once, Bonnie. Some live to grow into adults, and some don't." Mick gave Landon a stone cold look. He relaxed his grip, but kept his hand on the boy's shoulder.

"Will you tell me this," Bonnie asked, "have you hurt that girl?"

"I slapped her a couple of times when she deserved it. Does that count?" Mick trained the gun on Bonnie's chest. "You and me could have gotten along if you weren't so bitchy. You've got a beautiful set of knockers, you know, but they won't look so great with bullet holes in them."

"Wait! Please don't shoot her, sir. Ted ... or Mick ... or whoever you are. She's just worried about Sunny. We both are." Landon's mind was spinning. It suddenly went back to when Sunny told him she wouldn't sleep with another man unless she loved him. Holy shit. He couldn't stand it if her grandfather had been the one. He would kill him if he was, and if he only could.

Mick moved to the door. He opened it a crack just as a work van pulled into the parking lot. The side door opened and Poon stumbled out. "Wahoo! We kicked ass, Grandpa!" Poon had a guitar case in one hand, and a square bottle in the other. "Until the next time!" Mick could see an older guy driving. The man saluted Poon.

"Nice job, old friend," the driver said. "Get yourself good and drunk. You've earned it." He honked the horn twice, and then drove the van out of the lot. Poon staggered to the picnic table, put the guitar case on the ground, and stood next to Sunny. She was sitting there with her head in her hands.

"What's the matter, little girl?" Poon asked. He picked a plastic cup off the ground and poured it full. "Want a drink?"

Mick closed the room door. Poon complicated things.

Damn ... was there anyone left that he wouldn't have to kill?

42

Tony's man gave Henry three sheets of paper. He pocketed them, left, and checked into his usual skid row hotel. He read the papers in his room. He memorized them, and then flushed them down the toilet. There wasn't much information, but then Henry didn't need much. What he didn't have provided to him, he had the skills to obtain.

The hotel he used for planning was a dump with the smell of stale cigarettes and quickie sex. The people that came around Henry knew better than to breathe a word about any of his activities. They avoided his eyes as he passed through the lobby. He had a reputation.

Fear makes a wonderful insulator.

He put some porn on the cheap TV. The sights and sounds of grunting, depraved idiots faking love helped him concentrate. The bondage scenes were his favorite. Ahh, porn to think by. His eyes watched the grainy screen, but his mind was hard at work. From down the hall he heard the sounds of live people pursuing the same activities. Their noises only added to his intensity.

He summarized what he knew. Mick had definitely been in Jacksonville. He might have a young girl and a good looking reporter with him, or one or both of them might be dead. He had made a connection with Mobley, whose body had now been fished out of the Trout River. Mick most likely got fake ID from him before that happened. Richie and Tank were both history. Mick was in a stolen boat that he would get rid of as fast as possible. Yes, the boat was the key. That was enough.

Sunny Florida, here I come.

The Red Roof Inn was a single story, low-rent motel. The lobby was dark and small. In addition to the front desk, there was a pair of upholstered chairs and a coffee table holding a few outdated magazines. A wooden rack held brochures advertising the area's attractions. There was a coffee pot on a table against the wall. A handwritten sign said, "Fifty cents. Honor system." The coffee was charcoal black and cold.

Sam signed the register and took the heavily wrapped package that the desk clerk handed to him. The older man was nervous and shy. He checked to make sure Sam had filled out every blank on the check-in card. Satisfied, he said, "Have a nice stay," and looked down at the counter. He busied himself pushing around some papers.

Sam's room was in the back of the motel. It had a musty smell, and the carpeting was from a previous decade. The king-sized bed was covered with a bright, flowered spread. A cheap picture of a bullfighter hung on the wall. Sam clicked on the TV and pulled back the curtains. He had a wonderful view of a large green dumpster.

The gun was a nice, nine millimeter Beretta. There was a small box of cartridges, too. Sam loaded the gun and put it on the table beside the bed. He got his shoulder holster out of his bag, and put it on. It was time to call Toes.

Sam dialed the number on the card. It was answered on the second ring.

"Yeah?" The voice was low and gravelly.

"This is Sam Jeffers. I was asked to call."

"You on a clean phone?"

"I guess so. I'm using the one in my motel room. I just checked in."

"Give me the number. You'll get a call back."

Sam did as he was told, and hung up. He went in the bathroom to piss, and as soon as the stream was flowing, the phone rang. Sam shook off and hurried to the phone unzipped.

"Hello."

"Sam. You know who this is?"

"Yes, sir." The evil whisper of Tony Toes was unmistakable.

"There's been some trouble. I haven't caught up with our friend. Sam, I want to see him real bad."

"Yes, sir. I know."

"You got a friend, the woman. I think she might be of some help. You in touch with her?"

"Not right now, but I hope to be soon." Sam thought, I just hope she's still alive.

"I think you should reach her. You see, Sam, she is likely to be the one that will be able to find our friend. You find her, or you find him. Either way, you do me this favor. If you don't, Sam, I'm going to have someone come visit you. Understand?"

"Mr. Cicarella, I'm doing my best. I understand the situation and I will help you, you know that, but I. . ."

"No buts, Sam. No buts, no excuses. Find them, call me, and then stay out of the way." The line went dead.

A call like that definitely upped the ante.

Sam called Frank at the paper. When he got through to him, "Frank. It's Sam. You got anything for me?"

"You got your package, didn't you?" Frank asked.

"Oh yeah. Thanks. It's perfect. What I meant was, are there any new developments?"

"Yeah, there are. Two more bodies were pulled out of the river. Both shot." Sam held his breath. He was hoping that Bonnie's wasn't one of them. "The first one was Gerome Johnson, black, a giant and a native Texan. The other one was Paul Mobley." So that's why the call from Toes. "Mobley was renting the boathouse. No luck on finding the boat or Parsons yet. The theory is that after he wasted the three of them, he took the boat down the St. John's River. That's part of the Intracoastal. It leads right to the Atlantic. The cops, the state troopers, the Marine Patrol... hell, probably the Navy and Air Force are looking for him, but he could be anywhere by now."

"That's our boy." Sam said. "Thanks, Frank. I'll be in touch." He broke the connection and went to the window. He gazed at the dumpster while he tried to come up with a plan.

Less than a hundred miles away, a tan Ford, station wagon was cruising south on Interstate 10. Henry kept the car on cruise control at exactly seventy miles an hour. He had been driving all night. He took another cross-top, Dexedrine tablet and watched for the next exit. A cup of coffee on top of the pill would make sure that he would stay alert.

The drab appearance of the car was intentional. Henry valued anonymity. He felt it was crucial to his success. The prisons were full of hot-shot hit men that thought they had to wear flashy suits and drive expensive cars. Henry had a two year old Cadillac at his home, a nice place that no one knew about, but he preferred the Ford when he was doing a job.

Despite its poor origins, the tan wagon was a wolf in sheep's clothing. The stock engine had been swapped out for a 427 cubic inch, V8 monster that could propel the Ford through the quarter mile in roughly ten seconds. The car's

262

high end was pushing a hundred and forty miles an hour. Racing tires and rack and pinion steering kept the wagon on the road. Another benefit of the vehicle was the hidden compartment Henry had built beneath the floor in the luggage space. A high powered hunting rifle, a German machine pistol, three grenades, and a shoulder-fired rocket launcher all nestled nicely in their fitted spaces.

Henry turned off at the Lake City exit. He pulled into a Denny's, and used a pay phone to call Tony's guy. The man told him exactly where Tank and Mobley had been found. He learned that two cars were found left at the dock. Mick was on a boat. That was the thread he had to follow. He went into the restaurant and ordered a coffee to go. There was a display of local maps. He selected one of the greater Jacksonville area.

Yeah, finally him and Mick. This was going to get very interesting.

This was going to be fun.

43

Poon set his bottle of Flora de Cana on the picnic table, and sat down next to Sunny. He put a comforting hand on her shoulder. "Hey, Sunny. It's me, Uncle Poon. Look here."

Sunny raised her face, and looked at the old musician. There were tears drying on her cheeks, but Poon pretended not to notice. He lifted her chin.

"Little girl, we rocked the house tonight. We killed 'em!" Poon drained his cup. He was flying high. "Kirk said he'd have us back whenever we wanted, and next time, he'll pay us! I was glad you showed up, you and Landon. I like that boy. You two make a nice couple." He filled his cup from the bottle on the table. "It was like old times, Freaki, Woodsy, Grandpa and me. It was great. Hey, you can have a drink if you want. I'd never tell your grandfather."

"You can tell Ted to go to hell. Give me that drink."

"Whoa now, Sunny. What's up? Where did that come from?" He picked another cup up from the ground, and poured a small amount of rum in it. He put it in front of the girl.

"I'm just dumber than I thought I was," she said. She picked up the cup and tossed down the rum.

Inside room fifteen, things were tense. Mick was wavering. He couldn't decide whether to kill Bonnie and Landon right in the room, and then try to get Sunny away from Poon and into to the Voyager, or to load everyone, the whole mess of them, into the RV and take care of them out on some quiet, lonely road.

He wasn't sure how pissed off Sunny was. She was damn mad, but was she mad enough to turn him in? If he clipped Landon, she probably would. If she did, she would go to prison, too. Goddamn women. They sure could complicate things.

"You two get in the bathroom." Mick pointed with the gun. Bonnie and Landon did what he asked. When they were inside the room, he pulled the door closed and braced it shut by wedging the wooden chair under the door knob. Then he cut a length of cord from the venetian blinds and threw it on the bed for later.

Mick leaned against the bathroom door, tapped on it with his gun, and spoke through it. "I'm going out to get Sunny. If you ever want to see her alive again, you'll stay right where you are until I get back. If you're not here, or there's any funny business going on, the girl is dead, and you will be, too."

He went to the front door and cracked it open again. Goddamn it! There was a police car sitting in the parking lot. There was a uniform cop talking to Poon and Sunny at the picnic table. Mick scrambled to get the other guns out of the canvas bag beneath the bed. What the hell? Could Sunny have called the law on him already? He made sure all the pistols were loaded. He wasn't going back to prison. If they came for him, they had better have a whole lot of guns and a fleet of hearses.

Mick laid the weapons in a row on the bed. He turned out the light, and cracked the door open again.

"Poon, you're preaching to the choir. I hate to see the place go, too." The cop was young, about six feet tall with ginger hair and a crooked smile. He wore a bulletproof vest under his shirt that made him look larger than he was.

"Damn it, Randy, the Shallow Dive has been around here longer than I have, and I've been picking up sandspurs in this town for twenty years." Poon's face sagged with the weight of reality. The teenage girl sitting beside him stayed unusually silent.

"I know, man. I spent a few weeks in this place when Connie and I separated. Most guys that live on this island have stayed here at one time or another. The place has its history," the cop put his hands on his hips, "but no matter what we want, it's coming down. I'm sorry, old friend, but you and anyone else that's hanging out here, will have to be gone in two more days. I'll be checking. Don't make me take you in."

"This is the first place I stayed when I wandered in here on A1A. It's one of the reasons I stuck around." Poon hung his head sadly. "I bought my first bag of pot here. I *sold* my first bag of pot here. I must have gotten laid here a hundred times. They're vultures, Randy." Poon was feeling his rum and protested disgustedly, "All those fuckers care about is money."

"You won't get an argument from me, Poon, but that doesn't change anything. You know I've got a job to do. Two days now, out you go." Randy nodded at the pretty young girl sitting with Poon, and got into his patrol car. He waved once, and pulled out of the drive.

Mick watched the patrol car drivel away. The cop couldn't have been after him. He would have had a battalion of backup. He eased the door open, looked all around, and stepped out. He held a gun by his side as he walked quickly to the picnic table. Sunny looked up as he was coming. She stood up to leave.

"Sit your ass back down, Sunny." Mick demanded, showing the gun. "And you stay where you're sitting, Poon."

266

From the tone of his voice, there was no question that he meant business. "We're going to get a few things straight. Then we're going to my room and join my other guests."

"You better. . ." Sunny started.

"Zip it! You've said enough." Mick shifted his aim back and forth from one of them to the other.

"Now Poon," Mick began again, "you might have heard of Michael Jason Parsons, the serial killer. Well, I'm him. Sunny will confirm that, I'm sure. I'll tell you right now that I don't kill because I want to. I kill because I don't mind doing it. I kill just to make my life a little easier. So, if you like living, I suggest you make my life as problem free as you possibly can."

Poon was sobering up fast. He was staring at the gun. "OK, Ted."

"What was that cop doing here?" Mick asked him.

"He was telling me I got to get moved out in two days because of the demolition order. Me and anyone else still staying here."

"He didn't ask any questions, or say anything else?"

"No. He's a friend of mine. He checks up on me now and then. He's just trying to keep me out of trouble."

Mick looked at the girl. "Sunny, I don't know why you've got such a burr up your ass. So what if I got more money than I told you for that damn guitar. You going hungry? Are you naked? I don't see you sleeping on the beach. No! You ought to be kissing my ass instead of giving me shit. I could have left you to face a murder charge back in Ragley."

Sunny scowled at him. She clasped her hands on the table.

"I want the two of you to walk over to my room and get inside. The door is unlocked." He motioned in that direction with the gun. Sunny and Poon got up and started across the lot. Mick followed, looking in all directions as he walked.

When they entered the room, Mick quickly checked the chair holding the bathroom door. It was still in place. He locked the outer door and pushed past Poon and Sunny to stand by the bathroom. "Anybody home?" he said.

"Can we come out now?" Bonnie's voice was tentative. She didn't have a clue what might happen next.

"Yeah. You're the boss, Ted." Landon said. He didn't know what name he should use for the man. "We just need to get some air. We're suffocating in here."

"Are you OK, Landon?" Sunny called.

"We're fine, just crowded."

Mick took the hunting knife from the sheath at his back and held it in his free hand. A seventeen year old kid in love might try something foolish. He kicked the chair free from the door. "All right, come out holding your hands over your heads. Try anything stupid, and you'll die right here, right now." He held his weapons at the ready.

Landon led Bonnie out. They had obeyed Mick's command. They both had their hands clasped above their heads. The killer quickly sheathed his knife, and then patted them down to see if they might have picked up some kind of weapon. They hadn't, though Mick knew he could find ten things in any bathroom that would help him kill.

That was the problem with kids today. They showed no initiative.

44

Sam and Henry were doing the very same thing in very different places. Sam was examining his map while drinking a cup of coffee at a downtown Starbucks. Henry, on the other hand, had spread his map on the hood of the Ford wagon in a rest area a few miles west of the city.

Sam checked in with Frank, but there was no news from overnight. He reluctantly called Jack at the Times-Picayune. Julie put him straight through.

"So, what have you got?" were the editor's first words.

"Yeah. Hello, Jack."

"Come on, give. What's going on over there?"

"Three dead bodies, but none of them Bonnie."

"Is Mick one of them?"

"No. Two mid-level mobsters from Texas, and the librarian. It looks like Mick took them all out."

"Then where is Bonnie?"

"You have to face it, Jack. She could be dead. If she's not, she's somewhere trying to deal with a real psycho."

"What kind of answer is that? I'm paying you good money to find that woman."

"Yeah, I'm living it up at the Red Roof Inn. I drove right to it in my fucking Fiesta."

"When you deserve better, you'll get better. What are you planning to do now?"

"I'm going to play a hunch."

"A hunch? Is that the best you can do?"

"A hunch got me this far, Jack. I don't see any easy answers coming down the pike."

Jack spoke calmly, but forcefully, "Find her for me, Sam. Do what you do best . Go find her. Get to it."

"So long, Jack."

Yeah. Do what I do best. Sam went back to his map.

Henry was making phone calls, too. His first was to the Jacksonville Police Department, homicide division. It was too easy. He passed himself off as a Detective Jake Lewis from the Galveston P.D. homicide division. He claimed to be following up on the shooting deaths of two local Galveston hoods, Gerome Johnson and Richard Castilano.

The detective that took his call was very helpful. In less than ten minutes, Henry knew everything the cops knew about the shootings. He also knew how the investigation was going—not well—and the ongoing strategy. The troops were saturating both sides of the Intracoastal. Mick had stolen a boat, and it had to be somewhere along the St. John's River. At least, they were sure it was. After he got a full description of the boat, an older, Chris Craft cabin cruiser, a thankful Henry hung up and returned to his map. He studied it for a few minutes, paying particular attention to the area around the Trout River. He then called Tony's man in Galveston.

"Yeah?" the gravelly voice answered.

"The fox is on the trail," was all Henry said before he hung up.

No one knew Mick the way he did.

In Galveston, the stocky, black haired soldier was approaching Tony's table in Antonio's. He stopped a respectful four feet away. Tony looked up from his plate of ravioli and motioned to him. "Come." He wiped his mouth carefully with his linen napkin.

"Excuse me, Mr. Cicarella, but we have word from Henry."

"What did he say? I want the exact words." Tony leaned towards the messenger.

"He said, 'The fox is on the trail.'"

"That's it? The exact words?"

"Yes, sir."

"OK. That's good." Tony shooed him away, and then leaned back. Good for Henry. He was expensive, but with the possible exception of Mick, he was the best.

He turned to one of the big men seated at the bar. "Joey. Get me some red wine over here. I need a little something for the digestion."

Sam found the crime scene without any trouble. He stayed on 95 until he crossed the Trout River Bridge. He then took a quick right onto the off ramp. It led to the Trout River Road where he turned right. The scene was only a short way down the winding two-lane.

There was yellow crime-scene tape across the driveway of a large stucco house with a tile roof. He could see two police cars and an evidence collection truck further down the landscaped drive. Sam pulled the Lincoln in, stopped at the tape, and turned off the engine. In a couple of minutes, a uniformed cop approached the car. He was in his mid-twenties, and he walked with the swagger of a rookie. Guarding a crime scene wasn't a prestigious job. Sam rolled down the window, letting the delicious cool air from the AC escape.

"You can't be parking here, mister," the cop advised.

Sam offered him his private investigator ID. "I know, officer. I'm just trying to get a handle on what happened." The cop took the ID and looked it over. He nodded, and handed it back to Sam.

"There's a big time man hunt on. I can tell you that much. We don't need an out of town PI to screw things up. You better move along."

"OK. I understand, and I will, but can you tell me what the boat looked like that was stolen?"

"You know about that, huh? Well, I guess it doesn't matter. It was an older, white Chris Craft, cabin cruiser. It was big enough to handle the ocean, if that's the way the perp decided to go. Once you're in the Intracoastal, there's all kinds of possibilities."

Sam nodded. "Mind if I sit here a minute and look over my map?"

"Take a few minutes, but then you have to be moving on." The cop turned and walked back down the drive.

Sam got out of the car and spread his map on the hood of the Lincoln. Jacksonville was the largest city in area in the country. Tracing his finger down the Trout River, Sam could see the connection to the St. John's River. The St. John's could take him to the ocean at Mayport. The task force was blanket searching everything in that direction. But Mick had always succeeded by doing the unexpected. He knew how to hide. What if he had gone upstream instead of downstream? He studied his map more carefully. This time he stabbed his finger on a place that interested him. He smiled, folded his map, and got back in the Lincoln. He had another hunch.

Sam spotted the sign for the Wish and Fish RV Park as he was driving the Trout River Road. He was on the opposite side and upstream from the crime scene. He pulled onto a gravel drive, and into a haphazard collection of old RVs scattered around. He could see a short dock where several outboards and a couple of canoes were tied up.

Sam stopped at a wooden building by the dock. There was a hand painted sign above the door. It said, "BAR, STORE, OFFICE." He parked and went in. A grizzly, balding man with an enormous gut was working the small bar. His Jim Beam T-shirt sleeves were rolled up to the shoulders. There were jailhouse tattoos on both biceps. Behind the man, green fish netting was draped across the ceiling. There were beer signs and stuffed, freshwater fish hanging on every wall. A large ceiling fan pushed humid air around.

"What can I do you for?" the man asked.

"I'll take a beer, a Bud, and a little conversation," Sam replied.

The man pulled a bottle of beer out of a cooler. He popped the top, and set it in front of Sam. "Beer's two bucks. Conversation is likely to be more expensive."

"Fair enough." Sam put two singles and two twenties on the bar. The man took the singles. Sam put his finger on the twenties.

"Anyone pull a boat in here yesterday? A Chris Craft cabin cruiser?"

The man rubbed the stubble on his chin. "Nope. If you look out that far window, the only boats we have here are those three outboards, and a couple of canoes. This is the end of the summer season. It's too soon for the winter folks. We haven't stored anything in a week or two."

Sam pushed the first twenty across the bar. "If I wanted to hide a boat, how would I do it?"

The man swept the bill off the bar, and leaned on his elbows.

"I don't know how you'd do it, but I'd sink it."

"Yeah. I guess so." Sam sipped his beer. A sunken boat wouldn't leave a trace.

"But you'd have to get it out to the St. John's. The water is too shallow in the Ribault. It would stick up above the surface like an island." The man thought for a minute. "To hide a boat around here, you'd have to either trailer it away somewhere, or put it in a boathouse. There's plenty of those around. You could probably find an empty one."

Sam pushed the second bill halfway across the bar, but held on to it. "You know of any empty boathouses nearby?"

"Yeah, sure."

Sam released the bill, and waited as it was pocketed.

"The third house up the road from here belongs to the Colemans. They've got a dock with two boathouses back to back. They keep a bass boat in one, but unless they've rented it, the other one is empty."

"Would they be home now?"

"I doubt it. They live in Michigan. They just come down for the winter, or maybe for a few weekends to do some fishing. The Pickens live across the road from them. They keep an eye on the place."

Sam finished his beer. "Third house up, huh?"

"Yeah. You can't miss it. There's an old RV parked in the yard. They used to store it here until they got all tight ass."

Sam pulled out of the Wish and Fish and turned right. The third house sat back from the road among a group of twisted oak trees. He couldn't see the dock, but the mailbox read "Coleman" in faded black paint. It was stuffed full of junk mail. There was a tan Ford station wagon parked in the yard, but no RV.

Sam drove the Lincoln onto the property and killed the engine. He stepped out into the heat and looked around. The 1950s, three bedroom, clapboard house was closed up. It looked vacant. The curtains were drawn, and the yard needed mowing. Sam wiped the sweat off his forehead, and walked through tall grass and weeds to the right side of the house. When he reached the rear corner, he could see a man out on a short dock closing the door to one of two boathouses. The creek was narrow here. The houses on the other side were clearly visible. Most, like this one, appeared vacant.

The man on the dock started walking toward the yard and Sam. He was medium build, pasty white, and wore glasses. He was wiping sweat out of his crew cut as he walked up the dock. When he neared the creek bank, he noticed Sam. He kept walking, and called out, "Can I help you?"

Sam took out his ID and offered it to the man. "Maybe," he said. "This your house?"

"Sure is."

"You Mr. Coleman?"

"That's me," the man replied, smiling. He took Sam's ID. "The place isn't in the best shape right now, but I'll be getting it straightened out pretty quick. I've been away."

"I almost missed it. I was looking for your Voyager."

"Oh. My wife took it into town to get some work done on it."

Sam nodded. "The manager at the fish camp said you might be able to help me," he said. "I'm looking for a stolen boat. It was taken downriver. I think it might have been driven up this way."

The man handed the ID back to Sam. "Wow, Galveston, Texas. You sure came a long way to find a boat. I wish I could help you, but we just got in a few hours ago. I haven't seen anything."

"I knew it was a long shot. Do you know if any of your neighbors might have an empty boathouse?"

"Tell you the truth, my wife and I just come down occasionally for some river fishing. I don't know people around here very well. I do know there are plenty of boathouses on this creek. It's nice. You don't get the water skiers and the big wakes like you do on the St. John's." The man started walking toward the front of the house. Sam strolled along. They walked together into the front yard. The man stopped in the shade of one of the oak trees.

"Fishing pretty good around here?" Sam asked.

"Not bad, but say, if you don't mind, I've got to get started on this yard."

"Oh sure. I'm sorry. I think I'll try and see if anyone else around here might have seen something. Thanks for your time."

The man smiled. "Yeah, well good luck. I hope you find what you're looking for." Sam turned and stepped toward the Lincoln.

Something was wrong. The man was wearing a white shirt and hushpuppy shoes. Not exactly the right dress for working in the yard. He glanced at the station wagon. Oh shit. It had Texas tags . . . Tony Toes!

Sam spun around and was met violently. The smaller man hit him flush in the temple with a gun butt. He fell to his knees. A vicious karate kick in the face left him sprawled in the grass, bloody and dazed. He rolled to one side and wiped the blood out of his eyes. He shook his head. His vision cleared enough to see the man standing over him with a pistol pointed at his head. He didn't bother reaching for his gun.

"I don't know who you are, cowboy, or give a shit why you're here," the smaller man snarled. His finger tightened on the trigger, "but you are in my way."

That last night with Colleen was great, Sam thought. Her new tits really are spectacular.

Then his lights went out.

He never heard the sound of the shot.

45

Henry searched Sam's body. He took the keys to the Lincoln and his gun. He grabbed the dead man under the arms and dragged him around the house to the dock, and then out to the boathouses. If he hadn't been phenomenally strong for his size, he could never have done it alone. The long hours in the gym were paying off.

He put the corpse in the bass boat under the tarp. At this location, it might stay there for weeks before it was discovered. Dumped in the river, it would be found much sooner. He made sure both boathouses were locked before he walked back to where the Ford and the Lincoln were parked.

So, there was a Voyager RV missing. That was interesting. He started the Lincoln and drove it through the grass to the backyard. He parked it among some spreading oaks, and tossed the keys in the river. He returned to the Ford, got in, and drove to a gas station near the interstate. He filled up his gas tank. When he paid, he got plenty of quarters for the pay phone. He pulled the wagon beside the telephone booth, fed the phone, and called the usual number. When the phone was answered, he said, "I need to talk to him direct. I'm at a pay phone. I'll wait thirty minutes." Henry gave the man who had answered the number. He repeated it once, and then hung up. He walked into the station and bought a soda. By the time he got back to the phone, it was ringing.

"I'm here," Henry said.

"Talk to me." It was the unmistakable voice of Tony Toes.

Henry gave the short version of the morning's events. He asked Tony who the PI was and got a quick answer. "He's someone I know, but he's no loss. Don't worry about it." Then the boss asked, "Was there a woman with him?" Henry said no. Tony told him there might be a redheaded reporter from New Orleans snooping around. If he ran into her, he should use his own judgment. Henry asked Tony to get his Florida connections to trace an older Voyager RV registered to the Colemans on Trout River Road. He needed a description and a plate number. He would call back in four hours. The men hung up at the same time.

In New Orleans, things were as chaotic as ever.

"Julie! You or Colleen heard anything from Bonnie yet?" The city editor was shouting across the newsroom.

"No, Jack, not since you asked me fifteen minutes ago."

"What about Sam?"

"Same answer, Jack. Want me to call his office again?"

"Yeah. Call his office. Call the lousiest dives in Jacksonville. Call the National Guard. Just find him!"

Julie got the number of Sam's office in Galveston and made the call.

"Jeffers Investigations. This is Angie."

The voice was sweet. The woman sounded young. Julie would bet her vacation time that she was good looking. "Hi, Angie. This is Julie at the Times-Picayune in New Orleans. I'm calling for my boss, Jack. He's the city editor."

"Oh sure. I sent some invoices to you guys last year."

"That's right. I'm the one that got them paid. Angie, I really need to find Sam. Do you know how to reach him? My boss is blowing a gasket."

"He can join the club. I haven't heard from Sam in three days. I've left twenty messages on his phone, but he won't call me back. I'm about ready to lock the doors and go home to a nice guy and a very tall cocktail."

"You and me both. Oh, has a Bonnie Fitzgerald called there for Sam?"

"I know Bonnie. I think Sam was kind of sweet on her for a while, like he was on a lot of us. But no, she hasn't called, either."

"Drink one of those cocktails for me," Julie said.

"A couple. I'll let you know if I hear from either one of them. Bye."

Bonnie and Poon sat on one bed. Landon and Sunny sat on the other. Mick stood by the door covering them all with one of the nine millimeters. The other guns were back in the canvas bag. It was on the floor at his feet.

"Are you going to kill us?" Landon asked in a quivering voice.

"Of course he is," Sunny spit out, "that's what he does." She took her boyfriend's hand. "He's a psycho."

Mick stepped forward and slapped her hard in the face. Landon made a move to jump up, but as he did, the barrel of the gun cracked across his forehead leaving blood in its path. Landon was knocked back down. He leaned forward, and pulled a fold of the bedspread to the wound. Sunny clutched him to her.

"Mick, for god's sake. They're just kids!" Bonnie protested.

280

"And they won't get any older if they don't do what I say." He was angry and unsure of what to do. It was a bad combination.

"Can I go get my bottle, Ted?" Poon asked. In spite of Mick's violent actions, the alcoholic musician was too drunk to realize the seriousness of the situation. He looked at Mick, pleading with his bloodshot eyes.

"You just hang in there, Poon. You'll get your rum soon enough. This is what we're going to do. I'm going to open this door, and we are all going to file out one at a time. We are going to stay together in a group and walk to that RV out there. We will all get in it. Anyone gives me any trouble, you will all die, any trouble at all. So, any questions?"

There weren't any.

Mick opened the door a crack and looked out. The parking lot was deserted. There was no one in the hammock or hanging around the picnic table. The time was right.

He opened the door all the way, and picked up the bag of guns. "Let's go," he demanded. He gestured with the pistol in his hand. Sunny and Landon stood up. She had a perfectly defined, pink handprint on her cheek. The boy was bleeding heavily. Sunny took the pillow case off the motel pillow and held it to Landon's forehead. She gave Mick a look full of hate as she moved out the door with Landon leaning on her.

Bonnie and Poon followed. The group gathered on the concrete walk outside the room. Mick was locking the door when they heard the loud revving of a powerful motorcycle engine.

Looking up, a single blazing headlight was swinging into the entrance of the Shallow Dive. It moved like a laser, stabbing into the darkness like a spear of steel. The heavy cycle was swerving to and fro as it sped nearer the middle of the parking lot. Suddenly, the bike's speed increased and it roared straight at them. Mick pushed the group against the wall, stood in front of them, and raised the pistol.

Before he could shoot, the motorcycle began to skid. Even though the bike's rider fought to keep the machine upright, it slid across a patch of oily pavement and crashed onto its side with sparks flying. The rider was thrown onto the grainy asphalt, and he rolled across it three or four times like a rag doll. The cycle's momentum kept it sliding until it smashed directly into the left rear of the Voyager. The rider managed to untangle himself from his torn shirt and crawl a few feet. The end of the chrome rod that had held the cycle's mirror was protruding from his chest. He grasped it with a torn and mangled hand as his head dropped face down onto the asphalt. He lost consciousness in a spreading pool of purple blood.

Mick looked at the mess with violence on his mind. He was going to kill someone. He could tell from where he was standing that the RV wasn't going anywhere any time soon. The wrecked motorcycle was wedged beneath it. The Voyager's rear tire was destroyed. The frame looked bent. The rear axle was broken and hanging beneath the wheel well. The back taillight was smashed, and glass shards hung from its frame.

So much for plan A.

It would take hours just to remove the remains of the motorcycle from the Voyager's undercarriage. He unlocked the door to fifteen again and stepped aside. "You people get back in here. Do it now!"

Bonnie, Landon and Sunny went into the room. They were trying to process what they had just witnessed. Poon hung back. He wore a sheepish look.

Why the hell not, Mick thought. "OK. Go get your bottle, shithead."

"Thanks, Ted." With Ted watching him closely, Poon ran to the picnic table and grabbed his bottle of rum. He clutched it to his chest and hurried back. He took gulps from it as he slinked into the room and sat down on the wooden chair.

Mick left the door open so he could keep an eye on his captives while he walked over to the wreck. He took his heavy work boot and turned over the body of the motorcycle rider. He was covered in dark blood, and he wasn't breathing. His wife wouldn't have to worry about where he was any more. Donnie was finished.

What lousy luck. The last thing the asshole ever did in his life was to screw up Mick's plans.

The sound of a police siren cut through the night. Someone must have heard the crash and reported it. It didn't sound like the law was very far away. Mick hurried back to fifteen. He went in and locked the door. The others were scattered around the room. Bonnie and Sunny were on one bed, Landon was on the other, and Poon was slumped in the chair.

"Listen up," Mick began. "You people are here because of your own damn stupidity and bad luck. The last thing I ever wanted was to have a bunch of goddamn civilians to worry about. There are going to be police here in a minute. They will be knocking on this door. Before they do, I'm going to tie you up and gag you. You are going to stay quiet and stay still until they are gone, and I can get us out of here."

"I want you all to know, I may kill somebody every now and then, but I always do what I say. You can ask Sunny if you doubt me. Just you remember that."

It's a lie, he thought, but you remember it.

Mick opened the little toolbox he had brought in from the RV. He took out a roll of duct tape. He had all his captives stay seated, and he began taping their wrists together behind their backs one by one. He was finishing the job on Landon when he heard the police siren in the parking lot as it faded out. A car door opened, and then slammed shut. Mick went to the window and pulled the curtain a few inches to one side. There was a patrol car parked near the picnic table with its red and blue lights still flashing. He recognized the cop that was talking to Poon earlier. He was squatting down in the parking lot beside Donnie's body.

Mick hurriedly tore strips of tape and slapped them over the mouths of his captives. "All of you get in the bathroom," Mick ordered. The four of them jammed themselves into the six by eight foot space. Landon and Sunny stood in the bathtub, Bonnie sat on the toilet and Poon slumped to the floor. Mick closed the door and wedged the chair under the door knob again. He put his gun in the back of his waistband by his hunting knife. Then he adjusted his glasses and pulled his cap down low. He turned out the lights in the room, opened the door, and stepped outside.

46

A sheriff's car with its lights flashing squealed into the parking lot and parked. Mick pulled Poon's old lawn chair closer to the door to number fifteen, and sat down. A deputy in a tan uniform got out and walked to where the beach cop was talking into a hand-held radio.

"Yeah. Send a bus, but there's no hurry. The rider will be DOA.... Right. It's Donald Hawkins. He's a local. I'll tape everything off, and then check for witnesses."

The cop released the button on his hand-held and turned to the deputy sheriff. "Hi, Tom. We've got a nasty wreck here. Looks like the guy on the Harley was drunk. He turned into this lot for some reason, and then lost it. He must have been doing fifty when he went down. Not much less when he slid into the RV."

"What a mess. You want to run this one, Randy?"

"I guess so. I got here first. I know the guy that was driving the bike. His name was Donnie Hawkins. You've probably had dealings with him, too. He's had a couple of DUIs, a domestic disturbance, and several public drunks. I think he's been spending a lot of time here."

The deputy said, "There's no other cars in the parking lot. I doubt there are many people staying here."

"You've got that right. The place is going to be torn down in a couple of days. It's nothing but a crash pad now."

Randy noticed Mick sitting on the walk in front of number fifteen. "Tom, if you'll tape off this end of the lot, I'll talk to that guy over there. Call the medical examiner, too, if you will." The deputy nodded and walked toward his patrol car.

Randy walked to where the man was sitting. Mick greeted him. "Hello, officer. Nice night for a bad accident, huh? Is that guy dead?"

"It's a bad one, that's for sure . . . yeah, he's done for. Tell me, mister, did you see what happened? Is that your RV?"

"No sir. I don't know whose it is. I was about to go to bed when I heard this loud crash. I knocked my glasses off the nightstand reaching for them. By the time I found them and got dressed, I could see the lights from your police car in my window. That's when I came out. I didn't see the accident when it happened. I guess I just wanted to see if I could help." Mick was calculating how quickly he could crush the cop's windpipe with a finger thrust.

"So, you didn't call it in."

"No, sir. I don't think the phone in the room works."

"Probably not. If that's not your RV, though, how did you get here? There aren't any other cars."

"I hitchhiked down 95 from Savannah looking for work. A finish carpenter gave me my last ride from a rest stop north of Jacksonville. He let me out at the 312, A1A intersection." Mick was thinking on his feet, making it up as he went along. "It was getting dark and I needed a cheap place to stay. The man at the liquor store by the McDonald's told me to try this place. Well, here I am."

Randy made a few notes on his pad. "And what's your name, sir?"

"Mobley, Paul Mobley." It was the first name that came into his head. Mick realized his screw-up as soon as the words left his mouth. He knew that he had made a big mistake. Why had he given that name!

Randy jotted the name down in his pad. "Thanks for your time, Mr. Mobley. I'm afraid there will be some activity in this parking lot for a good little while. It might be hard for you to sleep."

"Ahh, I sleep like a baby, officer."

"Sir, you are aware that this motel is going to be torn down in two days, aren't you?"

"Yes, sir. I'll be long gone by then. I'm just happy to have a free bed for the night."

"Tomorrow at noon, you be out of here."

"You can count on it, officer."

"Well then, good luck, and good night."

The officer walked down to room nine. There were no lights on, but he knew his friend Poon had been squatting in that room. He knocked on the door and called out, but there was no response. Poon had to be either passed out or wandering around somewhere. Either way, he couldn't have witnessed the carnage.

Randy walked back to the accident scene. The deputy had strung yellow tape around half the parking lot. A boxy, red and white ambulance pulled in and parked. A white, St. John's County car followed it. A quick meeting was held near the Voyager, and then the various agency personnel began performing their duties. Randy took measurements that identified the place the bike went down and the distance to the collision with the RV. He took a dozen pictures of the damage, and another dozen of Donnie's body. He summarized his conversation with Mr. Mobley on the incident report he had on his clipboard.

Dr. Suhas, the medical examiner, finished his initial inspection of the body. He took lots of photos of it, too. Then he OK'd the ambulance driver to load it into the ambulance for transport to the county morgue. The deputy called a clean-up crew to sweep up the debris from the wreck. The fire department wasn't needed because there was no spilled gasoline to wash away.

Randy sat in his patrol car and finished his report by the dome light. He knew he would have to notify Donnie's family that he was dead. He put his clipboard on the passenger seat, shook his head at the uselessness of it all, and drove out of the parking lot.

He hadn't gone far before his car's number was called on the radio.

"Car 21, Car 21, this is dispatch, come back."

Randy knew what to expect. "This is 21. Go ahead."

"Car 21, the chief wants you to proceed immediately to 606 Second Avenue to request a Hawkins family member identify the victim of the accident at the Shallow Dive Motel. The body is in route, and shortly will be at the county morgue."

"Roger that, dispatch. Will do. Car 21 in route and out."

Fifty minutes later Randy was leaving Donnie's house. The notification went as he had expected. After asking his wife to sit down, he just said it. "Donnie is dead." He gave her a brief summary of what had happened. The man's wife was shocked at first, then the finality of it hit her, and she neared hysterics. She screamed about her kids, about how she should have done more to help him, about how she wouldn't be able to survive without him. How could she take care of the family? Randy let her scream until she was too tired to continue. He sat beside her on the couch and let her lean on him.

The children woke up during her crying and yelling. They came shyly into the living room. She clutched them to her. They all cried together. They were still grouped that way on the couch when Randy left. He would send a car for her in the morning to take her to the morgue.

As he walked toward his patrol car, a man came out of the house next door. "Hey, officer, aren't you here to take the report?" he asked. He was a big, balding man in a pair of sweatpants and no shirt. He was barefoot.

"Sir?"

"It's that turd, Donnie Hawkins. Early tonight, he stole my motorcycle right out of my driveway. I watched him from the window when he took it. It wasn't two hours ago. I'm pressing charges. I want my damn Harley back."

Not now, you don't, Randy thought to himself.

47

Back at the Shallow Dive, the parking lot was nearly empty. Dr. Suhas left as soon as he OK'd the body to be moved. The ambulance driver and his EMT loaded Donnie into the ambulance, and pulled away to drive the body to the morgue. A clean-up crew was putting the last of the loose debris in the back of a county pickup truck. They normally would have hosed the blood off the parking lot, too, but you could smell a good hard storm coming. The rain would take care of it. They finished their duties. Then they threw their shovels and brooms in the truck bed, and drove off for the city landfill. A tow truck had managed to winch the remains of the Harley out from under the RV. Two men maneuvered them onto a trailer. The driver waved as he headed for a local junkyard. The bike would wind up as scrap. The deputy sheriff was the last to leave. He rolled up his yellow tape, got in his patrol car, and headed for the sheriff's office to fill out his paperwork.

Mick let the edge of the curtain fall closed. He had been watching the activity in the parking lot for nearly two hours. He turned and sat on the bed to think.

Henry was having a Perrier, and watching the local ten o'clock news on the TV. He had taken a room at the Hampton Inn in south Jacksonville. He planned to go after the RV and Mick in the morning. The room was large, with two queen beds, a nice dresser, and a thirty-two inch, flat screen TV. He used the remote to tune the TV to the local news.

Henry finished his water and dropped down to the floor between the beds. The room wasn't set up for his usual, extensive work out, but he would do what he could. He started with one-handed push-ups. He did fifty with each arm. Then he rolled over to do his one hundred crunches. He was at about sixty when something the news anchor said caught his attention. He stopped in the middle of his exercises, and sat up to listen.

"... bizarre accident proved fatal to a St. Augustine man. Donald Hawkins, forty-six, was speeding on a Harley Davidson motorcycle in the parking lot of a Beach Boulevard motel. He evidently lost control and slammed into a parked Voyager recreational vehicle. There was extensive damage to the RV, and the motorcycle was a total loss. Police suspect that there may have been alcohol involved. Due to the location and the high rate of speed, an unusual attempt at suicide has not been ruled out. We will be following up on this story as more information becomes available. And now, Amanda has the weath ... "

Henry tuned the man out and contemplated what he had just heard. Could he be that lucky? Tony's man had said there were a hundred and thirteen Voyager RVs registered in Florida. There were about thirty just in the five surrounding counties. The one registered to the Colemans was an old, 1990 model, white with green stripes down the sides. The license plate was RV 6731. He decided to check out the one involved in this accident.

Henry got through to the TV station without too much trouble. He posed as an RV dealer that hoped to buy the damaged vehicle, repair it, and then turn it for a profit. He first asked if it was stolen. He was assured by the intern that answered that the station had checked with the police. The RV wasn't on the BOLO list. Henry asked if they had a plate number. The intern told him to hold while he looked at some pictures that were faxed to the station. They were using them until they could get some film.

"We only have one photo of the back of the RV that shows the license plate," he said. "I can tell it's a Florida plate, but the numbers are very blurry. They start with 'RV,' but I think they all do. There are four more numbers ... a six, then a seven or a nine, maybe an eight and then a one."

The match wasn't perfect, but Henry doodled with the numbers on a pad by the phone. With a few minor alterations, they could be the ones he was looking for. He was willing to bet he had hit the jackpot. He thanked the intern profusely and hung up. He felt the thrill of the hunt building. He was going to need another map.

Henry smiled at the beauty of random circumstance. Karma was bull shit. Good things happen to bad people, too.

If Henry had listened to the rest of the news, he would have heard the weather girl's warning that a tropical storm was bearing down on the area from the south. It displayed winds upwards of sixty miles an hour with heavy rains. The storm, as yet unnamed, was moving northward at ten to twelve miles an hour. It was expected to reach Jacksonville sometime tomorrow evening.

Angie hadn't heard from Sam since he arrived in Jacksonville. She was seriously starting to worry. The pile of telephone messages was growing. Some of them offered good opportunities. The two other investigators that worked for Sam were both just making busywork for themselves until they could get their next assignments. Bonnie hadn't called the office either. She had been out of touch for days now, too.

Angie put away her nail polish and carefully dialed Colleen at the Times-Picayune. She reached her on the first try. "Hi, hon, it's Angie from Jeffers Investigations again. Any word?"

"Nothing, Angie. This isn't like Bonnie. I'm getting really worried. She hasn't called Jack, either, and he is making life miserable for his assistant and the rest of us. I don't know what to do." Colleen arched her back slightly. She returned a salacious smile given to her by a passing city hall reporter.

"OK, then, let's stay in touch." A disappointed Angie hung up. She had scarred the polish on her dialing finger.

It was after midnight when Adam Pickens pulled his SUV off Trout River Road and into his driveway. He had been driving non-stop for five hours after attending his niece's wedding in Atlanta. His wife and two daughters were sound asleep. He considered waking his wife and leaving the kids to sleep in the car, but then he decided to wake them all so they could help unload. He was amazed at the amount of luggage three females could assemble for a four day trip. The SUV was packed like a can of sardines.

Adam woke his wife, Nancy, and she woke the girls. They all grumbled, but they wanted the comfort of their own beds. They hurriedly began carrying the baggage into the house. Nancy and his daughters were already climbing in their beds when Adam took the last suitcase into their home and set it on the living room floor. He had a full day of catch-up tomorrow. He locked the door, shut off the lights, and joined his wife.

48

The air in the five by eight foot bathroom was stifling. Bonnie was sitting on the toilet trying to hold back tears. She hadn't cried since she was a teenager. Poon was passed out on the floor. Behind the shower curtain, Sunny and Landon turned back to back in the tub. Sunny was blindly clutching at the duct tape that was wrapped around Landon's wrists, and he was doing the same thing in an attempt to remove hers. Sunny was silently wishing she had let her nails grow.

The pair was making progress. One layer of the tape on Sunny's wrists had torn halfway through. Suddenly they heard the chair being pulled free from the door. It opened, and Mick was standing there silhouetted by the light from the bedside lamp. His gun was in his hand. "Out," he said. Bonnie stood, wiped her eyes, and stepped over Poon and out. Mick reached into the room and grabbed Poon by his shirt collar. He dragged him into the room with one hand, and let him fall to the floor. He went back in and jerked the shower curtain back. "You two," he motioned to Landon and Sunny, "get out here." The pair nervously stepped out of the tub and complied.

Bonnie sat on one bed. Sunny and Landon sat on the other. Poon curled into a ball on the floor. He began to snore softly. Mick took the chair. "It's time to go nighty-night," he said. "The parking lot has been busy for a long time. Until it's completely empty for an hour, you are all going to take a nap. After I decide that the coast is clear, I'll get you up. Then we'll all get out of here. Maybe we'll all leave alive, maybe not. Now lie back on those beds and keep quiet."

Mick was dead tired. He would have to sleep soon, or he was sure to start making mistakes. He sat in the straight chair with the gun in his lap. He closed his eyes.

Five hours later, the morning sun streamed through the thin curtains and woke Mick up. He was instantly alert. He quickly surveyed the room.

Poon hadn't moved. He was still curled up on the floor. A thin line of drool dripped from his lips down his chin to the carpet. Sunny and Landon were on the far bed now, lying back to back. Bonnie was on the bed nearest the door. All three of them looked asleep. Mick pulled the curtain slightly aside and looked out the corner of the window. The parking lot was deserted. It was still early enough that few people would be out and moving around. It was a good time to move.

"Wake up, all of you. We've got places to go. This is the last day for this shithole, and good riddance. I've lived in better cells than this. Let's go greet the morning." Mick shook each of them except Poon. He took his knife and began cutting their bonds. When it was Sunny's turn, he was amused to see the tape on her wrists was ragged and very nearly torn through. "Nice try, little girl, but you don't get the prize this time." The little bitch was sure persistent.

"You can pull the tape off of your mouths, but don't be making any noise."

He bent over Poon and checked his breathing. He left his mouth and his wrists taped.

Sunny and Landon looked at each other with disappointment. Landon looked like he might cry. Sunny looked like she would like to kill someone. Mick could see that the two of them together could be trouble.

"Rub your wrists and stomp your feet to get your circulation going again. They won't be free for long."

Mick established an observation post at the window. The captives stretched and rubbed themselves. "What kind of plan do you have now?" Bonnie asked. "Your rolling home isn't going anywhere." She threw the crumpled tape she had removed from her mouth on the floor.

Mick was happy to respond. "First, we're going to get dressed for the beach. This is Florida. We have to get in the spirit of things." He laughed. "Sunny, you put on your shorts and a T-shirt. Landon, you look all right in your board shorts. See if you can get Poon up. Miss Reporter, I'm cutting the legs off your slacks so you'll look more casual. Everybody move!"

Sunny went into the bathroom to change. Landon squatted beside Poon and began shaking his shoulder. The old man moaned a little, but he didn't wake up. Mick knelt beside Bonnie, and used his hunting knife to cut her slacks into ragged shorts. She thought his hand lingered on her calf, but she was so frightened that she couldn't be sure of anything.

When Sunny came out of the bathroom, Mick had them all sit in a line on one of the beds. "Time for accessories," he said, as he began duct taping their wrists again. This time he bound them in front. He taped Landon and Sunny, but he left Bonnie's hands free. She had to look like his girlfriend. When he realized Poon was still on the floor unconscious, his hands still taped behind his back, he bent and taped his ankles tightly together. There was no way he was going to carry him with them.

Mick stepped into the bathroom, dragging Poon. He wrestled the man into the tub. Then he rolled him face down and hog-tied his ankles to his wrists. He picked up two motel towels and took them back into the room. He draped one over Sunny's taped hands, and one over

Landon's. "Gee, it will be nice strolling down to the beach for a swim."

He hated leaving the extra guns, but he knew it would look strange to be carrying the lumpy canvas bag. It would also tie up his gun hand. He took the book out of the bag, put it in his pocket with the fake IDs, and kicked the bag holding the guns under the bed. He took a final look out the corner of the window. Seeing no one, he opened the motel room door.

Mick ushered his captives outside. Landon and Sunny were in the lead, with Bonnie and Mick following. The group marched through the parking lot. They crossed Beach Boulevard and walked down Sixteenth Street. It only took minutes to reach the stairs leading down to the beach. During the walk, Mick kept Bonnie's elbow tightly in his grasp. He wanted them to look like a couple. He needed her hands to be visible, but he didn't want her doing anything to draw undue attention.

They filed down the treated wood stairs, past a section of sandy dunes heavy with waving sea oats. The sun was over the horizon, but not high enough yet to produce relentless heat. As they neared the ocean, they could hear gulls chattering and the crashing of heavy waves on the shore. They were greeted by a startling view of a very dark green Atlantic that was generating large waves. Mick could see the dramatic crashing of seawater onto the protective rocks a few hundred yards away. Above them, billowing gray clouds moved rapidly across the sky. A brave surfer, too far away for them to identify, was sitting on his board outside the breaking waves.

The breeze was brisk along the shore. There was a faint smell of ozone in the air. The fishing pier was to their left, but no fishermen were visible. Brown and white sandpipers darted to and fro in the ocean's tidal pools. They were chasing flashing minnows. Their movements seemed more frantic than usual.

"Storm coming," Landon stated, nodding at the darkening sky. "I wish I was riding those waves."

"You wish you were doing anything but what you're doing. Quit your whining," Mick ordered. He guided his captives away from the pier and southward along the edge of the churning water. It was still early, and the beach was nearly deserted. There was only one couple jogging south, and an older women with a short ponytail walking her dog in their direction. As she approached, her shaggy little terrier strained at its leash, trying to sniff the party.

"Don't mind Tippy," the woman said. She looked very familiar. "He just ... oh, hello there!" The woman recognized Mick. "I read the Lincoln biography." She smiled. "You were right. The author did a fine job."

"Glad you liked it," Mick managed to say, while keeping the group moving.

"I missed you at the book club," the woman called to their backs as the group moved away. It would have been nice if he could have gone, Mick thought. Books could be so exciting.

His plan was to walk the group down to one of the beachside motels, search the parking lot, and steal a vehicle that could hold the four of them. He hated moving in a herd, but he couldn't see any other way. This wasn't a safe place to waste them. He couldn't afford to leave any witnesses around, especially not here. Really, not anywhere.

The sun had moved high enough off the horizon to look like a hazy orange ball bouncing over the Atlantic. It was starting to send dagger-like heat waves into the white

298

sand, and onto their unprotected skin. The seaweed that had washed onto shore was beginning to give off its pungent odor.

Bonnie and Sunny suffered in the sun the most. They were very fair, and they could quickly feel a slight burning sensation on their cheeks. The group walked in the froth at the edge of the water. The cool liquid felt good on their hot feet. They had covered nearly a mile and a half when Mick saw a sign for the Holiday Inn. He turned the group, and they walked to a set of stairs marked "Guests Only!" At this time in the morning, Mick didn't expect anyone to be watching the stairs for trespassers.

He was right.

49

He woke at seven thirty in the morning. Randy felt too tired to be starting another shift.

The night before, it was after one o'clock when he finished his reports on the accident. When he got home, his wife was waiting up for him. The candles were lit, and she was wearing his favorite, a white silk negligee. They hadn't been very romantic lately. Any other time, Randy would have been very grateful for the chance to indulge in some playful lovemaking, but he was exhausted from his double shift. His performance wasn't his best. He knew that his wife was disappointed.

Today he had to work traffic on A1A during the morning rush hour. He had to escort a funeral at eleven, and then make sure no persons were inside or hanging around the Shallow Dive at one. Working as a policeman for a small town like St. Augustine Beach meant wearing a lot of hats. Thinking about that, he remembered that he needed to pick up some metal polish to shine his uniform insignia, and the badge on the front of his cover.

Randy parked in the shade of a red oak tree that grew next to the sidewalk on "A" Street. The speed limit was only thirty miles per hour. Most people ignored it. Randy thought that the limit was too low, but he didn't make the traffic laws, and he rarely observed them. He took the radar gun out of its case and set its calibration.

Randy left for the funeral at ten thirty. He had stopped twelve drivers, and ticketed seven. Some of the other cops thought he was too soft. He thought they were too fond of power. A ten mile, over the limit ticket cost the driver a hundred and fifty dollars. It didn't seem fair.

The funeral parade was over by eleven-thirty. Randy drove to the F.A. Cafe and had a light lunch. He ate his Caesar's salad and chatted with Benk, the cook and owner of the place. They talked about getting together to play golf, but they both knew it was doubtful they would ever get to play. Both of their schedules were brutal.

In Jacksonville, Henry was eating his complimentary buffet breakfast at the Hampton Inn. He skipped the eggs and bacon, and chose instead a muffin and a plate of fruit. He did indulge himself with two cups of coffee. He normally avoided caffeine, but when he was working, it was a necessary part of the job.

Henry was wearing his working clothes. His shirt was white and short-sleeved. His pants were tan, stay-press cotton. He wore a thin leather belt and hushpuppy loafers with white cotton socks. He prided himself on being generic. He was Mister Anonymous.

The hit man examined the Florida map in front of him. He traced Interstate 95 south to the town of St. Augustine. He planned to stop at a convenience store when he got on the road. He wanted to pick up a St. Augustine newspaper. In a small town, a traffic death as unusual as this one would warrant a two-column story. It would surely include the address where the accident happened. That would be his starting point. He would pick up Mick's trail from there.

The Ford was parked under a palm tree at the end of the lot. Henry opened the tailgate, and after carefully looking around, pulled up the carpet and the panel that concealed his weapons. He selected the machine pistol to compliment his nine millimeter Beretta. He took an extra magazine and put it in his pocket. Then he replaced the panel, and pulled the carpet back in place. He closed the tailgate and got into the car.

It was a lovely day for a drive.

Randy finished his lunch, paid his bill, and walked out to his patrol car. He checked in with dispatch to let them know he was on his way to the Shallow Dive. He was surprised to get a "forthwith" from the dispatcher. What could that be about? A "forthwith," was a special order that meant he was to drop everything, and get to the office of the Chief of Police as soon as possible.

Randy put on the patrol car's flashing lights. He was less than two miles from the station. In six minutes, he was walking through the entrance door. He nodded at Liz, the elderly dispatcher working this shift behind the reception desk, and walked past her to the door of the Chief of Police. He knocked, and a voice yelled, "Enter!"

The St. Augustine Beach city commissioners hired James Hobbs as Chief of Police after he retired from the Orlando Police Department. Hobbs was a big man, over six feet tall, with silver hair and a booming voice. He had the belly of a beer lover, and hands that could grip a basketball. He had a fine, twenty-two year record in the larger city. It included extensive training and experience in all facets of police work. He grew bored with golf and fishing soon after retiring, and in spite of the meager salary, he was happy to renew his career in the relatively quiet town of St. Augustine Beach.

"What's up, Chief?" Randy asked as he walked into the office.

"I was reading over your report from last night's accident, Randy. I think we may have something big on our hands."

"What do you mean? Hawkins was drunk, stole the bike, and bought the farm in the Shallow Dive parking lot. We've dealt with him before. Can't say that I'm surprised. Not much else to it that I can see."

"Yeah. You're right so far, but what about your witness?"

"There weren't any actual witnesses. One guy heard the crash."

"Right, Paul Mobley. Is this the same Paul Mobley that the Jacksonville cops pulled out of the river two days ago? The same Paul Mobley that they think was whacked by none other than Michael Jason Parsons? The same Michael Jason Parsons that has been killing his merry way across the country, and is now somewhere on the east coast of Florida?"

Oh shit, Randy thought. I knew that name sounded familiar.

The chief didn't wait for an answer. He pushed a photograph across his desk to Randy. It was a mug shot of Parsons.

The hair was different. He wore glasses and had a goatee, but goddamn it, it was the same man.

"I don't know what to say, Chief. This is the guy I talked to last night."

"Ever notice those wanted posters on the board, Randy? A bulletin came in here over a week ago warning that Parsons and a teenage girl he has taken hostage might be heading this way. Now we know he came right into our own backyard. I want you to get back-up, and then get over to the Shallow Dive. Parsons is too smart to still be there, but try it anyway."

"Right away, Chief. I'm sorr..."

"Just go!"

Randy practically ran out of the office. He stopped at the reception desk. "Liz, I need every officer you can reach right now!" He remembered the girl. "And have an ambulance on standby."

"Wow, Randy. What's going on?" she asked.

"We may have a shot at one of the most notorious serial killers ever. Who can you get for me?"

Liz could tell from Randy's tone that this was serious business. "I can bring in the two cars on patrol, but you'll need more help than that. I'll call the sheriff's department and the Flagler P.D. I'll have all the manpower available here in thirty minutes. I'll warn the hospital that we might need a bus."

"Great, Liz. Do all you can as fast as you can."

50

The Pickens family slept late. When Adam woke up, he could hear his wife in the shower, but none of the jarring music, sibling squabbling, or other noises that his daughters typically produced. He crawled out of bed and pulled on an old pair of Levi's and a Jacksonville Jaguars T-shirt. He put on his worst pair of sneakers. If the grass wasn't mowed today, it would have to be bush-hogged. While he had the riding mower out, he planned to do the Coleman's yard, too. They paid him eighty bucks a month to keep the grass under control, and to keep an eye on their place. The extra money came in handy.

After a quick breakfast of cereal with blueberries, Adam thanked his wife with a pat on the butt, and went out to the garage. He put gas in his red Toro riding mower, and backed it into the yard. As he cut his first row, he glanced at the Coleman's yard across the road. He realized that their RV was missing. Oh hell, that wasn't good. He shut down the mower, and hurried into the house.

An hour and a half later, he was finishing cutting the last patch of tall grass near his mailbox when a police car pulled up. A thin young officer wearing sunglasses and holding a clipboard got out of the car. He walked to the spot where Adam stood by the mower.

"Good morning," he began, "I'm Officer Burton. So, you've got a missing RV?" He took his glasses off.

"It's not actually mine, officer. My name is Adam Pickens. The RV is my neighbors'. I keep watch on their house for them when they're up north." Adam pointed at the Coleman house across the road. "Their RV has been parked right under that oak tree in their yard for nearly a month."

"You're sure they didn't move it themselves? Maybe come down for a visit or something?"

"I'm sure, officer. I've been up in Atlanta with my family for a few days. We got back last night. When I came outside this morning, I saw the RV was gone. I called the Colemans right away. They're the ones that asked me to get in touch with you."

Adam asked the policeman into the house. They sat down with glasses of iced tea. He gave Officer Burton a description of the Voyager and the license plate number. The officer made some notes on his clipboard, finished his tea, and stood up to go.

"I'll turn in this report, but first I think I'll check the house. There might have been a break-in, too." The officer put his glasses back on and left.

Officer Burton pulled his squad car into the Coleman's drive. He got out and walked completely around the house. There was no sign of any kind of break-in or vandalism. The doors and windows were closed and locked. All the curtains were pulled.

The back of the house faced Ribault Creek. There were a couple of red oaks in the backyard. The ground sloped slightly down to the water. There was a late model Lincoln parked under one of the trees. That seemed strange. Burton called in a description and the plate number on the car. He learned that it was a rental, still in good standing, rented to a New Orleans newspaper. He examined the car through the windows as well as he could. He didn't see anything suspicious.

306

There were twin boathouses forming a "T" at the end of a short dock. A large blue kingfisher sat on top of one of the pilings, looking for a minnow to have for lunch.

Officer Burton decided to check out the boathouses. When he reached the end of the dock, the doors to both of them were locked. There wasn't any evidence of a break-in, but there was a smell coming from one of them that was unmistakable. Burton had smelled it once before during the worst day of his professional career.

This would be the second worst.

The officer choked back bile, covered his nose with his hand, and hurried off the dock. He went back to his police car and called the duty sergeant. While he waited for the detectives from homicide, he tried to cough the odor of death out of his throat.

The parking lot at the St. Augustine Police Department was full. Along with the civilian cars and two unmarked Fords in the lot, Randy counted his and two other police cars, three sheriff's cars, and a lone, black and white cruiser with "Flagler County Sheriff's Department" painted on its sides.

Nine uniformed men and two detectives in plain clothes, gathered at the entrance to the station and faced him. The chief stood beside him on the station steps in front of a blackboard on wheels. Randy began his briefing by introducing the chief and himself. As he looked over the troops, he remembered that he had often argued that a SWAT team would never be needed in a town this small. Damn, he would have welcomed one today.

"Here's the run down, officers. We have reason to believe Michael Parsons, currently near the top on the FBI's ten most wanted list, may be holed up in a local motel not two miles from here. He may have one or more hostages." The anxious surprise showed on the men's faces. They were used to the general run of petty crimes, not murder.

"The Shallow Dive Motel is scheduled for demolition tomorrow at noon. He knows the structure has to be cleared today, and he may have taken off already. If he hasn't, we're going to take him down. He has killed an estimated forty people. He will be heavily armed. This man is extremely dangerous, and we've also got the hostage possibility to worry about."

A stocky sheriff's deputy asked, "How do you know he might be there?"

"Because I saw him face to face last night. He sat in a lawn chair and chatted with me." Randy was embarrassed. He smiled nervously, and turned to the blackboard to change the subject. He pointed to several strategic areas on a roughly drawn diagram of the motel.

"Check your weapons. All of you put on your vests. We will go to the motel in a convoy. I want to take the right end of the building." He pointed out room fifteen. "Parsons was sitting outside this room last night. There is only the one entry point. I want you two detectives to back me up at this door. The rest of you spread out. Two of you be sure to take the other end of the motel by the office. We want him hemmed in. Have the riot guns handy, but don't shoot unless you are sure any hostages are clear. We will have to be covering the whole place, and this guy is no stranger to gunfire."

Chief Hobbs spoke up, "Good luck to you, men. I'm counting on you to get this right. Bring home the bad guy." He turned around and went back in the building.

"OK, let's hit the cars. We'll meet at our rendezvous point on Sixteenth Street. I'll give you final instructions then. Be careful out there." The men dispersed into their various vehicles.

As the chief walked past dispatch, Liz waved him over. "We have a new communication from the Jacksonville P.D. The RV that was hit by the motorcycle here last night was stolen from a house on a Trout River tributary approximately two nights ago. They found the boat that Parsons took to get away from his last killings there. It had another unidentified body in it. They think Parsons was the one that drove the RV here."

"He did. All our guys are going to the Shallow Dive to arrest him right now." Hobbs started towards his office, and then turned back. "Bring Jacksonville up to speed, Liz. Tell them we will keep them advised as to our progress, and call on them if need be." He didn't want any jurisdictional challenges to screw this up. "Oh yeah, and find out the story on their latest victim."

With Randy's car in the lead, the convoy pulled to the side of the road at Sixteenth Street and Second Avenue. They were a block from the Shallow Dive. Randy informed all of the law enforcement people of his plan. He and the two detectives would proceed on foot. When they were in position, Randy would give the remaining officers a radio signal to speed into the motel parking lot. They were to stop their cars in a spread formation. The officers were to get out of their cars and take cover behind them. Randy and the detectives would then try to get Parsons to surrender. If he refused, they would gas the room and force him out. He would probably come out shooting.

The plan worked perfectly, except for the fact that Parsons was long gone. When he and the detectives were in place, Randy called in the cavalry. In minutes the parking lot was thick with cars, and there were nine guns trained on the door to room fifteen.

Randy and the detectives made their challenge at the door. There was no response. There was no noise or any other indication that there was anyone in the room. Ignoring the gas, with a high swift kick, Randy broke the door lock. The three men burst into an empty room. One of the detectives checked the bathroom. "I've got a dead body in here!" he shouted. At least that's what he thought. Poon was hog-tied, face down in the tub. He wasn't moving.

Randy pushed his way into the bathroom with the detective. He saw his friend in the tub. He put his hand on Poon's neck and felt a slight pulse. "He's alive. Quick! Get an ambulance."

It only took four minutes for the ambulance to arrive. Randy had Poon sitting up in a chair when the attendants rushed in the door. He had pulled the tape from his mouth and cut free his wrists and ankles. He was wiping the crusted drool off of his shirt. Poon's hands and feet were blue from the lack of circulation, and he was still drunk.

While the attendants worked on him, Randy was asking, "Poon! Listen to me." He slapped his cheek lightly. "Where did the man go that did this to you? Was there a girl with him? We've got to find him before he hurts someone else. You've got to help us."

Poon coughed and looked up at Randy. Recognition slowly appeared across eyes that threatened to spill blood. He swallowed, and managed to get the words out, "Ted did it, Randy. He got us all."

Randy knew that "Ted," must be the alias that Parsons was using. The attendants had a gurney at the door now. One of them helped Poon stand up.

"Did he have a girl with him, Poon? Tell me!"

"Yeah, Sunny." They were strapping Poon onto the gurney. "And he's got guns and Landon and some woman, too." The gurney was pushed to the ambulance, and Poon was loaded in. He waved a swollen hand weakly as the attendant closed the double doors.

Across the road in the municipal parking lot used for the pier, Henry put the 7power binoculars down on the seat next to the morning's St. Augustine Record. He smiled. It amused him to watch these Keystone Cops scramble around hoping to catch Mick. It would take a lot more experience than these hayseeds had to figure out where his rival could be. He turned the key partway in the Ford's ignition. The radio came on, and he tuned it to a local rock and roll station. How appropriate, he thought, as "Sympathy For The Devil" blared from the speakers.

He would listen to the Rolling Stones, and wait until the local law finished their clown act. Then he would continue his mission.

51

"Jack!" Julie called over the general din of the newsroom.

"Yeah!" he replied.

Julie hurried around the divider and put both her palms on her boss's desk. He lifted his eyes from the copy he was marking up and said, "So, talk to me."

"You've got Angie, Sam's secretary, on line two."

"What's she want? Does she have news?" he asked, reaching for the phone.

"It's hard to tell. She's devastated, Jack. She's bawling. Talk to her." Julie stood back from the desk, but she didn't leave.

"Yeah, Angie. This is Jack. What's the problem? What do you know?" He looked at Julie with consternation.

A shriek and loud crying came over the line.

"Whoa, honey. You have to calm down. Talk slowly now. I can't understand you."

Amidst her crying, Angie gasped out, "The Jacksonville police found Sam's body. He was murdered! He's dead, Jack. My Sam is dead."

Thoughts flooded Jack's head. Goddamn it, Jeffers was a good man. He was a hard nose, but a good man. That Parsons is one vicious prick.

"Angie, are you at home? Is there anyone with you?" The girl could only sob. "Listen, Angie. I'm going to find out what I can about this. I want you to stay home, or go home if you're not there now. Get a friend to stay with you. I'm going to put Julie back on the phone. You tell her if there is any way we can help. I'm really sorry, Angie." Jack motioned to Julie, and she went back around the divider.

Jack picked up the phone receiver, switched to line one, and dialed the number of the Jacksonville Times-Union. He maneuvered through the switchboard, and Frank answered his extension on the second ring.

"Hello? This is Frank."

"It's Jack, Frank. What the hell happened over there? I've got a hysterical secretary on my other line."

"Sorry to tell you, Jack, but your boy is dead. His body was found in a fishing boat kept in a boathouse on Ribault Creek. The adjoining boathouse had the cabin cruiser that Parsons stole inside it. Jeffers was hit by a pro, Jack—a double tap—one between the eyes and one behind the ear just to be sure. The gun I gave him wasn't found."

"How did they know it was him?"

"His wallet was still on him. No attempt at all to clean up the scene. Lots of blood found in the grass in the front yard. That's where they think he got it. There was a rented Lincoln with his name on the papers pulled into the backyard. His wallet hadn't been touched. It had credit cards and over three hundred cash in it. It wasn't a robbery, Jack."

"I know what it was."

"No fingerprints, but you wouldn't expect any."

"Shit, Frank, was there a woman found, too? A redhead?"

"No. No one but Jeffers. He was close to something, Jack. He must have been very close."

"Yeah, but he's still dead, and I'm still missing my top reporter." Jack was running his fingers through his thinning hair. This business was getting nastier and nastier.

"Can't help you there, buddy, but is there anything else I can do?" Frank paused. There was no response, and he went on, "There is one interesting thing. The cops are looking for an RV they think was stolen from the scene by Parsons. It may be the one that was involved in an accident south of here last night. They've sent a couple of detectives down to St. Augustine to check it out. Other than that . . . "

"Yeah, I understand, Frank. You've done all you can. I owe you."

"Anytime, my friend. I'm sorry there isn't better news. I'll talk to you later."

"Yeah, later."

Line two was free again. "Julie!" Jack yelled. "Get Colleen over here, and break out the tissues."

The Jacksonville Police Department was a mess. Half of the law enforcement personnel in the county had wasted a full day searching the banks on both sides of the Intracoastal Waterway. It was just a lucky break that led them to the boat on the Ribault and another dead body. This one was a guy from Galveston, too. There was something to that connection.

A newly promoted detective named Swanson offered to call his contact in the Galveston P.D. to see what he could find out. Problem was, when he was connected to homicide and asked for Detective Jake Lewis, there was no such animal. His colleagues were quick to point out that he had been scammed, most likely by a newspaper reporter.

The RV involved in the crash in St. Augustine was their only lead. A veteran of the homicide division offered to take Swanson along to get some experience while he checked it out. He gathered together what information and pictures of Parsons they had. Then the two of them went down to the garage and checked out a dark blue Crown Victoria. They took the keys, and then they stopped at the armory to check out a shotgun.

"Think we'll need this?" Swanson asked.

"I'd rather have it and not need it, than need it and not have it," was the answer. "It's about an hour to St. Augustine. Rookies have to drive."

Randy called dispatch and had Liz patch him through to the chief.

"We missed him, Chief. The men all performed well, but Parsons has flown the coop. We did find a hostage that we put in a bus for the hospital. That's something. A few of us are going to go through the whole building just to make sure. I'm cutting the rest of the men loose."

"That's too bad, Randy. I was hoping . . . Well, when you finish your search, tape the place off for demolition. It goes at noon tomorrow. Then head back here. we'll hash things over. Good work on the hostage."

"Right, Chief." But a real fuck up on the killer.

Randy gathered the men and dismissed all but the other two beach police. The parking lot was now occupied by three patrol cars and the wrecked RV. The remaining cops worked their way through the motel room by room. Randy opened the door to room nine. He knew that was where Poon had been staying. He wanted to make sure none of his friend's possessions were destroyed.

He needn't have worried. Except for a guitar case leaning against the wall, the room was almost bare. There was no linen on the bed. The nightstand was missing, and the cheap lamp was sitting on the floor. There was a lighter patch of wall where a painting might have once hung. There was no TV.

Randy went through the dresser drawers. He tossed the few shirts and a couple of pairs of cut-offs that he found onto the bed. He walked into the bathroom and picked up a toothbrush, a tube of toothpaste, and a disposable razor. He was turning to leave when he noticed a yellowing newspaper clipping that was scotch-taped to the cracked mirror. It was a photo with a caption beneath it. He carefully peeled back the tape and took the clipping into the room where the light was better.

I'll be damned, he thought, as he held the paper near the window. It was wrinkled and stained, but Randy could easily make out its content. There was a podium in the foreground that was decorated with ruffled bunting. Behind the podium, holding a large plaque, stood a smiling, much younger Poon. He was clean shaven, had a decent haircut, and he was wearing a tuxedo. To his right were three more men similarly dressed. To his left, a beautiful, dark haired woman stood with her hands on the shoulders of two teenage girls. They were beautiful, too, and obviously twins. The three of them were wearing lovely cocktail dresses. They were smiling proudly at the man at the podium.

Beneath the picture, the faded printing said, "The National Commercial Builder's Association honors its past president, Wa . . . " The bottom corner of the clipping was torn away.

Randy put the yellowed paper in his pocket. He tied Poon's clothes in a knot and put them by the door. He picked up the guitar case and laid it on the bed. When he opened it, he found a nice, older Martin D-28. He took the newspaper clipping out of his pocket and slipped it under the guitar's strings. Pleased, he closed the case. He took it and the bundle of clothes out to his patrol car. The two other cops were waiting there.

"All clear, Randy." They nodded at each other in agreement.

"OK, guys. Tape off the property, and then go back to your regular assignments. Thanks for your help." Randy planned to brief the chief at the station. Then he wanted to go to the hospital and check on Poon. He had the two officers sign his patrol sheet. Then he left.

It took the officers about twenty minutes to finish up. When they had, bright yellow tape surrounded the whole parking lot. They had posted caution signs along it.

After a last brief look around, they wiped the dust off their shoes with a piece of abandoned bedding, got in their car, and drove off.

"It's about damn time," Henry mumbled.

52

Mick halted the group at the top of the stairs. They were on a small wooden deck leading to the swimming pool of the Holiday Inn. They were looking across the pool at the rear of the motel. The sun was hot on their backs. There was a strong smell of chlorine.

It was still mid-morning. Only a few people were scattered about, reading or chatting in lounge chairs. A handsome teenage lifeguard was wiping off the vinyl straps of some of the chairs at the far end of the deck. A storm front was expected. He was checking out the sky as he worked. An elderly couple slathered in sunscreen was soaking in the shallow end of the pool. A thin oil slick surrounded them. Four or five kids with noses white with zinc oxide splashed in the kiddie pool. They were playing Marco Polo.

Mick put his gun in the back of his waistband next to his hunting knife. He guided his captives around the north end of the deck onto a concrete walk that curved through palm trees planted along the side of the building. They followed the walk until it ended at a sea grape tree that shaded a gate to the parking lot. Cars filled the lot that stretched across the front of the property.

"So far, so good," Mick said. "If you people can keep from screwing up, you might get out of this alive."

Fat chance, he was thinking.

Mick opened the gate and stepped aside. He kept his grip on Bonnie's arm as Sunny and Landon moved past them. Then he pushed the reporter through the gate ahead of him.

318

"Be careful now, children. Uncle Mick is going to find us a ride." Mick herded his captives to a place beside a galvanized fence that defined the corner of the parking lot. "You stay here. If any one of you moves, you will all pay the price." Mick gave them a casual smile and a mock salute. Then he moved between the first two rows of cars in the parking lot. He walked casually, glancing into the cars as he strolled along.

"Landon!" Sunny whispered urgently. "Quick, stand in front of me. Block my hands." Sunny had spotted a sharp point on the twisted wire that attached the fence to the fence post. Bonnie watched without much hope as Sunny scraped her hands against the wire. The point hit the duct tape holding her wrists. She forced her hands to drive themselves against the fence over and over. Each time the pointed wire ripped into her wrists, but it was ripping the duct tape, too. Blood was beginning to soak the towel that Mick used to disguise her captivity. Finally, with one last thrust, the tape parted. Sunny's hands were free. She clutched the towel tighter to quench the blood flowing from her wrists. She looked around for Mick.

He was four rows over now. Apparently, none of the closer vehicles had met his requirements. He wanted a car or van that could easily carry all of them without attracting attention. Sunny turned Landon so she could try to free him, but Bonnie whispered, "Watch out. He's coming back!" Sunny wrapped the towel back around her wrists as Mick approached. He walked with purpose over asphalt that was beginning to show shimmers of heat.

"It's been nice everyone, but it's time to go. I'm going to hotwire that green Chrysler minivan in the fifth row. We'll all get in it, and go for a long, long ride." He pointed at the vehicle. "Bonnie, once I get the van started, you're going to drive. Landon, you ride shotgun. Sunny, you'll be in back with your dear old granddad." He took Bonnie's arm and shuffled the group towards the fifth row.

When they got close to the minivan, Mick let go of Bonnie and used his hand to shield the glare on the side window. As he bent over, his golf shirt pulled up, exposing the knife and gun at his back.

Sunny never thought about it. If she had, the delay might have killed her. She threw the towel off her wrists. In the same motion, she snatched the gun out of Mick's waistband. She stepped back against the car parked beside them. She pointed the pistol at Mick's head. He knew immediately what had happened. He slowly turned around and faced her.

"Go, Landon. You two go. Just run!" She was shouting. She held the gun with both hands to keep it from shaking. Bonnie and Landon were stunned.

Bonnie reacted first. She let out an involuntary cry and ran for the walkway back to the pool. Landon started to say something, but Sunny cut him off. "Go! I mean it, get out of here!" She glanced at him. He could see the determination in her eyes.

"Are you sure? I can maybe help." The words were right, but his voice was shaking. Sunny could sense the terrible fear he was feeling.

"I'm sure. Now go!"

Mick was watching the boy to see what he would do. Landon stepped back a few steps. Then he turned, and ran as fast as his bound hands would allow him.

There were no other people in the parking lot. It was just the two of them. Mick leaned back on the green van. He folded his arms across his chest.

"Now what, Sunny?" he asked, as if he was curious to know her favorite color. "You going to turn us in? You want to go to prison, Brenda Rose?"

"It's going to happen whether I like it or not," she said. "The end of my road started back in Ragley. I guess it finishes right here."

Mick looked around the parking lot. "It doesn't have to, you know."

"So you say." Sunny was feeling mixed emotions. Fear was the strongest. "I've got the gun. What can you do?" She shook the weapon at him.

"You ought to know by now that I can take that gun away from you before you even know it. I could crush your windpipe. I could walk away while you suffocate on your own blood."

"I do know that. I'm trying not to think about it."

"You've got to make a decision." Mick locked eyes with her. He leaned forward. It was the moment of truth. He was so close. He reached out, and Sunny saw her reflection in the pupils of his eyes. She looked away.

He was a monster, a man with no feelings. He could kill her and forget he ever knew her. She remembered when she saw the pocket knife sticking out of her granddad, Charley. But she also remembered how good it felt when she stabbed the hunting knife into Santos. She let the hand with the gun fall to her side. Then, slowly, she brought it back up.

She handed the gun grip first to Mick.

Sunny was finally able to cry. The dam burst. Her shoulders shook, and she shielded her face with her hands. Huge sobs slipped between her fingers and she pressed her face against Mick's chest and hugged him.

He was unmoved. "You never took off the safety. That was bush league. It could have gotten you dead. If you're going to be a killer, you can't make mistakes like that." He put the gun back in his waistband. "No need to truss you up anymore. We're going to have to ride out this shit storm together. Wrap that towel tight around your wrists. You're dripping all over the place."

Sunny stared at the asphalt, and pulled away from him. "I think I hate you," she said defiantly.

"Most do," Mick said.

"But I can't forget that you saved me. All the mean things you do, the way you order everyone around and don't care about anyone, the way you can murder someone and then stop for ice cream. The plain fact that I'm no different to you than any other annoying thing you can find to maneuver and manipulate . . . none of that changes the fact that you saved me."

"Whoop-tee-doo." Mick made a little circular motion with his finger. "Now, let's get going. Your friends are probably calling the cops as we speak."

"Aren't you going to steal a car?"

"Not now. Your little stunt calls for a change of plans. Your friend the reporter is right now off doing her thing. She'll have the law here in a few minutes. Any car I steal from here will be on the BOLO list before we get ten miles. I've got to do something original, something they won't expect."

Mick started walking towards the entrance to the motel's driveway. He stopped and turned to Sunny. He reached behind his back and took the hunting knife in its sheath from his waistband. "Take this." He handed it to her. "I know you know how to use it. You might have to." He turned back and the two of them walked past the Holiday Inn entrance to Beach Boulevard.

Bonnie was babbling at the young lifeguard. She had run down the walkway to the pool deck, and rushed up to where he was wiping off the top of a white plastic table. She grabbed him by his forearms and tried to speak. The mixture of fear and urgency was making her unintelligible.

"Lady! Calm down," the puzzled boy pleaded. "I can't understand you. What's the matter?"

Bonnie looked over her shoulder. She took a big breath and released her grip on the lifeguard's arms. She consciously slowed her speech. "There is a convicted serial killer in your parking lot. He has been holding three people hostage. Two of us escaped. He is still holding a young girl. She is in terrible danger!"

Landon ran onto the pool deck then. He saw Bonnie talking to the lifeguard. He didn't want any part of that. Landon wanted his old life back. Killers and cops, knives and guns, love and duct tape, fear . . . fuck all that. Before he met Sunny, his life was a breeze. He wanted that normal life back.

He didn't even slow down. He kept running across the deck onto the stairs and down them to the beach. He looked at the wild, powerful ocean as if it could comfort him. Landon shrugged away the towel and tore at the duct tape holding his wrists with his teeth. He jogged up the beach towards the pier, never looking back.

The lifeguard steered Bonnie into one of the lounge chairs. "OK, lady. I'm going to call 911. You stay right here. I'll be back in a minute."

As he hurried away, Bonnie called to him, "I need a phone!"

53

The Jacksonville detectives were hot and grumpy when they arrived at the St. Augustine Beach police station. The AC in their unmarked car crapped out before they left their own jurisdiction. Rolling down the windows of the Crown Vic only brought hotter air into the car.

Randy pulled his patrol car into the station parking lot right after them. The two cars parked side by side. The men nodded to each other and entered the station together. The detectives stopped at reception. Randy went straight to the chief's office. The boss was sitting behind his metal desk, sifting through a stack of reports.

"I can't believe I talked to that asshole, Chief," Randy began. "I looked him straight in the eye, and then I let him bullshit me and get away."

The chief dropped the papers on his desk and looked up. "Parsons isn't some kid on a stolen bicycle, Randy. He's made fools out of half the cops in this country. You missed him, so now you have to get smarter." The chief stood and walked to his window. The sky was darker than he liked to see it, but his window looked out on a nice, one acre pond surrounded by pines and oaks. He always meant to fish in it, but he never did. There must be a bass or two in that pond, he thought.

There was a burst of static, and then Liz announced over the intercom, "Detectives from Jacksonville P.D. to see you, Chief."

"Send them in," the chief said without moving.

Randy was ten minutes into briefing the men when Liz once again interrupted. "I've got a hot 911, Chief. It's one of the hostages. She's free. A lifeguard is with her at the

Holiday Inn pool. She says she's OK, but I'm sending a bus anyway."

"Yes! That's great, Liz." The chief slapped the top of his desk. "Go, Randy. Get over there!"

"We'll go with you," the older detective said. He and Swanson stood. "Yeah. Come on. I'll fill you in on the way." The three of them rushed out of the station as Liz was ordering the other two cars on patrol to proceed immediately to the Holiday Inn.

When the detectives got into Randy's patrol car, they noticed the clothes and the guitar case. "You play on duty?" Swanson asked.

"No, not hardly. That stuff belongs to a friend of mine. This psycho put him in the hospital."

Mick and Sunny looked both ways when they reached Beach Boulevard. They didn't have much time to find transportation. There was a landscape crew trimming the azalea bushes around a condominium clubhouse across the road, and a family standing by a bench fifty yards to the south of them. The father was waving at a yellow bus that was approaching.

"That bus. It's a shuttle!" Mick exclaimed. "Come on." He grabbed Sunny's hand and pulled her to where the family—a man, wife, and two small boys—were beginning to climb on board. They followed the family onto the bus. The father handed a few bills to the driver and guided his family to the rear. The radio was playing salsa music. The boys hopped like bunnies to the back seat of the bus.

The driver was a grossly overweight Hispanic wearing a Greek sailor's cap and a tan uniform. The patch on his shirt identified him as "Carlos." He gave them a big smile and said, "It's a dollar each, folks. Best deal in town."

Mick paid the man, and they sat together on the first seat on the right side of the bus. Where the shuttle went didn't matter, as long as it took them away from the Holiday Inn. Carlos closed the door, and the little bus headed north on Beach Boulevard. The "whap, whap, whap," of an approaching helicopter could be heard above. A crooked bolt of lightning raced across the darkening sky. Sunny was glad they were no longer on foot in the worsening weather.

A mile and a half up the road, Henry was using his binoculars to check the Shallow Dive again. He was losing his patience. He had been trapped in his sweltering station wagon for nearly two boring hours. He shut off the radio for fear it would run down the battery. There was a very competitive volleyball game going on in front of the car between teams of four young women each. The girls were college age and pretty. They wore only bikinis and head bands.

Henry watched them with curiosity. What did men see in females? The women ran and jumped across the sand court, shouting and laughing the whole time. They were silly. He had never cared for sex with women, or men either, for that matter. It seemed like a ridiculous way to waste time. You get all sweaty and tire yourself out without any benefits. What was the point? He would rather have a good hard work-out and then enjoy a fruit smoothie.

Henry resumed his watch on the Shallow Dive. There was one lousy cop still sitting in his patrol car next to the wrecked RV. He was hunched over, writing on something he held below the window. The volleyball game was ending. Soon Henry was going to have to change parking places or risk becoming conspicuous. He was tempted to take out his sniper rifle. With one easy squeeze of the trigger, he could explode the cop's head and turn his neck into a crimson fountain.

At last the officer straightened in his seat and started his cruiser. He drove slowly through the parking lot and exited on the far end. Henry sat up and took the machine pistol out from under his seat. He checked the clip one more time. He put the pistol in a red gym bag he carried for that purpose. He was sure Mick was in the wind, but he wanted to be ready for anything. He opened his door and stepped out. As he did, two beach police cars and a sheriff's cruiser came screaming past on Beach Boulevard. Their lights and sirens were full on.

What the hell? There was only one thing that would demand that strong a response. Mick had been spotted somewhere close by. Henry decided to follow the police cars. He hurriedly climbed back into his station wagon and started the engine. He quickly drove to the exit of the parking lot. Before he could pull out, a yellow shuttle bus stopped to pick up a young couple standing at the side of the road. The two of them climbed the steps and paid for their ride. The bus was blocking Henry's exit while the couple took their seats. He leaned hard on the horn, and the passenger in the front seat turned and faced him.

Goddamn! It seemed impossible, but Michael Parsons was thirty feet away, staring right at him! He was wearing glasses and a ball cap, but it was Mick.

The men recognized each other at the same time. Mick jerked his gun from behind his back and pointed it out the window. Henry dug his machine pistol out of the gym bag and raised it. The men locked eyes, but neither of them took a shot. They were pros, and the scene was just too public.

54

Carlos, unaware of the confrontation, closed the bus door and drove on down Beach Boulevard. Horns didn't bother him. He liked his job. He enjoyed driving and singing along with the radio.

The clouds above him were darkening quickly. He decided to turn on his lights. A weather alert had interrupted one of his favorite songs twenty minutes ago. A serious tropical storm was on the way. He hoped to finish his shift before the bottom fell out. The little bus was like a kite in a strong wind.

Mick managed to get his gun concealed in his shirt without any of the other passengers noticing. Sunny questioned him frantically with her eyes. He pulled her close to him and spoke softly into her ear, "Bad news, little girl. That was one nasty mother in that station wagon. He's coming after us. I've worked with him before. Except for me, he's the best there is. I think I know why he's here, and he's the kind that will get the job done or die trying. We've got to make sure he does." Sunny strained to hear Mick's voice. "He's too close to us. You take this." Mick reached inside his shirt and took the small brown diary out of the bag holding his IDs. He handed it to her. "I hope I'll be taking it back from you, but if shit happens to me and you're still alive, get this to your reporter friend. She'll know what to do with it."

Mick slipped past Sunny. He stood up in the aisle and casually walked toward the back of the bus. He leaned so he could see out the rear window. Sure enough, Henry's tan Ford was right behind them. Large rain drops began to hit the windshield as he returned to his seat.

The police cars and the ambulance arrived at the Holiday Inn at the same time. Randy led the others into the lobby where they found the manager, desk clerk, and the lifeguard all standing around a pretty redheaded woman seated on a couch. The woman was speaking into a cell phone.

"He was going to kill me, Jack. He had some surfer kid and Brenda Rose, too. The girl is tough. She got the drop on him and held him at gunpoint while the surfer and I escaped. She saved my ass. Now, hers is on the line."

Randy pushed his way past the others to stand beside the woman. "Lady," he began, but Bonnie kept talking.

"I don't know where they are now. I checked the parking lot. There's no trace of them."

Randy leaned in and took the phone out of the woman's hand. He disconnected the call. Bonnie looked up at him angrily. "That was an important call!"

"I'm sorry about that, lady, but I need to know who you are and where I can find Michael Parsons," Randy spoke with authority, "and I need to know now."

"My name is Bonnie Fitzgerald. I'm a reporter for the New Orleans Times-Picayune." She fluffed her hair with her fingers. "I was sent to Jacksonville on assignment. I've been looking for Parsons and the girl he took hostage."

"How did you wind up here?" the older homicide detective asked.

"Parsons kidnapped me. I saw him kill two men. He made me drive a stolen boat up some creek and hide it, and then he brought me here in a stolen RV. Brenda Rose was staying just up the road in a cheap motel."

"She wasn't a hostage?" Randy asked.

"It's hard to explain. She wasn't locked up or anything, but he has some kind of hold on her. He called her Sunny, and he called himself Ted." Bonnie touched the duct tape residue around her mouth with one finger. "He has a set of fake IDs, but it isn't complete. There is still some work to be done on it. He and Brenda Rose were staying at a shitty motel called something like the Dive Inn."

Randy noticed that the woman's wrists were swollen. "You need these EMTs to check you out?" The ambulance attendants had just entered the lobby.

"No, I'm fine. I just need to pee, and then get back to my phone call."

Randy sent the detectives back to the parking lot to see if they could learn anything. He called dispatch and had Liz patch him through to the helicopter operated by the sheriff's department.

"Perkins! This is Randy. Can you hear me?" The chopper's engine noise made communication difficult.

"I got you, Randy. What am I looking for?"

"A tall man, sandy hair, probably wearing a cap. He's about sixty. He has a teenage girl with him. They were on foot in the Holiday Inn parking lot not ten minutes ago. You might see them if they haven't stolen a car."

"OK. The weather is getting rough, but I'll scan the area as long as I can. I'll fly a three mile circle. Over and out."

Randy told the motel manager to notify the guests that they should check their cars. Swanson came running into the lobby. He was breathless, but managed to say, "We've got a witness. A guy working on the lawn across the street saw an older man and a young girl get on something called the Sunshine Bus."

"Great!" Randy exclaimed. "That's a bright yellow shuttle that people catch for short trips around town. It travels down Beach Boulevard towards Old Town. We can stop it. We've got to stop it! You get going while I let dispatch know. That's good work." He told the manager he didn't have to bother the guests.

Bonnie was listening intently. As Randy moved away, she grabbed the lifeguard's arm. "Do you have a car? I've got to follow that bus."

"Yeah, but I have to go back to work."

"Screw that. I'll give you five hundred dollars to take me." She pulled his arm against her breasts. "Come on, I need this."

The lifeguard paused, then smiled at the beautiful redhead. "It's a red Toyota pickup. I'll get the keys."

As they hurried out the front doors of the motel, the sky turned ugly. The clouds were passing from gray to black. A bolt of lightning split the sky with a crash. They made it to the pickup just as the rain began to cascade down in marble sized drops.

Mick knew his ultimate test had arrived. On the one job he did with Henry, the two of them speculated about which of them would triumph in a final showdown to the death. They would find out today.

Mick was trying his best to examine the road ahead. The rain was heavy now. Swoops of the windshield wipers gave only limited visibility. The height of the bus let gusts of the growing wind shift it slightly from side to side. He wanted to be the one to pick the battleground, and he needed to do that fast. He and Sunny were trapped on the bus. The sooner they could get free of it, the better.

Carlos stopped singing and turned off the radio. He was growing nervous. He turned on his emergency lights. He was responsible for eight passengers, and he didn't like the way the little bus was moving in the increasingly powerful wind. He also hated trying to drive with such poor visibility. He radioed in to the central office, and told them that he was going to find a place to park while he waited out the worst of the weather.

The conscientious driver crept ahead slowly. He made the gradual turn onto A1A, and drove with his right side wheels on the shoulder of the road. He cautiously continued until he was able to see the large red and white sign for the Alligator Farm and Zoological Park. The facility was on the left side of the road. It was a popular tourist attraction that displayed reptiles, birds and animals. The park could hold hundreds of people.

Carlos turned across the highway and into the large parking lot. Cars with their bright lights on were lined up at the exit to leave. People that had been enjoying a day at the open air zoo were caught off guard by the storm. Most were soaked. They were heading back to their motels and house rentals to get dry and escape the storm's fury. Crashing thunder was rolling across the angry sky above them.

The driver stopped his bus in an open area at the rear of the parking lot, hopefully safe from falling branches and trees. Mick looked out the window at the swirling wind and rain. He couldn't see far, but he didn't see the Ford. He hoped Henry had missed the turn in the storm.

The oaks and palms around the lot were twisting and bending. Debris was starting to blow across the pavement. The storm was bad for the tourists, but maybe not so bad for him. He made a split second decision and grabbed Sunny's hand. He stood and pulled her up. He stepped behind the driver. "Get that door open!" he shouted, over the roar of the storm.

Carlos was shocked by the request. "You can't go out in this. If you don't get struck by lightning, a tree will fall on you!"

Mick shoved the gun in the driver's face. "I said open it." He shifted the aim of his pistol and fired a carefully placed bullet through the bus's short wave radio. "Now!"

Carlos jerked back from the madman. He broke out in a sweat, his butt clenching on the vinyl seat. He grabbed the handle that opened the door and pulled. A sudden flood of driving rain blew into the bus. Mick pushed Sunny down the steps and out into the storm. Carlos slammed the handle to shut the door. He let out a swallowed gasp.

The pair was soaked through immediately. They bent over, and scrambled arm in arm to the partial shelter of the flapping awning at the park's entrance.

55

Sunny was scared. The cops and the storm were bad enough. Now they were being stalked by a professional killer. She didn't have any idea who it was that was hunting them, but she knew that if Mick thought he was good, he was very good. This is going to be my life, she thought. I'll always be running from someone.

But then, today could be the end of it.

The double doors to the entrance of the park suddenly swung open behind them. A pale, frightened looking man in a heavy raincoat came rushing out. He turned and locked the doors. He was soaked immediately.

"I'm closing. We're closed!" he shouted into the wind. The man brushed past them. Shielding his eyes with his hand, he charged into the rain. Before he had gone fifty feet, they lost sight of him in the growing turbulence of the storm.

Mick stared at the doors through the water dripping off of his cap.

Liz was standing up behind the reception desk. This was the most excitement she had seen in her twenty years as dispatcher. The sheriff's chopper called in to tell her that he didn't have any luck spotting the targets. The storm had arrived in full force now. He was going to head back to the airport. The wind, rain, and lightning made flying too dangerous.

The chief was standing at the glass entry doors to the station. The rain was now in sheets. He couldn't see the other side of the parking lot. "The weather bureau has named the storm," Liz said. "They're calling it tropical storm DeDe." That meant the winds would be consistently over thirty-nine miles an hour and could climb to seventy-nine. There would be tree and roof damage, downed power lines, and some flash flooding.

"This mess is all I need right now," the chief complained. "I've got every man I can grab chasing the Sunshine Bus. Even Mother Nature is giving me a hard time."

Only minutes later, the two beach police cruisers called in. They had both driven all the way into the historic district searching for the Sunshine Bus. They found nothing.

"Damn it!" the chief exclaimed, as he overheard the call. "That bus didn't just disappear. We need that chopper!" Right on cue, with a deafening crash, a bolt of lightning raced across the sky and struck a transformer on the utility pole at the corner of the police station parking lot. Liz and the chief both flinched. Sparks flew from the metal box in a fiery display. "Shit!" the chief cried as he surveyed the damage. He ran out of the building into the driving rain to move his personal, vintage Pontiac convertible out of danger.

Henry knew that he had lost the bus. Even though he had followed squarely behind it for a couple of miles, when the true fury of the storm hit, he was completely surprised by how badly it blinded him. He wasn't familiar with the roads, and he couldn't risk having an accident. He managed to cautiously pull into a pizza restaurant's parking lot. He was sitting there now, cursing the weather, and letting his fury feed his desire to kill.

The street lights along A1A were operated by electric eyes. Henry watched them turn on automatically in the darkness caused by the storm. Then minutes later, they went off again when lightning took out an island transformer.

Bonnie's college kid was a good driver. He talked too much, but that was a small price to pay for someone that knew the town as well as he did, and he wasn't afraid of a little rain. Chasing this story had almost killed her. She was determined to have her byline on a full page work-up that would put her in contention for a Pulitzer, and Jack would pay.

The Toyota pickup had oversized tires, a four wheel drive transmission, and a bank of flood lights mounted on the roof. The truck's fancy accessories were the kid's attempt at being ultra cool, but they actually were helping to keep them on the quickly flooding roadway. They passed many cars pulled to the side of the road that either couldn't see the next hundred feet of their lane, or were afraid of flooding their engines.

"I've been wanting to give this baby a good road test," the lifeguard shouted. Bonnie could barely hear him above the noise of the wind and the slap of his windshield wipers. She just smiled and nodded. She was peering through the storm, hoping to catch a glimpse of a bright yellow bus. The sky was so black that the automatic activator had kicked on the powerful rotating beam from the lighthouse. It was the only break in the darkness as it swung across the tumultuous sky.

Randy was trying to talk to a group of people standing under the roof of a small gazebo in the historical plaza at the foot of the Bridge of Lions. They were bunched together in a feeble attempt to escape the wind and rain.

He gathered several of them into a huddle. He had to shout to be heard above the weather. He asked them about the Sunshine Bus. The plaza was one of its usual stops, so all of them were familiar with it. Some had been waiting for the bus to take them home when the storm hit. None had seen it pass. They guessed that it had suspended operations due to the weather. If that was true, the little shuttle bus was still somewhere on the island. He might have a shot at Parsons yet.

Randy hurried back through the torrents to his patrol car.

56

Mick leaned back. Then, as he thrust forward, he high-kicked the park doors at the handles. He had to do it three times, but finally the heavy wood around the latch splintered, and the doors crashed inward. He grabbed Sunny's elbow, and dragged her into the building. There were no working lights inside. The dim light from the large windows was all they had to see by. Mick pushed the entry doors closed, and wedged a plastic chair against them.

They were in a reception area where admission tickets were sold. There was a ticket booth, and velvet ropes to direct the customers. The walls were varnished pine decorated with wildlife posters. Heavy beams crossed the high, white-plastered ceiling. There was a large map painted on one wall depicting the whole zoological park.

Sunny sat down on a padded bench and squeezed the water out of her shirttail. Mick examined the posters and studied the map.

The Alligator Farm was created back in the late eighteen hundreds. It had expanded and increased its offerings each year since. The posters showed anacondas and pythons, spider monkeys, exotic birds, and albino crocodiles. Mick was more interested in what potential the place had for escape. Not only was the law after them, but now Henry was chasing them, too. That meant that staying alive and free was going to be a whole lot tougher, and more dangerous.

He went to the far end of the room where patrons exited reception to enter the actual zoological park. He pushed open a thick oak door, and was met with a blast of howling wind and rain. The panicked calls of hundreds of frightened birds and animals assaulted his ears. He jerked the door closed, and leaned against the wall to try and think. The crack of lightning and the loud booming of thunder sounded overhead.

Mick asked Sunny, "You doing OK, little girl? How are your wrists?" He didn't give a damn if she was doing OK, but he was starting to form a plan. She might prove useful. "Easy to see why Landon called you Puddles." He pointed to the rainwater on the floor by her feet. He walked purposefully to her and grasped her chin. "In a few minutes, we're going to have to get back into the weather."

She jerked her face free, and then she scowled at him. She wiped drips off her forehead with her palm and said, "I can take care of myself. I can handle anything you can." She was a cocky little bitch. Mick granted her that much.

He got a firm grip on the door to the park's interior. Fighting the wind, he eased it open a few inches until he could see out. The heavily treed grounds were a chaotic scene of twisting oaks and blowing leaves and branches. Captive animals pressed against their fencing. Birds flew blindly into the wire of their cages. A wet monkey ran screeching past the door. A large pond close by was churning with masses of dark green reptiles. Mick could see the snapping of their jaws as the confined alligators reacted franticly to the wildness of the storm.

Mick saw a small shelter through the rain that was situated past the alligator pond. It was about fifty feet down a flagstone path. The shelter held several rows of bleachers and a wooden podium on a raised stage. The podium had blown onto its side. There was a door to the rear of the stage that accessed a small concrete block storage building. That was where he planned to start.

Mick pulled the door closed until he heard the latch firmly engage. Then he went to stand by Sunny. At the slightest break in the weather, they were going into the zoo. He studied the wall map while he waited.

Bonnie's newest admirer was driving so slowly that she felt like they were crawling. Still, his Toyota was one of only a few vehicles moving. Nearly everyone else had parked for the duration of the storm.

"I always wanted to be a newspaper guy," he said loudly against the noise of the storm. "Think it's too late for me?"

Bonnie looked over at him. Yeah. Over the hill at twenty-three. He was cute, and he didn't appear retarded. He wouldn't have any problems getting a good ride out of life. But why would he think because he could write a complete sentence and knew how to use spell check that he could be a newspaper man? Could confidence to the point of ignorance send you on your way to a successful career as a reporter?

If it was that easy, Bonnie would be retired. She would be living in one of those beautiful places Mick talked about. She would be relaxing on a white sand beach, sipping margaritas, and ordering her servants around.

Bonnie reached over and patted the lifeguard's cheek. He was sweet, and she loved the ripples that his muscles made across his stomach. It was at that moment that the black sky faded to dark gray, and over her faithful boy toy's shoulder, the parking lot of a widely advertised tourist attraction became visible.

"Stop, stop!" Bonnie screamed. "There it is."

On their left, beyond a group of oak trees, the back end of a yellow bus could be seen. It was parked well off the road, nose to the parking lot fence. The lifeguard pulled to the side of the road. He stopped the pickup. They both studied the parked shuttle bus.

"Can you tell if anyone is in there?" Bonnie asked. She pressed against him to better see out his window.

"This weather is crap. I can't see inside it, but I would bet whoever got on that bus is still on it. It's a mess out here, not a good day for a stroll." The lifeguard's hand casually fell on her thigh. The squeeze he gave it wasn't so casual.

"Honey," Bonnie cooed, "you're an amazing driver. I'm looking forward to maybe spending some fun time with you later, but right now I'm working." She took his hand from her thigh and pulled it to her right breast. She rubbed it across the nipple. The kid was so clueless that he pinched it, much too hard, and then let Bonnie guide his hand back to the steering wheel.

Now that she could see the bus, Bonnie didn't know what to do. She wasn't fool enough to confront Mick without an army behind her, but the longer she waited, the more time that he could be escaping. She decided to call the local police. Damn it! The weather had knocked out her phone service.

Randy was moving at a snail's pace in his patrol car. He left his siren off, but turned on his flashing lights. He glanced over the railing as he crossed the Bridge of Lions and began retracing his route on A1A. The river was dotted with whitecaps. The sailboats moored in the harbor were straining at their lines. There were hardly any cars on the bridge. It was a good thing. He could barely see the lines on the road through the dense rainfall. The second police car was following him. He just hoped it wouldn't drive into his rear-end. The weather was causing so much static on his police radio that Randy gave up trying to let dispatch know what he was doing.

Little by little, Randy proceeded up A1A. He had gone about a mile through the storm, when he saw a red pickup truck parked on the opposite side of the road. The truck began flashing roof-mounted spotlights at him. He pulled his cruiser over to see if someone needed help. A woman got out of the passenger side of the truck, and ran towards him through the rain. It looked like the reporter that had escaped from Parsons.

Randy leaned over and unlocked his passenger door. The woman jerked the door open and jumped into the cruiser, bringing a hard gust of wind and rain with her.

"It's here. Right over there in that parking lot." The woman was pointing towards the Alligator Farm. "That's the bus. The yellow bus that Parsons got on!"

Randy looked past the woman. He could just make out the rear end of the shuttle.

"I don't know if he is still on it, but no one has gotten off that bus in the last five minutes." She was wiping the rain from her eyes. She tried to smooth her red hair.

"Stay here," Randy told her. He hurried out of the car. The other cruiser had pulled up behind him. Randy ran back to it. His fellow officer rolled down the window and Randy shouted for him to follow him back to the other car. They both returned to Randy's cruiser.

Inside, with the windows closed tightly, the dripping men could talk. They had to come up with a plan, a good plan, that would put Parsons behind bars.

"We need backup," the junior officer began.

"Sure we do, but how are you going to get it? The radio is no good. Cell phones are out, and while we're here shooting the shit, Parsons is going to get away. I say we have to go after him."

"Yes! Do it!" Bonnie exclaimed from the passenger seat. She would get the exclusive.

"Look lady, we have enough on our plate without you chiming in. Stay quiet and stay put." Bonnie looked indignant.

Randy turned to face the junior officer. "This isn't training. Check your gun, and keep in mind those are real bullets. I'm going to approach the door of the bus. You're going to stay ten feet behind me with your back against the side of it. There are civilians in there. Don't fire a shot unless you are damn sure it's Parsons you're going to hit. Now, let's go."

Randy pushed his door open, and ran into the rain.

57

Doctor Barringer was worried about his newest emergency room patient. The man's condition was questionable. His hands and feet had been so tightly bound during his abduction that the blood circulation to them was totally cut off. It would be touch and go as to whether he could save the man's fingers and toes.

As he was massaging the patient's swollen fingers, the man suddenly began to shake violently. The patient was having a seizure. Barringer quickly grasped both sides of his patient's head to keep him from injuring his neck. A security guard that was in the hall ran in and pinned the man's arms. The doctor shouted for a nurse to bring a sedative. When she arrived, he directed her to give the man the shot in his bicep. In seconds, either the seizure passed, or the shot worked. The man's movements gradually subsided and his muscles relaxed. He began to sweat buckets.

"I know this guy," the nurse said. Her name was Sarah. She was blonde and pretty, in her forties, worked out, and looked great in her pink scrubs. Barringer liked working with her. She was confident, and much more capable than the younger nurses.

"He plays guitar and sings in local bars over on the island. I think they call him Poon."

"Nice name," Barringer commented. "What are his vitals?"

"Pressure is fair, 145 over 110. Pulse is a little fast." She put her palm on Poon's forehead. "He's getting clammy."

"Think he's a heavy drinker?"

"I'd say that's a sure thing. He's got a bit of a reputation," Sarah answered.

"The police said he's been tied up for ten or twelve hours. That long without a drink for an alcoholic, I'd say he's going into the DTs. That would explain the seizure."

"No argument here," Sarah said. She wiped Poon's face with a hand towel.

"Let's get him admitted. When he's settled in, get him on a saline and alcohol drip. Without it, he could stroke out, or even have a heart attack. Give him about an ounce of medicinal alcohol an hour until we can safely wean him down."

"He'll like that." Sarah smiled at the irony. She knew Poon much better than she was letting on.

Mick was judging the storm by the howl of the wind. He thought he could detect a slight lessening in its ferocity. "Sunny, get ready." He walked over by the exit door.

The girl stood up and walked fearlessly to his side. Her clothes and shoes were soaked. She stood motionless as Mick grabbed the door latch. As soon as he turned it, the wind jerked the door open and slammed it back on its hinges. Mick broke into a run, straight into the storm. Sunny was close behind. The rain pelted their faces like buckshot. Mick pulled his cap down as low as it would go and kept running.

The two of them ran past the large alligator pond, and finally reached the meager protection of the partial shelter. They pressed themselves against the wall of the storage building. Mick checked the door knob. The door wasn't locked. He opened it, and they both dashed inside. Mick slammed the metal door.

The storage building was small and dark. A lot of the noise of the storm was muffled inside its block walls. Mick found a light switch, but when he tried it, nothing happened.

It took a minute for their eyes to adjust to the dim light admitted by a small window high on one wall. The space they were in was used for storing tools, feed, and medicine. There were stacks of fifty pound, feed sacks on the floor. A series of shelves held bottles and plastic containers of salves and pills. One wall was fitted with pegboard with hooks for holding hand tools. Mick looked this wall over carefully. He saw a possible component to his very sketchy plan. He reached over a work bench, and took down a long handled, heavy duty bolt cutter.

According to the park map, there was a gated entrance for heavy equipment at the very rear of the property. He had to make sure he could get through that gate before he wanted to bet his ass on it.

The wind was definitely dying down a little. Mick lowered the volume of his voice some. "I'm going to check a possible way out of here. If it's clear, I'll be back in less than ten minutes. You be ready to move. I've got a diversion in mind. As soon as I can put that in place, we'll haul ass."

Mick didn't wait for Sunny's comment. He gripped the bolt cutter tightly, opened the door, and ran back out into the storm.

It was a struggle running through the unfamiliar park in the middle of the storm. Branches were breaking off the trees and falling around him. The rain stung his eyes, and it was hard to move in his soaked clothes. He nearly collided with a hard-running ostrich that had escaped its walled area. Howling monkeys, baboons, and all kinds of birds clung to the stronger branches still left in the

346

trees. Mick ran past a huge aviary filled with panicking parrots. Then he passed a long low building with a sign that said "Reptile Domain." He crossed two wooden bridges. One went over a pool of juvenile alligators. The second spanned a pool holding the largest salt water crocodile in captivity.

At last, he located the equipment gate in the tall chain link fence at the very back of the park. It was partially hidden by a growth of climbing vines. He pulled a section of the wet, bushy vines free. That exposed a padlock holding a chain that secured the gate. Using the bolt cutters, he cut the chain. With great effort, he managed to pull the gate open. He left it that way, and went back for Sunny. When he reached the storeroom, he jerked open the door. She was standing there waiting.

"Follow me!" Mick shouted, "Don't let yourself fall behind."

Instead of running back towards the gate, he went straight to the large alligator pool by the door where customers entered the park. The agitated alligators were climbing over themselves, whipping their tails and snapping their jaws.

There was a wooden railing around the pool. Heavy wire fencing ran from the top rail down to the ground. Mick didn't hesitate. He used the bolt cutters to slice a section three feet across out of the fencing. Even before he had finished the last cut, gators were pushing to get out of the enclosure. An angry seven footer charged through and lunged at Sunny. She screamed and jumped back. Mick ran to a second gator pond and repeated the process.

The rain was definitely slowing up now. It was getting easier to see. Some of the birds were starting to calm down. Mick led the way in the direction of the equipment gate. Before they reached it, Mick kicked in the door to the Reptile Domain. "Don't move," he told Sunny. He ran to the far end of the building. He turned around and as he ran back, he used the heavy bolt cutters to smash every one of the glass cases used to house some of the deadliest snakes in the world. A king cobra, a timber rattler, a coral snake . . . these killers and more crawled to freedom.

Mick turned around at the door. He saw a black mamba and a cottonmouth slithering in his direction. He left the door wide open, and pulled Sunny onward on the path. They crossed the two bridges; Mick cut a heavy lock and set the mammoth crocodile free. Hurrying on, they reached the gate in a few minutes. They went through, and Mick pushed it closed. He did his best to disguise it by pulling vines and fallen branches over it. His quick efforts would have to do.

The two of them hurried along outside the zoo's tall fence.

The beam from the St. Augustine lighthouse swept periodically through the dark of the storm. The rain and wind seemed to be lessening slightly. Henry turned on his windshield wipers for a few minutes. He strained to make out the gray stucco building that housed the pizza restaurant that he was parked beside. A downed palm tree lay between his car and the building. All manner of refuse was scattered across the parking lot. He had been confined to the same spot for over half an hour. He had to get moving again.

The Ford wagon drove away from the pizza place and crept up A1A as fast as its bright lights would allow. Henry didn't like the risk required, but settling things with

Mick was all he could think about. He managed to cover about a quarter mile when the flashing lights of two parked police cars appeared through the rain. Henry pulled to the side of the road. He had to learn what was going on. He used his binoculars to try to pierce the curtain of raindrops. As he watched through a blur, two cops in raincoats stepped out of the lead patrol car. Then they hurried into a large parking lot. Beyond them he could see the yellow bus.

Yes, finally.

58

Randy approached the bus with his weapon at the ready. When he got close enough, he could hear children crying over the sounds of the storm. He positioned himself in a crouch with his back to the bus so he couldn't be seen through the windows. He signaled the policeman behind him, and carefully moved towards the door of the shuttle.

He was preparing to kick in the door, when it suddenly opened. Randy aimed and nearly fired at a large Hispanic man that stumbled down the steps. The man saw the police officers. "Help us! Please help us!" he pleaded. "There are women and children on my bus." Carlos gasped for breath. "He shot my radio. I was afraid. I waited, but I had to try and get help."

"What about the tall man, the man with the gun? Is he still on the bus?"

"No. No, he took the girl and dragged her into the storm. They got off the bus about ten minutes ago."

Randy pushed past the man and boarded the bus. He saw a middle-aged man and a frightened woman sitting on the back seat trying to console two young boys. "Thank heavens!" the woman exclaimed. A teenage couple was huddled together on another seat. The girl was sobbing. Randy walked the length of the aisle to be sure there was no one else on the bus.

"You are safe now," he shouted. "An officer will stay here for your protection until we can get transportation for you." Randy got off the bus and looked around. He motioned for the other officer. He told him to stay with the passengers.

The rain was slowing now. Where could Parsons have gone?

He tried his radio. Thankfully, it was working again. He gave dispatch an update on the situation, and asked for all the help Liz could muster. In a few minutes, he began to hear distant sirens heading in his direction.

Bonnie stood shivering by the rear of the bus. She was eavesdropping for all she was worth. "Damn, that Mick is smart," she grumbled. "They missed him again."

The black skies were gradually changing to gray. Henry watched the activity on the bus through his binoculars. The bus driver and a ginger-haired cop were talking in the aisle. The driver sat down in his seat, and the cop stepped out into the rain. A sheriff's car turned into the parking lot, followed by another beach police cruiser. A highway patrol vehicle and two more sheriff's cars showed up. It was going to be tough tracking Mick with all those idiots in the way.

Henry adjusted his binoculars and swept the area. The rain was easing into a drizzle. His visibility was improving. He focused on the entrance to the tourist attraction. In the midst of that storm, Mick would have had to take shelter. The cops must have come to the same conclusion. He watched as the whole group of lawmen moved to the double doors that led to the admissions center.

His suspicions were confirmed after the men examined the entry doors. He saw the law enforcement officers take out their guns. The beach cop seemed to be in charge. He kicked at the doors until one of them opened slightly. He pushed it the rest of the way, and led the other men inside.

Mick might have fixed the doors to look like he was inside the park, and then made his way through the storm to another place. It wasn't like him to get himself trapped. Henry started the Ford and drove slowly past the park.

Randy cleared the admissions center and addressed the gathered troops. "They were here. There are fresh rainwater puddles by the bench and near the exit door. It's been kicked in, so they're most likely somewhere in the park. The weather is still too bad for the chopper, so it's up to us to find them." He turned to the large map painted on the wall. He roughly divided the park into three sections, and assigned men to search each of them. "I don't need to tell you how dangerous Parsons is. You spot him or the girl, get backup before you make a move. Let's go, and be real careful out there."

Randy stood aside and opened the exit door. A sheriff's deputy stepped through.

"Oh shit! Help!" he screamed. He shoved his way back into the building. A five foot alligator was firmly attached to his left leg. The gator's tail was whipping left and right. His jaws were clenched on the man's calf. "Help me! Get him off!" the deputy yelled. Most of the men jumped away, but Randy fell on the gator and trapped his tail between his legs. The highway patrol officer grabbed his head and attempted to wedge his pistol barrel between the thrashing gator's jaws. The move didn't work. The gator held on. Blood began to soak the deputy's pants leg. Luckily for the bleeding man, the angry reptile decided to spread his fury around. He released his first victim, and snapped at the highway patrolman's free hand. The officer managed to catch hold of the gator's snout, and hold the jaws of the reptile closed. Between he and Randy, they wrestled the gator to the door, and threw him back outside. Randy slammed the door, but not before he saw a ground that was teeming with angry, scrambling alligators. Some were huge. How in the hell could they search for Parsons in that?

Mick and Sunny followed the fence as it curved around the property. It was difficult going. Their clothes were heavy with rainwater. Sandspurs snatched at their legs. When the perimeter fence made a sharp turn at the road, Mick stopped Sunny beside a huge, white oak tree. He peered around its trunk through the drizzle.

He could see the parking lot and the shuttle bus. There were half a dozen cars from various law enforcement agencies scattered around. Some still had their colored lights flashing. The powerful periodic beam from the lighthouse made crosses in the sky when it hit them. The double doors at the park entrance hung open. Good. Mick wished his trackers a fun time playing in the park. It might even be feeding time.

He took Sunny's hand, and they ran across the street into the relative safety of the wooded grounds of an elementary school. They ran past several brick buildings and a small playground. The grass was mowed. There were lots of oaks covered in moss scattered around the grounds. There was a swing set, a see-saw, and a jungle gym. Adjoining the playground at the rear was a large soccer field. They stopped and hid inside a messy public restroom at the edge of the field. It smelled of industrial disinfectant and had the usual graffiti on the walls.

"We shouldn't be here," Sunny told Mick, looking very serious.

"Yeah, I should be in Guatemala," he replied.

"No, I mean we're in the ladies' room," she laughed. She was making a joke, something she couldn't remember ever doing.

Mick had to smile at that. He moved to the door and looked out. The lighthouse beam was still making its rounds through the drizzle. Sunny was looking at herself in the mirror and shaking the water from her hair. Mick thought for a moment. "You know anything about that lighthouse?"

"Just that it's old, and plenty of people take pictures of it."

He took another look outside. The rain was stopping. A few rays of sunshine peeked through the thinning clouds. They needed to move. "Well, little girl, let's you and me go play tourist."

Henry turned left on A1A. He drove a block, and turned left again. He was in a residential area. There were houses on his right, and the Alligator Farm on his left. He could see the high, landscaped wooden fence that surrounded the zoological park. He drove slowly, studying it until he saw a section of fencing that was covered with newly fallen branches. Henry parked the station wagon. He got out into the mild rain. He walked to the fence and discovered the camouflaged, chain-link gate. Its padlock was cut. He began carefully examining the sandy soil around it. The gate had recently scraped the ground while being shoved outward.

Aha. There they were, a pair of footprints that moved from the gate to the strip of ground running along the fence.

Excellent.

Henry went back to the Ford and opened the tailgate. There was no one around. He lifted the rug and the fitted top of the secret compartment that held his weapons. He wanted to be prepared, and he wasn't sure what situation he would find himself in during the next few hours. He removed the sniper rifle, two grenades, and another fifteen shot clip for his machine pistol. Satisfied, he buttoned the hidden compartment back up, and loaded his equipment onto the back seat. He got back in the wagon, turned it around in a handy driveway, and headed back to A1A.

As he drove, Henry wondered how long it would take the incompetent cops to realize that Mick would never allow himself to get trapped in a confined space. They were probably searching the inside of the area inch by inch, while Mick was heading for open spaces. Shame on them, but good for him. He wanted the showdown between the two professionals to be private.

What about the girl? Henry had no idea why Mick hadn't wasted her long ago. When the time came, he would enjoy dealing with her, and he wouldn't waste time doing it. No big deal.

The residential road swung away from the fence before it met A1A. At the intersection, though, Henry looked to his right. He could see where the fence ended its enclosure of the park property beside a large tree. The parking lot was crowded with official cars and TV trucks. There were lots of people milling around. The sun was breaking through the clouds and the rain was over. Directly across the road from that spot was a school.

Henry smiled. He drove across the intersection and parked the Ford a couple of hundred yards down another residential street. The school grounds were empty due to the weather. He checked his pistol and set its mechanism for three round bursts. He grabbed one of the grenades from the back seat, and got out of the car. He walked quickly, his hushpuppies squishing with each step.

When Henry reached the school, he searched among the single story brick buildings, looking for any sign of a break-in. There weren't any. When he neared the rear of the school property, he walked through a small playground and came upon a soccer field. The area was flat and open, but there was a concrete block restroom building on its closest side. The simple structure looked like a possibility.

Henry approached the small building with caution, but when he reached the door marked "Men's Room," he didn't hesitate. He pulled open the door and rushed in. He held his silenced pistol in front of him. He planned to eliminate anyone or anything he might encounter.

But the room was empty.

He checked each stall to be sure, and then he stepped out. He took a deep calming breath, and then entered the ladies' room the same way.

59

Chief Hobbs drove his cruiser into the parking lot of the Alligator Farm. He was immediately surrounded by TV and newspaper reporters. He climbed out of his cruiser and managed to push his way through the forest of microphones that the jostling news people thrust at him. They were still shouting questions to his back as he reached Randy by the entrance to the admissions center. He was standing with a wet, but attractive, redheaded woman.

"They saw me just get here. What do they think I know?" the chief wondered out loud. "Talk to me, Randy."

Randy briefed the chief on everything that had happened since he spotted the bus. He introduced Bonnie, and then explained that she had been one of the hostages, and also had been the one to locate the shuttle bus and point it out to him.

The chief only nodded. "What about the civilians? Anyone hurt?" he asked.

"Just shaken up. There were two kids on the bus. They were upset, but they've calmed down now. They think that getting kidnapped was cool."

"And Parsons? What about that son of a bitch?"

"As far as we know, he's still in the park, and he still has the girl. The Jacksonville boys have their SWAT team in route. Every lawman in three counties is either here or on the way. We have the whole park surrounded."

"Then we've got him," the chief said.

"It looks like it, but there's one big problem, Chief. Parsons let all the wildlife loose in the park. We've already had a man attacked and injured by a good sized alligator.

It's going to be tricky going in there. I put a call in to Marine Patrol and the Florida Department of Wildlife. Our guys aren't going to be able to handle the situation on their own."

The chief nodded in acknowledgement. "Keep me informed," he said, and he walked back to where the reporters were gathered.

"Is he always that friendly?" Bonnie asked.

"Give him a break. He has one heavy load of shit on his mind."

Bonnie noticed that the street lights were back on. A few minutes later, the emerging sunshine caused the electric eyes to turn them off again. She looked around the parking lot for someone else to interview. She already had lots of good stuff the other media people wouldn't have. This story was hers.

She walked back to the Toyota pickup. Her lifeguard buddy was sitting on the hood. He looked at her sheepishly. "Lady, if you don't need a ride anywhere, I've got to get back to the Holiday Inn and see if I still have a job. I could use that five hundred, too."

"I'm going to stick around here. I'm sorry, but Parsons took my purse. You'll have to give me your address. I'll have my boss send it to you."

"You never told me that," the boy complained. "I could have messed up my truck. I might lose my job."

"Yeah, but you haven't yet, sweetheart. You can play the hero card. " She patted his cheek. "You'll get your money. I promise."

The lifeguard went into the truck and brought out a stub of a pencil and a fast food bag. He tore off a piece of it and scribbled down the information. He handed it to her. "I'm going to be counting on the money for rent. Don't fuck me over." He touched her on the cheek, got into the truck, and quickly drove off.

Bonnie crumpled the slip of paper and dropped it on the ground. She had to borrow a phone and call Jack. She might be able to make today's deadline.

The houses around the school and soccer field were nice, middle-class homes. They were ranch style, faced with brick, and each had an attached, two car garage. It was an established neighborhood, and there were plenty of full grown trees. The yards displayed oaks draped with Spanish moss, the occasional long-needle pine, and scattered palms. The bushes were trimmed. The flower beds were weeded. Mick and Sunny walked on the edged sidewalk, stepping over branches brought down by the storm. The clouds were parting now. The sun was breaking through. They could smell rainwater mixed with oil on the pavement.

Ahead of them, the lighthouse tower stood dramatically above the surrounding oaks. It was less than a quarter mile away. Mick was leading them straight towards it.

They passed a sign pointing to their right for The St. Augustine Yacht Club. Beside it was another that pointed left to the Lighthouse Museum entrance. They were only a few hundred feet from the massive structure. They had to look almost straight up to see the top of it. The base was painted in bold white and black stripes. The area at the top was red. That was where the huge lens that magnified the rotating beam of light was housed.

They walked into the empty parking lot that served the museum. They passed a bronze plaque erected by the St. Augustine Historical Society. It told of the construction of the current lighthouse in 1874. The original structure was built on this same site by the Spanish in 1589. It was the first lighthouse ever built in the New World. The plaque stated that the height of the tower was 174 feet.

"Think you can climb that thing, little girl?" Mick asked, looking upward.

"I can if you can," Sunny replied.

"It's the best place to survey the whole area. The cops will never suspect it, but if the guy hunting us sees it, he'll have to check it out. It's the high ground."

There were two structures at the base of the tower. One was a frame house that looked like it might hold offices. The other was a brick home that had to have been built for the lighthouse keeper. It now held the museum. When word about tropical storm DeDe came over the radio, both of the buildings were closed and shuttered. Other than a few smaller trees that were down, the buildings appeared to have suffered only minimal damage. A few shingles were missing from the smaller building, and a shutter hung at a crazy angle on the front of the museum.

There was a picket fence at the rear of the museum, and a walkway to the base of the tower. Mick looked around and didn't see anyone. He kicked the latch on the gate and it broke easily.

"After you," he said gallantly.

Henry knew he was on the right track. There was a puddle on the floor of the ladies' room that hadn't begun to dry. He checked the stalls for good measure. No one was in them, but he couldn't have missed his targets by much. He stood in the restroom doorway to scout the area.

There were no cars in the school parking lot. He doubted that Mick could have stolen one from there. The houses on the adjoining street all had garages. The cars owned by these people were locked up tight due to the storm. Maybe he could have gotten away on a bicycle.

He wondered if Mick had killed the girl. He would have. She had to be a problem for him. A good hit man traveled light.

He walked back to his car. He was trying to put himself in Mick's place when he glanced up. Directly ahead of him, towering above the oak trees, was the lighthouse that had been sending out rotating beams of light during the storm. He picked up his pace.

His trusty Ford started easily. Henry drove down the road focused on the lighthouse. If Mick hadn't found transportation, he would seek to command high ground. He would want to oversee the whole area. There was nothing higher on the island than the lighthouse.

Henry drove very slowly, checking the yards on both sides of the road. He approached a very nice, heavily treed park on his right. The entrance to the lighthouse complex and museum was on his left. He drove past a sign identifying the properties, and continued driving until the road made a sharp left turn. Henry parked on the side of the road. He got out and opened the back door. He picked up the sniper rifle and a grenade. He took off his windbreaker and wrapped it around the rifle. He closed and locked the car doors, and walked back the way he had come.

If you're here, Mick, it's you and me.

60

The ambulance driver was more than earning his pay. His siren was blaring and his lights flashed as he made his fourth trip over the 312 bridge that day. Fortunately, Flagler Hospital was located immediately past the bridge. The trips to the island were short ones. His EMT was in the back giving a shot of anti-venom serum to their passenger. The odds of it saving the man's life were slim.

Doctor Barringer and a team of two nurses met the bus at the emergency room's back entrance. The driver backed his vehicle up to the off-load area and killed the engine. He could hear the rapid shouting at the rear of the ambulance as the gurney holding his passenger was pulled out of the back. "Fifty year old male. He's in shock. Blood pressure 75 over 50. Pulse slow and getting slower. He's fading fast!"

Barringer bent over the gurney and pressed his stethoscope to the man's chest. "Not good," he reported. "Get him to trauma as fast as you can." The team hurried off, pushing the gurney in front of them.

In spite of admirable efforts by Barringer and his team, the patient didn't make it. No one bitten on the neck by a black mamba ever had.

Bonnie was trying to bring Jack up to speed. He was very sweet and caring at first, but once she convinced him that she was safe and unharmed, he reverted back to his sarcastic, bombastic, and demanding self. She calmed him down by threatening to hang up and give the biggest story of the year to another paper. She could sense his blood pressure rising, but he kept silent.

362

"Parsons is still on the loose. He has the girl, Jack. The cops have him trapped inside this nightmare of a zoo where he's let all the freaking animals loose. One man had half of his calf bitten into chunks by a pissed off alligator. A wildlife specialist is on his way to the hospital because some kind of poisonous snake dropped out of a tree and bit him on the neck. A state trooper had to have over thirty stitches in his forearm because a damn spider monkey freaked out when he tried to capture it. Did you know that monkeys bite?"

"Who cares, Bonnie? What about Parsons? Are they going to get him?" Jack was salivating into the phone.

"He's smart, Jack. These small town cops don't realize what they're up against. They average one murder here every couple of years."

"Goddamn it, Bonnie, this is big. I'm going with a prelim in today's edition. I know you don't have copy, but I want to get the scoop. Give Colleen what you've got. We can fill in the blanks tomorrow."

"What's your lead?"

"'REPORTER TAKEN HOSTAGE ESCAPES, KILLING SPREE CONTINUES.' I'll do it in a 28 font, top right of the front page."

"I'm OK with that, but you're just going to get the bare bones."

"I understand, just don't rest on your laurels. I want all the story you can get me ASAP. You stay all over this thing for the duration," he demanded. "I'm going to hold the right column on the front, and a whole inside page for tomorrow's edition."

"I can handle that. I've never had a chance at a story as whacky as this one, and it's not even close to finished. You're picking up the tab for everything, right Jack?"

"This time, I'm not even going to bitch. You just make sure you deliver."

"This is all mine, Jack. Don't you forget it."

"You'll get a byline above the fold. I promise."

"Bye, boss. Kisses." They both hung up.

Jack felt that he probably should have told her about Sam, but shit, she had work to do. Bonnie needed to concentrate. A paper didn't just print itself.

The chopper was finally flying. Randy could hear its distinctive, "whack, whack" sound as it was nearing the zoological park. Damn, did they need it! No one knew for sure how to corral all the dangerous wildlife that was going berserk inside the park enclosure. There were already three casualties, and Parsons was still hiding somewhere in the chaos.

Another team of wildlife experts was gathered at the door. They were dressed in heavy duty camouflage overalls and wore rubber hip boots. They each had a forty-five in a belt holster, and carried a shock stick. They looked completely prepared, but so had the man that Randy knew had just died in the emergency room.

Snake bite . . . a goddamn snake bite!

The leader of the group raised his hand as a signal to be ready. He dropped it, shoved open the door, and led his troops into the park. Randy could hear them cursing immediately.

It would take two full days before all of the escaped animals and reptiles could be recaptured and controlled. Randy would have a totally different picture of the situation by then.

Henry was approaching the lighthouse complex with extreme caution. He took advantage of the many oak trees with low hanging branches and moss to hide his movements as he carefully made his way through the museum parking lot. He wasn't sure he would find Mick in the lighthouse, but his hunch told him he would. He always trusted his hunches. They usually paid off.

Once near the access, Henry used the scope on the sniper rifle as a substitute for his binoculars. He scanned the entire area. The buildings were unoccupied and secure. The metal roof on the museum was giving off a slight hint of steam as the sun grew more prominent above. The grounds were very wet and devoid of any sign of people. It wasn't until Henry turned his search skyward that he felt the thrill of discovery.

He moved the focus of the scope from the striped lighthouse base up to its bright red top. What he saw there seemed too good to be true. Oh yes, there was his elusive prey. Mick was facing away, looking out over the city, standing squarely in his cross hairs at the rail that circled the giant glass lens. Henry's immediate thought was to jack a shell into the rifle's chamber and end Mick's life. So much for their rivalry. With one gentle squeeze of the trigger, it would be over.

He quickly retreated from that thought. Killing Mick was a very special event. It had to be done face to face. He wanted Mick to die knowing that he lost to the best. Henry needed to witness the acceptance of defeat in the fading spark of his old competitor's eyes.

He lowered the rifle. He looked for a way to get into the lighthouse without being seen. When he saw one, he smiled and eased his way back to his car.

Bonnie wanted dry clothes and a drink. She sweet-talked a nice looking radio announcer while he was breaking for commercial. He was doing a live, on-the-scene report of the supposed, last free minutes of Michael Jason Parsons. She convinced him to loan her his car. He was glad to do it. He knew he would be tied up at the Alligator Farm for hours. When the sexy redhead returned the car, she would owe him. She was smart, and tasty in a naughty kind of way.

Bonnie took the announcer's keys and used them to unlock a mustard yellow, six year old Chevrolet. God, she couldn't wait to sit in her own Mustang again. She started the car, switched on the radio, and drove to the stop sign at the exit. Of course, her new friend's report was coming through the speakers. Why would he listen to anyone else? She switched the radio off.

Bonnie was a little turned around with all the confusion. She wasn't sure which way it was back to the Holiday Inn. As she was thinking, she saw a pale, thin man walking through the drizzle across the grounds of an elementary school across the road. That was strange. He wasn't even wearing a raincoat. Was everybody crazy in this town? Or . . .

Bonnie drove across the road, and parked the Chevy at the curb under a spreading oak. She wasn't five hundred yards from where she had borrowed it. From her sheltered location, Bonnie watched the man pass through the school grounds, and walk towards a small building beside a soccer field. He seemed to be approaching it cautiously.

"Oh shit!" she yelled out loud. The man had pulled a huge handgun out from under his windbreaker. The guy wasn't Parsons. She knew Mick was wearing shorts, and he was much taller. Who in hell was this guy? The man charged into a door on one side of the building.

Bonnie had no idea what to do. Obviously this guy had some connection to Parsons. Events like those of the last two days didn't happen by coincidence. She rubbed the places on her face that were irritated by the duct tape. She had a great story. Was it worth risking her ass all over again, just to make it a better one?

Yeah, goddamn it, it was.

When he woke up, Sarah was sitting in an upholstered chair beside Poon's hospital bed. He had sagging bags under his eyes, and he badly needed a shave. He blinked, and tried stretching his arms until he felt the needles and tubes. "Gee," he said, trying to focus his bleary eyes on Sarah, "am I in heaven? Are you an angel?"

Sarah had to laugh at that. He was such a dog. He would chase women from the grave if he still could.

"No, Poon, you're here in Flagler Hospital. We're trying to save your guitar picking fingers. You've got some trouble with your toes, too. They aren't as bad, though."

"Sarah, is that you?" Poon recognized her voice before he could see her clearly. He wiped his eyes with a bandaged hand, dragging tubes across his chest with the motion. "You must have come in here just to save me."

"Not really. I was just ending my shift when you showed up. How did you get yourself hog-tied?"

"That is a long story, sweetheart. I only remember parts of it."

Sarah knew that the hangover and need for a drink were going to hit him at approximately the same time. They did.

"Can you find me a drink, Sarah? I'm starting to get a little shaky." She took Poon's hand. She could feel it trembling. The DTs were on their way.

"I've just put you on an alcohol drip, Poon. You've already had a seizure. How did you let things get so bad?" She stood and went to check the bag that held mixed saline and medically purified alcohol. Gravity was feeding the liquid into Poon's vein.

"Life happens, Sarah. I watch it carefully, but it just keeps happening."

"Listen, I'm upping the alcohol for you to three ounces an hour. I'm coming back in two hours and reducing it again. Enjoy it while you can, but don't mention this to a soul. Barringer is a good guy, but he'd have my license for this."

Poon smiled at her and relaxed. He could feel the change in his intake immediately. Sarah bent over him. She kissed his cheek. "No break dancing either," she said. Then she left his room.

61

Henry didn't pay any attention to the old yellow Chevy. It passed him when he parked by the side of the road. He did notice that there was a lone woman in the car. Most likely she was picking up her kids after being stranded by the storm. He made sure the car was out of sight before he got out of the station wagon. He took his weapons out of the back seat, and set them on the hood of the car. He checked each of them carefully.

Henry briefly considered taking out the whole top of the lighthouse with his rocket launcher. He had only used the weapon once before, but he liked it. He had exploded an airplane for Toes. A foolish bush pilot thought he could steal from the mobster while bringing in a load of cocaine. As soon as the plane was unloaded and ready to take off, boom! No plane, no evidence, and no one left to tell any tales.

Somewhat reluctantly, he decided to leave the rocket launcher in its space. He picked up the sniper rifle, a grenade, the machine pistol, and two extra clips. He re-wrapped the weapons in his windbreaker.

Henry headed back to the lighthouse. He had his plan. Five minutes later, he was standing in the shelter of a huge oak near the edge of the museum parking lot. He could see that there was only a fancy picket fence protecting the walkway to the door into the base of the light house. He checked his weapons one last time. He decided to leave the high powered rifle by the trunk of the tree. The machine pistol and the grenade would do the trick. His last confrontation with Mick would be at close range.

Henry knew he had his rival cornered, plus he had the element of surprise. He would creep silently up the stairs, and then catch Mick off guard on the walkway at the top of the tower. After a little sharing about old times, he would shoot Mick. Or maybe he would give him the honorable option of jumping off the tower on his own. After all, he was the closest thing to a friend that Henry had ever had.

Mick was the one that taught him that even though neither of them had the emotional ability to care for anyone, they could "admire." He remembered the contract they shared years ago. They clipped the owner of a high class art gallery in Dallas. The idiot had stiffed Tony Toes on a coke deal fronted to him. He had to pay the price. The hit was simple. Either one of them could have done it in their sleep, but Toes wanted them to get to know each other. They were his favorite assassins.

The gallery owner was surprised when he came home after a charity fashion show. He found Henry and Mick sitting on his living room couch. There was no conversation. That only happened with amateurs. They both stood. Without a word, they put a couple of bullets each in him. Then they dragged him to the bathroom and wrestled his body into the tub.

Before leaving the man's penthouse, he and Mick spent nearly an hour discussing the paintings that lined their victim's walls. What Mick taught him changed his way of looking at life. What Mick said was true. Even a psychopath could appreciate talent. Hired killers could admire true skill. Whether it was painting, hitting a golf ball, or accomplishing a nice, neat murder, it was invigorating to feel a warm connection with something positive.

Henry walked to the broken gate and pushed it open. It was ten steps to the base of the tower. He covered them quickly. He found that the lock to that door had been kicked in, too. He pushed the door open as quietly as he could, and cautiously entered the dimly lighted space.

Bonnie stood under a dripping gutter by the lighthouse museum. She was wiping drops from her eyes and peering around the corner of the building. She could see the strange man's movements, but she didn't have a clue what he was planning. She watched as he entered the base of the lighthouse. He had a pistol he held closely by his side. She checked her phone again, but it was wet and still not functioning.

Henry took each step on the spiral staircase with care. He had to remain perfectly silent to sneak up on a professional like Mick. The tower dimensions were tight. It was so tall that he couldn't see over the stair rail to the top. He held the German machine pistol in front of him and moved upward, one step at a time. Even his breath had to be controlled. He felt the tightening of his testicles in anticipation of the kill. He climbed the spiral staircase until even his very muscular legs were starting to protest. Fifty, a hundred, a hundred and fifty feet . . .

Finally, Henry saw a metal door at the very top of the stairs. It was standing open a few inches. He took the last few steps as quietly as he could, and then stood motionless on a woven wire landing just outside the door. He concentrated his focus, taking slow deep breaths. He held his pistol at the ready as he stepped back, and then placed a powerful kick on the door.

The door burst open and Henry screamed, "Freeze, Mick! Hands up, motherfucker!"

The person at the rail slowly turned around to face the attacker. The bill of the ball cap she was wearing was dripping water into her eyes. She brushed it off with one hand. The wet glasses she wore slipped off with her movements. Henry's gun looked gigantic. It was pointed straight at her face. "Stop! Wait!" was all she could say. She held her hands in front of her as if they could slow the velocity of a copper jacketed bullet.

What the fuck? Henry thought, as he realized the person wearing the ball cap wasn't Mick. A girl? He started to squeeze the trigger anyway, but a voice from behind him stilled his finger.

"Hello, Henry," Mick said calmly. "I thought you might drop by." He had slipped from behind the shelter of the massive lens of the lighthouse. "Long time, no see."

Henry froze. This couldn't be happening. He couldn't believe that Mick had tricked him. He kept his gun aimed at Sunny and spoke over his shoulder. "Be cool, Mick. You can't shoot me without me doing this girl. I'll kill her. You know I will."

"Right," Mick said, and then he pulled his trigger.

Henry's head took the bullet like a bomb. His brain was too dead too fast for his muscles to react. He dropped to the floor like an anchor. The machine pistol hit the deck and fired three loud rounds that ricocheted off the tower cap and into the sky.

"So long, Henry." Mick commented. "You were efficient. You just weren't the best."

Sunny shuddered at the sight of Henry's brains spattered on her. She turned and vomited over the lighthouse rail. Mick was pushing at Henry's body with his foot. It was nice to be a winner. He was surprised, though, that a pro like Henry could be brought down by such a simple trick. He must not have known about the girl.

"Sunny, when you finish tossing your cookies, can you give me a hand here?" He grabbed Henry's body and wrestled it into a sitting position against the railing. Mick took his gun and began beating in Henry's skull around the gunshot wound. That would slow down the ID of the bullet's caliber. Not really necessary, just good procedure. The sound of the pistol thwacking into flesh sent Sunny to the rail again.

Once she got it back together, Mick reminded her that Henry had very nearly put out her lights. That helped. Sunny managed to lift Henry's feet for Mick as they rolled the body over the railing. It took seconds for the corpse to hit the concrete below. As high up as they were, they could still hear the splat. The sound was that of a ripe melon dropped on wet concrete. Mick grinned. He was happy.

Winning was its own reward.

62

When Randy got the call, he was tying a tourniquet on the arm of a marine patrol officer. Liz had just learned that a shooting victim had been found close by at the lighthouse complex. Randy knew it couldn't be Parsons. He was still hiding somewhere inside the Alligator Farm. Whoever it was, she said he was very dead.

Randy told the EMT standing by to get the man he was working on to the hospital as fast as he could. The officer thought it was a cottonmouth that bit him, but it happened so fast that he wasn't sure. The man's hand had swollen to twice its normal size. It was a dangerous mess in the park. There were so many angry animals and snakes loose. It might take days to get the zoological grounds under control. Especially with Parsons in the middle of it.

Goddamn. What could happen next?

It only took Randy minutes to get to the lighthouse. He parked his cruiser in the museum's lot and got out. There was an elderly couple comforting a sobbing young girl by the walk that ran alongside the building. The three of them were facing away from a body that was splashed all over the walkway behind them.

"I'm here to help," Randy said. "You can calm down now. Tell me what happened."

The man was first to speak. "We're just trying to take care of this girl. We were in our car driving through the park looking for our cat. She spooked during the storm and ran off. As we pulled up to the museum entrance, a body came sailing off of the top of the lighthouse. We watched it fall the whole way. We rushed over here as this girl came running out. She told us that the man back there on the concrete tried to assault her."

"Is that right?" Randy asked. The girl was crying so hard that she had to struggle to answer.

"He tried to rape me!" she gasped. Her T-shirt was ripped, and her shorts were torn. There were exposed scratches on the tops of her budding breasts.

"I thought there was a shooting," Randy offered.

"There was!" the girl said. "He had a gun. He was holding it on me. When he grabbed me, we fought. I was sure I was going to die. He said he was going to kill me. The gun he had went off. It was like slow motion. The bullet went in that freak's head. The fucking rapist smiled at me, and then he just fell over the railing."

Randy sat the hysterical girl down on a bench by the walkway.

"My name is Brenda Rose Martin," she blurted out. "I was kidnapped by this crazy serial killer. Not this one, another one. He's kept me with him as a hostage for the last ten days. He's made me do horrible things. He left me here, and I know he'll come back to kill me. The guy that fell is one of his gang. He was supposed to watch me until the other guy got back."

Bonnie came running up to the pair. She was out of breath, and fought to gasp out words of comfort to the girl. She hugged the child to her tightly and smoothed her hair with one hand. "Oh, Brenda Rose, when I saw that body come flying off of the lighthouse, I was sure that it was you! But you're safe now. You're really safe. I'm so glad, sweetheart. You know you saved my life."

Randy knew that Mick wouldn't be coming back into all this. "Well, don't you worry now. No one is going to hurt you. I'm going to check the lighthouse, but I'll come right back. I'll stay here until we can get you to a hospital and get you checked out." The girl pressed her face to Randy's chest and hugged him.

"It was horrible!" she cried.

Randy looked over the girl's shoulder. He could see the body sprawled on the concrete. It was a splat.

No rush getting an ambulance this time.

63

Grandpa was tuning the Gibson, and Woodsy was hitting a few high notes on his harmonica. The group of locals that had come to witness the Shallow Dive being torn down were drinking hard at eleven o'clock in the morning. The Florida sun was getting hot enough to send rivulets of sweat rolling down their foreheads. The uniform of the day was Hawaiian shirts and cutoffs for the guys, short shorts and bikini tops for the women.

The group milled about, swapping stories about the old place, and drinking steadily. Most of them had spent some time at the run down motel during binges, split-ups, times of unemployment, or hiding from the world. Tammy was mothering them all. The crowd had gathered in the heat on the vacant lot across the road from the doomed motel. They all cheered when a green Volkswagen bus pulled up with Freaki Tiki driving.

Oh yeah. Poon climbed out of the side door wearing only a gaping hospital gown. He was holding a plastic bag of some kind of liquid over his head. A clear tube ran from the bag to the back of his free hand. He was barefoot, and there were bandages on both his feet and hands. There was a huge smile on his face. Tiki pulled a lawn chair out of his bus and set it by the curb for Poon. He set a bottle of Flora de Cana beside it.

Across the street on the Shallow Dive property, a huge Caterpillar bulldozer was being unloaded from a flatbed truck.

Sarah drove up in her convertible, and parked at the first empty space on the side of the road. She knew most of the crowd and waved to them as she hurried to Poon's side.

"You're nuts!" she scolded. "The hospital is going crazy. The intern that was in charge of you is likely to lose his job, and you're likely to lose a few of your digits."

"Isn't she beautiful?" her old friend asked the crowd. "I might need prolonged care." He grabbed Sarah's hand between his two bandaged ones. Before she could give Poon the cussing out he deserved, the bulldozer's diesel engine coughed to a start. There was no delay. The driver lowered the machine's blade, and his steel tracks rolled him into the first corner of the Shallow Dive. The heavy duty machine crashed into what was once the motel's office. The corner was taken out, and the section of roof above it collapsed upon the cage that sheltered the driver. A sad groan came from the sentimental observers.

The group was pissing and moaning and sharing sad tales of times gone by when a yellow and blue delivery van pulled up. The driver got out, and opened the van's back doors. "Come and get it!" he called. "Everything's on the house."

There was bar-b-que pork, beef, and chicken. There were trays of potato salad and cold slaw. There was even a keg of beer sitting in a blue plastic tub full of ice. The driver started drawing beers and passing them out to the crowd. Freaki Tiki began putting big helpings of food into foam containers and handing them out.

Poon was the first one to ask, "Where did all this great stuff come from?"

The driver gave him a silly card with a couple of raccoons on it. Poon opened it and read, "I made a deal with you. I'm sorry for the delay, but here's your bar-b-que. I'll never forget you."

The card was signed in a scrawl, Sunny Cathleen Cantrell.

Epilogue

The sky was crystal clear, and the tropical sun was shining on a magnificent view. In front of them, the multicolored colonial buildings on the slightly hilly island looked spectacular. Behind the tiny town, the larger volcanic mountains loomed over the island's shoulder.

Their red and white panga was the only motorized boat on the whole lake. Its sixty horsepower outboard motor moved them across the water at a fast clip. Their wake mapped their progress to the island, leaving a rolling white trail behind the wooden boat. They were returning from a shopping trip to the Guatemalan town of Elena on the mainland.

Bonnie was letting Sunny drive today. It was great to see the young girl so happy. She was quickly growing up. Her blonde hair waved behind her. Her new, crocheted bikini displayed her fine figure. The noise of the old motor was too loud for conversation, but for no particular reason, they both laughed occasionally.

As they passed, Bonnie waved at a fisherman in his painted canoe. He raised his stringer and displayed two nice lake fish, hoping for a sale. She waved him off. She had plenty of food in the woven straw bags in the bottom of the panga. The bags held tomatoes, squash, avocadoes, three dozen tortillas, and a fresh pineapple.

Bonnie took over the wheel and slowed the boat as they approached the island's community dock. Juan was waiting. He caught the line that Sunny threw him, and pulled the boat into its waiting space. "Hola, senoritas," he called. He was a slim, almond-colored man in his thirties. He had four children and was very grateful to have his job as the "assistant" to the Americans. "Let me help you with the bags."

Bonnie handed the three bags of purchases to Juan, and stepped out of the boat and onto the dock. She turned back and offered a hand to Sunny. The girl was so pretty now that she had learned to smile again. There was a constant parade of young Guatemalan boys anxious to show her the delights of Flores nightlife. She asked if she could date while they were staying in Flores, and Bonnie and Doug had agreed. After what she had been through, she deserved a little fun.

The women wrapped themselves in long embroidered scarves in respect for the more conservative Catholics living in Flores. They slipped on handmade sandals, and followed Juan off of the dock.

As the three of them walked up the cobblestone street to the classic colonial home Doug rented, the sound of his helicopter came from overhead. Good. He would beat them home. He had a contract for delivering supplies to the anthropologists working the least accessible sections of Tikal. Two trips a day to the Mayan ruin worked out perfectly. He was with them every night, and the money he made helped replace Bonnie's temporarily suspended salary. Of course, her Pulitzer money was in a New Orleans bank drawing interest if they needed it. Doug liked his new job. Traffic reporting was a drag without someone to flash him every once in a while.

Juan opened the door for Bonnie and Sunny. His wife, Rosalita, was waiting for them. She held a pitcher of tea. The short, dark-haired woman led them across the tile entryway through the living room to the balcony outside. It was made of hand-placed stone, and overlooked the lake. Rosalita placed the pitcher on a bamboo table, and went back to the kitchen for glasses. Bonnie and Sunny sat in wrought iron chairs, took off their wraps, and soaked up the sun. They looked over the lake and relaxed. They really were in a place close to heaven.

On a similar balcony on the other side of the narrow lake, he adjusted the focus on his telescope until he could clearly see the two of them. It was something that had become an afternoon hobby for him.

The reporter looked good today. She was getting a tan. Her red hair was growing longer, too. She smiled a lot, and she wore clothes that accented her figure. The intricate local embroideries suited her coloring, too. Today she hadn't changed after her boat trip to Elena. The bikini she wore was dark green. It should be gold, but he could adjust the color in his daydream. Through the powerful lens, she looked close enough to lick.

Their maid came out of the house and put glasses on a table in front of the two of them. She filled the glasses from a ceramic pitcher. Bonnie and Sunny were chatting like school girls.

"Come on, kiddo," Bonnie teased. "Give me the details. How was the big night?" Sunny had gone out to dinner with a handsome local boy the night before.

"Oh, you know. He was a sweetheart. In a way, it was my first time." The women giggled together.

Occasionally, as they sipped from their glasses, Bonnie glanced down at the side of Sunny's calf. When Bonnie was Sunny's age, a girl with a tattoo was automatically considered a tramp. Times were different now. If a young girl wanted a tattoo, it really didn't mean much of anything. Still, when Sunny wandered off on her own in Elena, Bonnie hadn't expected her to return with one. The girl was so happy and excited about it.

Bonnie would have chosen butterfly or a flower, something pretty and girly, but she knew Sunny well enough now to know she would always be a little different. For her tattoo, the girl had selected two blood red hearts, pierced by a single dagger.

His past companion looked older. She was very pretty now. He could tell that Sunny would be amazingly beautiful in a few years. Her hair was blonde again, and she didn't look so gangly. She was wearing a brightly colored, woven bikini with sandals. She was laughing at something Bonnie said. Later, he knew she would change into a peasant blouse much like the one the maid was wearing. The difference would be that Sunny always wore very tight shorts beneath her blouses. He could tell from the way she moved, that she kept a knife in their waistband at her back.

He couldn't help but admire her. Sunny had made it through a lot of tough shit, and the girl had learned from every bit of it. Mick drank contentedly from a glass of caramel-colored rum. He enjoyed watching the pair.

They were almost like family.

The End

Major Characters

Bonnie: top investigative reporter.
Colleen: Bonnie's assistant.
Donnie: alcoholic, hangs out at the Shallow Dive.
Doug: helicopter pilot. Boyfriend of Bonnie.
Freaki Tiki: musician, friend of Poon.
Frank: Jack's friend at Jacksonville paper.
Grandpa: musician, owner of music store.
Henry: hired assassin.
Hobbs: Chief of St. Augustine Beach PD.
Jack: Editor at the Times-Picayune newspaper.
Julie: Jack's assistant.
Liz: dispatcher, St. Augustine Beach PD.
Mick: escaped serial killer
Paul Mobley: prison librarian. Counterfeiter.
Poon: alcoholic beach bum, guitar player.
Richie: young hit man, Tank's partner
Randy: St. Augustine Beach police officer.
Sam: private detective hired by Jack and Bonnie.
Sunny: teenage girl taken hostage.
Tank: works for Tony Toes.
Tony Toes: Texas mobster

In Appreciation

I would like to thank the people of St. Augustine Beach for their help and inspiration on this project, especially Pat Payne, Michael Shartran, Jan Turney, Phil and Bonnie King, and Jessica Rambo Without them, it would never have become a reality.

About the Author

Walker Newton was born in Tampa, Florida, but spent most of his life traveling both domestically and internationally. He served in the U.S. Navy as a submariner before earning both a bachelor's and a master's degree from a Kentucky university.

His career involved all facets of real estate, culminating with the development of a small hotel chain and a large condominium project.

He is the father of twin daughters and grandfather of two. When he is not traveling, he makes his home in St. Augustine, Florida, where he writes both songs and fiction. His books describe generally many of his friends and favorite places.

35389047R00220

Made in the USA
Charleston, SC
08 November 2014